Selected material from
the Oxford Handbooks in Nursing series, Nursing: Study and Placement Learning Skills, and Clinical Nursing Skills: Core and Advanced

D1077914

Selected material from

the Oxford Handbooks in Nursing series, Nursing: Study and Placement Learning Skills, and Clinical Nursing Skills: Core and Advanced

OXFORD
UNIVERSITY PRESS

OXFORD

UNIVERSITY PRESS

Great Clarendon Street, Oxford OX2 6DP

Oxford University Press is a department of the University of Oxford.
It furthers the University's objective of excellence in research, scholarship,
and education by publishing worldwide in

Oxford New York

Auckland Cape Town Dar es Salaam Hong Kong Karachi
Kuala Lumpur Madrid Melbourne Mexico City Nairobi
New Delhi Shanghai Taipei Toronto

With offices in

Argentina Austria Brazil Chile Czech Republic France Greece
Guatemala Hungary Italy Japan Poland Portugal Singapore
South Korea Switzerland Thailand Turkey Ukraine Vietnam

Oxford is a registered trade mark of Oxford University Press
in the UK and in certain other countries

Published in the United States
by Oxford University Press Inc., New York

© Oxford University Press, 2011

British Library Cataloguing in Publication Data
Data available

Library of Congress Cataloging in Publication Data
Data available

Typeset by Glyph International, Bangalore, India
Printed in Great Britain
on acid-free paper by
Ashford Colour Press Ltd., Gosport, Hampshire

ISBN 978–0–19–964006–5

10 9 8 7 6 5 4 3 2 1

Contents

Chapters 1, 2, and 3 from *Nursing:
Study and Placement Learning Skills* — **1**

Chapters 2–3 from *Clinical Nursing Skills:
Core and Advanced* — **63**

Chapter 1 from the *Oxford Handbook of
Mental Health Nursing* — **141**

Chapter 2 from the *Oxford Handbook of
Children's and Young People's Nursing* — **203**

Chapter 1 from the *Oxford Handbook of
Learning and Intellectual Disability Nursing* — **243**

Chapter 1 from the *Oxford Handbook of
Midwifery*, 2nd edition — **269**

Chapters 1, 2,
and 3 from
Nursing:
Study and
Placement
Learning Skills

Edited by

Sue Hart

Freelance educator,
formerly head of CFP at Surrey University

OXFORD
UNIVERSITY PRESS

So you want to be a nurse

So you want to be a nurse *4*
Nursing is dynamic *5*
Nursing: the life-long journey *8*
The characteristics of nursing *10*
So how do nurses do all this? *12*
Summary *14*

So you want to be a nurse

The aims of this chapter are:
- To explain why nursing is a continually changing profession
- To demonstrate why developing effective strategies for learning and studying are essential for your career as a nurse
- To introduce three essential nursing skills sets: academic and learning skills; clinical practice skills; and professional skills

If you want to be a registered nurse, you need to be aware of the characteristics of the profession and to understand what your nurse education programme will demand of you. To be successful, a student nurse must reach the required standard of performance with regard to their professional behaviour, clinical practice skills and in their academic studies.

Student comment

"New students need to understand that they don't have to make their mark or show their potential straight away. I remember when I started, I wanted to prove how much I wanted this and how keen I was to get stuck in. The fact was I didn't need to right away because the uni just wanted us to settle in first and meet people. Relax is all I can say, and everything comes so much easier!"

Nursing is dynamic

If it was possible to travel back in time to the 1920s, what you would see of a nurse at work then would bear little resemblance to the nursing practice seen today. Nursing has evolved from vocation to career, and now has its own evidence-base and professional standards. This means nursing has its own body of knowledge developed over time, and clear ideas, guidelines and standards about what constitutes good nursing practice.

Figure 1.1 Nurses in the 1920s © Pie Powder Press

Developments in nursing are sometimes as a result of changes in the practice of another professional group. For example, a procedure once undertaken under general anaesthetic and requiring an overnight hospital stay for the patient, can now be performed as day surgery. This change has a 'knock-on' effect for nurses, as they need to understand the correct management of the patient following their treatment. To work with others, accept change and adapt is to grow into your practice. To resist change is to stagnate and, ultimately, to fail. If you seize the learning opportunities open to you now, you show your teachers that you are someone who looks as though they will 'fit' into the profession.

Why does nursing change all the time?

Imagine a conjuror performing a card trick. He fools the audience every time as the Queen of Hearts appears when they were certain, a moment ago, that he had put it back in the pack. Although quite difficult to learn, once mastered, such a skill can be rolled out at every performance, with little modification or development. On the contrary, constant change is a feature of the nursing profession, and to be successful, all registered nurses have to accommodate this fact.

The Nursing and Midwifery Council (NMC) code (2008) outlines the responsibilities and duty of care nurses have to their patients and clients. The public has the right to expect that the professionals nursing them are up-to-date with their practice, are competent and skilled to perform the tasks required, and are sufficiently knowledgeable to give the best possible advice and guidance. To illustrate some of the ways nursing has evolved, consider the following from each of the four fields of nursing practice:

Adult:
- A conscious adult patient would have had their temperature taken with a mercury thermometer placed under their tongue.
- A patient's care plan would have been completed by hand and stored in a paper folder.

Child health:
- Sick children in hospital were separated from their parents, with only limited visiting times.
- Before special-care baby units (SCBU), many premature babies (i.e. born before the full term of 9 months) struggled to survive.

Learning disability:
- Known as mental sub-normality nursing, this took place in long-stay hospitals, the largest of which would accommodate up to 800 or more residents (Korman and Glennester 1990).
- The more able residents were known as 'high grades' and often acted as assistants to the less able 'low-grade' residents.

Mental health:

- Large psychiatric hospitals were the place most mental health nursing took place, and not in the community, as now (O'Carroll and Park 2007).
- Care was once mainly custodial with nurses meeting only the physical needs of patients and not their mental health needs.

In order to respond to the changing need for healthcare, many educational opportunities are offered following registration. Most UK universities provide education for lifelong-learning, with opportunities to obtain higher degrees at masters and doctorate levels. Your pre-registration programme is just the start of an exciting career.

What changes ahead do we already know about?

At the time of writing, the NMC are reviewing the standards of proficiency for pre-registration nursing education and the first all-degree programmes are expected to be in place by September 2011. In the future there is to be a blend of generic and field-of-practice specific learning extending throughout the programme, with more field-specific learning increasing over time.

Fact box

It is because nursing and nurse education changes so rapidly that this book has the online resource. If you are reading this after September 2011, please follow this link to the necessary updates you need, www.oxfordtextbooks.co.uk/orc/hart.

Exercise 1.1

List 10 things that you think nurses of today do on a daily basis. Try to think beyond the obvious tasks (injections, bed pans, etc.). Also, do not just think about your own chosen field of practice. What do you think other nurses do? Refer back to your list when you have read Part 2 of the book.

Nursing: the life-long journey

Anyone planning to pursue a career that requires a minimum of 3 years full-time academic study and practice time before initial registration will have given a great deal of thought to the decision to apply for their course. When you were thinking of applying, you will have had your own thoughts about 'nursing' and what the course will be like, as well as your ideas of what it is that nurses 'do'. You may also have thought about the area of practice you would wish to work in once registered.

By now you will understand that over the next 3 years your goal is to learn, understand and develop the necessary nursing skills, and to acquire the essential knowledge needed to be successful in your programme of study and, in so doing, satisfy your teachers and mentors that you are a person 'fit' to be accepted on to the nursing register for your chosen branch.

What do you mean by life-long journey?

In the past, once an individual was accepted onto the nursing register their nurse education effectively ended, with the exception perhaps of the occasional training course. Commonly, nurses referred to their 'ticket', meaning their eligibility to practise. Much as having bought a train ticket to travel from London to Manchester, the 'ticket' was the key to the job; nurses were not required to keep up-to-date with developments in their work, in the way they are now. Why would this matter? Patients would then not be getting the best, most 'up-to-date' care that they deserved.

The situation now is very different. The pre-registration programme is considered to be just the beginning of learning, and definitely not all you need to know. Also, when in clinical practice in the UK, student nurses now have 'supernumerary status' (see Fact box below) stressing they are there as learners, and not as a regular member of staff.

Fact box

When as a student in your placement you are supernumerary, you are counted as additional to the established number of staff usually required for the area. This protects your time to be there to learn under the guidance of your mentor. Sometimes you will learn by observing and listening, at others by practising essential nursing skills.

The fact that registered nurses are required to keep up-to-date means that in the future, studying, reading journals and nursing text books, and going on courses will become an important part of your professional working life. You must have the evidence that you have done this in order to re-register every year with the Nursing and Midwifery Council. Failure to do so will mean that you will no longer be eligible to practise.

But I have only just started the first year!

Reading this as a new student you may feel we are leaping ahead some-what, but we do so with good reason. It is helpful to know this now so you can, from the beginning of your course, recognize the value of developing efficient study skills and competence in your clinical work, not only to be successful in your pre-registration programme, but to be successful in your career.

From student nurse to registration and beyond

In the first year of the pre-registration programme, shared learning between students from across all the future fields of practice takes place. It gives grounding in the skills and knowledge essential for all areas of nursing. The later years of the programme are to ensure you learn how to deliver and manage the nursing care and skills in your chosen field: adult, child, learning disability or mental health.

Following registration as a nurse, there should always be opportunities to pursue further learning. This is known as continuing professional development (CPD) or life-long learning. An example of this would be courses at graduate or post-graduate level (e.g. a degree or a Masters in Advanced Practice). Depending on your field of nursing, you could further your study in accident and emergency or coronary care nursing practice, community learning disability nursing, neonatal intensive care or caring for people with enduring mental health problems.

The characteristics of nursing

Nursing is a diverse (varied) profession. There is no easy answer to the question, what do nurses do? The role and daily working life of a mental health nurse working with patients with Alzheimer's disease differs significantly from that of a paediatric intensive care nurse or community based diabetic specialist nurse. Learning disability nurses mainly work with people who are not ill. So, why are there such nurses?

Despite these obvious differences, it is possible to identify common characteristics across the nursing profession and it is helpful to understand these as you prepare for what is ahead.

Teamwork: nursing is one of several healthcare professions

Whatever the field of practice, most nurses do not work in isolation, they come into contact with patients, other nurses and professionals. For example, a learning disability nurse may need to liaise with a psychologist regarding a client's behaviour; a child health nurse may need to discuss a case with a paediatrician (a children's doctor). Working well with others, communicating clearly, liaising and valuing their expertise are essential to the effective delivery of patient and client care.

Where do nurses work?

If at random you asked a hundred people in the street 'Where do nurses work?', the chances are that a majority would say 'in hospitals'. Yet where nursing care is delivered has changed over time, and more and more patients are being cared for in their own homes, in specialist units, hospices, community health centres and walk-in clinics. Chapter 7 includes more information about where nursing care is delivered.

What does the patient/client want?

What the public expect from the National Health Service and the staff who work in it has developed over time. Health education, 'expert' patients (Department of Health 2001) and the concept of patient choice, all feature in the modern health service. People are encouraged to engage in their own care, and to discuss and agree this with nurses. Today nurses often speak of working in partnership with their patients and service users (and not just in mental health and learning disability nursing but all fields of practice). Nurses practise 'with' rather than 'do things to' patients.

So how do nurses do all this?

> **Exercise 1.2**
>
> Pause a moment here and think about what you have just read. What do you think are some of the personal and professional qualities a nurse needs in order to perform their role effectively?

You may well have answered reliability, honesty, caring and good communication skills as some of the qualities, and there are many more. As you will have realized from the passages above, the willingness to face up to challenges, to communicate well, to liaise with colleagues and to be flexible are all important; but this is just the beginning.

Introducing the three essential skills sets

To be successful on the pre-registration nursing course it is fundamental that you understand the three essential skills sets, and appreciate why they are so important. It is because it is the evidence of your achievement in these areas which will, for the most part, indicate your suitability to become a registered nurse. Your success on the programme depends on you reaching a satisfactory level of proficiency in the following areas:

- academic and learning skills,
- clinical practice skills,
- professional skills.

Although listed above as three separate entities, in the 'real world' of nursing these skills overlap (see Figure 1.2). It is to assist your understanding as a pre-registration student in the first year of the programme that we present them separately here. Reading this book will help you to be successful in all three areas.

3. Professional
Standards required by
the Nursing and
Midwifery Council

1. Theory – that is the
academic learning and
understanding of the
subjects which
underpin nursing care

2. Practice – the
undertaking of clinical
nursing skills and
nursing care with
patients and clients

Figure 1.2 The three essential skills sets for nursing

The skills are equally important and you must achieve in all to be successful. The following introduces each individual skill set. Part 2 of this book explores them all in much more detail.

Academic and learning skills

As a university student and future registered nurse, you must be able to demonstrate through a variety of assessments that you have a basic understanding of the academic subjects underpinning nursing practice, such as biological science, psychology, sociology, nursing theory, ethics and care planning. It is vital that a registered nurse's actions are evidence-based. Also, as a student you will have to provide evidence (e.g. through reading nursing text books) to support your written work for the course. Chapters 5 and 6 will help you to develop the academic study and learning skills that you will need on the course. The second book in this series (Holland and Rees 2010) will help you to advance your skills in research and evidence-based practice.

Clinical practice skills

Clinical nursing practice (or 'practice') is the term that is used to describe the actual 'doing' of the nursing role. So whether you are supporting a patient to eat or drink, giving an injection, assessing someone who has a learning disability, working in an assertive outreach team in mental health, the 'doing' of these nursing skills is your practice. To be a registered nurse you must have the skills to perform your role. To be successful you must demonstrate through a variety of practice-based assessments, that you have the skills required to complete the first year and later the skills required for registration. Chapter 9 explains how you will learn in practice and Chapter 13 will help you to be successful in your practice assessments.

Professional skills

There are numerous differences between having a job and being a professional. Nursing is a profession. Once registered, you will be professionally accountable and responsible for your actions. The education and regulation of nurses, the existence of the nursing register, and 'The Code' (NMC 2008) are some of the strategies to ensure that only nurses who are fit to practise are able to do so. You will have a minimum of 3 years as a student nurse to show you can develop into the professional role. Chapters 14 and 15 explore nursing as a profession and outline what professional behaviour means.

Summary

Be confident. But also be aware the course can be challenging and this book is here to help. It tells you what you need to know to succeed. Settling in can take some time and Chapter 3 contains some healthy living and stress-busting mechanisms. It also gives advice about managing your money. The book will guide you through the essential skills sets to help build your understanding and give you the best possible grounding in the profession of nursing. Remember, if you can achieve the required standard in these three areas, you will be on the way to success. The first step to that success follows in Chapter 2, which is going to guide you through the first days of the course.

Top tips

- If you have been accepted on the course, celebrate—you have the potential to succeed.
- Settling in can take time.
- If you are worried or do not understand something, ask.
- The nurse teachers are on your side and want you to succeed.
- Focus on developing in all the essential skills. Being excellent in practice but failing your exam is not going to lead to success.
- Writing excellent essays but never arriving in your placement on time is not going to lead to success.
- Enjoy learning, and not just for the assessments.
- Treat people in your care as you would wish to be treated.

More advice

- You can find out much more advice to help you succeed in first year in *Nursing: Study and Placement Learning Skills* by Sue Hart from which this chapter has been taken.

Online resource centre

To make the most of the advice in this chapter, and to develop your knowledge and skills further, now go online to **www.oxfordtextbooks. co.uk/orc/hart/** to find advice from other students and explore the Nursing and Midwifery website, www.nmc-uk.org.

References

Department of Health (2001) *The expert patient: a new approach to chronic disease managementin the 21st Century.* The Stationery Office, London.

Holland K and Rees C (2010) *Nursing: Evidence-based practice skills.* Oxford University Press, Oxford.

Korman N and Glennester H (1990) *Hospital closure.* Open University Press, Milton Keynes.

Nursing and Midwifery Council (2008) *The code.*

O'Caroll M and Park Q (2007) *Essential mental health nursing skills.* Elsevier Sciences, Edinburgh.

Further reading

The following are novels, each opens up the world of the people they are about.

Bayley J (1998) *Iris: a memoir of Iris Murdoch*. Duckworth, London.
About a woman with Alzheimer's disease.
Faulks S (2006) *Human traces*. Vintage Books, London.
A novel tracing the development of psychiatry.
Haddon M (2003) *The curious incident of the dog in the night-time*. David Fickling Books, Oxford.
Written from the perspective of a 15-year-old boy with Asperger's Syndrome.
Picardie R (1998) *Before I say goodbye*. Penguin Books, London.
About the mother of 1-year-old twins who develops cancer.

Websites

Department of Health: **www.dh.gov.uk**
National Health Service: **www.nhs.uk**
Nursing and Midwifery Council: **www.nmc-uk.org**
Website about public services: **www.direct.gov.uk**

Welcome to the course

Welcome to the course 18
Before you start the course 20
Overview of pre-registration nurse education in the UK 22
How the pre-registration programme is structured 24
Students: how many on the course? 26
Starting the course 27
Your first day at university 28
Induction (introductory) activities 30
Other likely induction-period activities 32
Brief overview of subjects covered during the CFP 34
Other useful information 35
Summary 36

Welcome to the course

The aims of this chapter are:
- To suggest pre-course activities
- To show the structure of pre-registration nursing programmes
- To guide you on your first day and during induction

If you have been offered a place or have already started the pre-registration nursing course, think of this as your first achievement. Not everyone who applies is accepted, and if you have been, this indicates you have the potential to be successful. Well done, and welcome.

This chapter will explain how the course is likely to be organized from the first day, through the induction to the end of the first year. It also outlines the role of some of the people you will be meeting. Based on the experiences of students who have gone before, the chapter introduces some of the challenges you may face and how to get support.

Before you start the course

We asked a nurse teacher how they would advise a student who has not yet started the course.

Nurse teacher comment

"If you have been offered a place you will most likely receive confirmation of this by letter and you must reply to secure your place. Study everything you are sent and respond to any instructions. You may be asked to fill in paperwork re a CRB clearance or be asked to attend an occupational health appointment. Reading through what you have been given will help you to find your way around your course and help you to understand aspects pertinent just to your own university/place of study. Also see the University website. If you want to live in university accommodation, apply now or you risk being disappointed. If eligible, you should also have been advised to apply for a bursary and, if you have not already done so, go to NHS Student Bursaries **www.nhsbsa.nhs.uk**

Exercise 2.1

You have accepted your place on the course. Excellent! What can you do now to prepare yourself to start?

Read this book and others on a pre-course reading list. If your university offers a pre-start open day, do visit again. Ask questions. Some universities have online 'welcome' activities to bridge the gap between accepting your place on the course and actually starting. You will have been told if this is the case and have been given logon details.

A word about: Pre-course reading

The nursing department may have given you a reading list. If the books are not in stock at your local library, it should be possible to order them. When you buy books take care to obtain those recommended by your nurse teachers and ensure you get the latest edition (your bookseller will advise). If you are instructed to buy a particular text book (e.g. anatomy and physiology) there will be a reason. It could be that exercises in class are based on the text. So you must buy them or else you will risk disadvantaging yourself.

Students come to pre-registration nursing from a variety of backgrounds. You may be joining the course straight from school or following a gap year, a former career or job you have been doing for some years. However, one thing is for certain; in the next 3 years your life is going to be very different from what it was before. Consider some of the ways:

- You will be studying and learning a lot of new things.
- You will be meeting many new people.
- You may have moved a distance from home.
- You may now be living some distance from friends and family.

Also, it is unlikely that before starting university you simultaneously needed to work on an essay, be on placement late in the evening and then up for an early shift the next day. How will your family manage this, let alone you? For new students time spent preparing for the change in circumstances will help.

Although it will have been explained during your interview day, it may help refresh your understanding of what you will be doing during your course to read the following overview of pre-registration nursing.

Overview of pre-registration nurse education in the UK

Wherever you are studying, your course has been designed to enable you to achieve the necessary proficiencies as laid down by the **Nursing and Midwifery Council** (NMC 2004) to become a registered nurse. The nurse teachers at your university, and their nursing colleagues in practice locally, will have written the curriculum (i.e. the programme of study) that you will follow. The curriculum will then have been scrutinized and approved (validated) by representatives from the NMC, your university and local NHS Trust. They must be sure that the content of the programme can help you to achieve the year one outcomes for entry to the branch programme and, at the end of 3 years, entry to the register (see the NMC website at www.nmc-uk.org).

Required hours for the programme

There is no 'national curriculum' for nurse education but, as the standards for pre-registration programmes are national, it follows that, wherever you are studying, there are certain essential NMC requirements to be met. Adult nurses must also meet the **European Directives**. The NMC stipulates that the pre-registration nursing course is not less than 3 years or 4600 hours in length. Allowing for any interruptions (such as ill health), full-time students must complete the course in not more than 5 years from initial registration and part-time students within 7 years. It is possible to '**step off**' the programme and return later, as long as the maximum length of time is not exceeded.

The 3-year programme must be equally divided into 50% theory and 50% practice, and end with a 3-month period of clinical practice. It is usual that most of the 50% theory time takes place in the university, with some self-directed study. Normally the 50% practice time takes place in a variety of care settings in hospitals and the community. Up to 300 hours can take place in a university skills laboratory. In practice you will be required to experience 24-hour, 7-days a week opportunities.

At the time of writing, the NMC calls the first year of the pre-registration nursing programme, the **Common Foundation Programme (CFP)**. It is 12 months long and is the foundation on which the rest of the programme sits. It provides nursing students with learning opportunities in all four fields of practice (branches) and enables the acquisition and early development of essential nursing skills and knowledge.

See the online resource for this chapter where news of changes to the pre-registration programme will be explained after September 2011.

Entry to your chosen field of practice is by successful completion of the first-year outcomes required by your university, and by attaining the first-year NMC proficiencies (NMC 2004).

How the pre-registration programme is structured

Throughout the course you will be referred to as either being 'in theory', e.g. attending lectures, seminars or self-directing your own learning, or you will be 'in practice' being supervised by a mentor, experiencing nursing face-to-face with patients or clients, or undertaking other practice-based learning experiences, as agreed, such as a visit to a community learning disability or mental health service. When not in 'theory' or 'practice' you will be on annual leave, or possibly having a statutory day, such as a bank holiday. If you are sick, absent or on authorized leave, you will be doing so when you should either have been in theory, practice or on holiday.

Fact box: Modules or units of learning

Because what you need to learn to become a nurse is complex and varied, universities organize learning into discrete parts known as modules or units. These are independent units of study that combine to form your course. In year one you can expect to see titles such as 'Foundations of Nursing', or similar.

Figure 2.1 showing the theory/practice flow gives you an idea of how your first year may be structured. If you have it, refer now to the one for your course.

Your chosen field of nursing practice

We mentioned the four fields of nursing practice in the last chapter, and Chapter 11 says much more about them. On successful completion of the programme you will become a registered nurse (RN) followed by the field you studied, e.g. RN (Child). The four fields are of equal status.

A word about: Changing from your original field of practice choice

Most universities recruit students to join a particular field of practice and assume that students will not wish to change. In certain circumstances this may be possible, e.g. if you could do a direct swap with another student. If you wish to change, then tell your personal tutor as soon as you can. You may be asked to give good reasons so do your 'homework' before such a meeting is called.

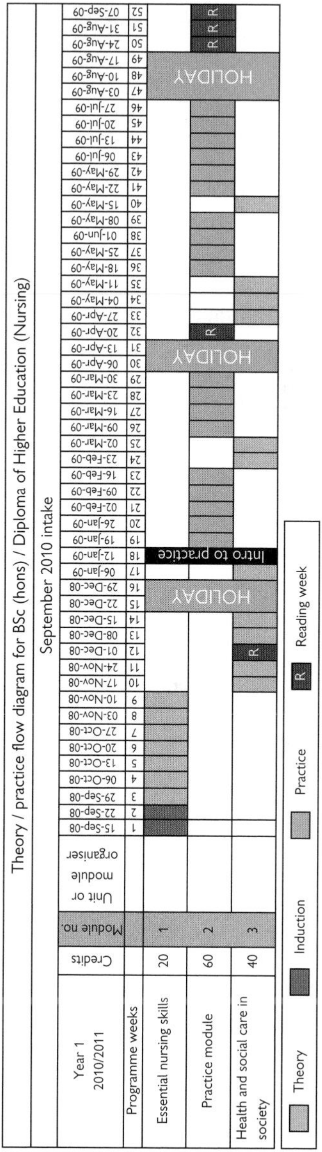

Figure 2.1 Example of a theory/practice flow diagram

Students: how many on the course?

How many students there are in your year group can depend on a variety of factors. For example, does the university have courses in all four fields of nursing at pre-registration? Some universities have one intake of student nurses every year, most often in September, others also have an additional mid-year intake in February or March. The autumn cohorts tend to be the largest.

If you are studying to be an adult nurse, invariably you will be a member of the largest group in your year. Adult tends to have the most students simply because more adult nurses are needed in the future workforce than nurses from the other fields of practice.

A word about: The number of students on your course

It is the future workforce planning needs of your local health care economy that determines the numbers of students being recruited for each branch. This is known as the **sponsored (or commissioned) number.**

Starting the course

We asked a number of current students what it felt like to start the course, what were some of the challenges they faced and how would they advise new nursing students to overcome them.

Student comment

"I think one of the most important things to tell new students, is not to worry, as everyone else is in the same situation, and to try to be proactive in meeting people and chatting to people in lecture theatres, although this does come with time. I am still meeting people now who I haven't spoken to before. It's important just to be friendly and to be yourself, as you're all in it together!"

"For the first couple of weeks I would want new students to understand the message that, even though there is a lot take in, and settle into, and the number of students you see every day can be overwhelming, this is probably one of the very few chances to get to know the place, make friends (and make use of the student union bar!) because soon it is shiftwork and deadlines, and the chances may be more limited than they were at the beginning of the year."

The next part of this chapter is going to tell you something about what to expect on the first day of your pre-registration nursing course and outlines some of the likely induction programme activities. As the students indicated, to feel rather overwhelmed is not unusual; this would be an entirely normal reaction. Even if you feel that others look more confident than you feel, they may just be masking their own 'first-day nerves'. People manage in different ways. What is true is that you are all facing the 3 years ahead, and being supportive to one another to settle onto the course is important.

Nurse teacher comment

"It may help you to know that the teachers in the nursing department at your new university are as pleased to see you arrive on your first day as you are to be there! They have invested a great deal already in getting you to this point and want to make you feel welcome and to support you to be successful."

Your first day at university

Whatever the circumstances, when large numbers of people arrive at the same time at any venue it requires careful organization. On arrival you will find people around to welcome you and point you in the right direction. If you do not immediately see them, look for signs directing you or follow the map/instructions that you have been sent. Planning your arrival for at least half an hour (if not more) before the start time is good. This will allow for delays or getting lost. It also minimizes the chances (and embarrassment) of arriving late. All universities manage their new intakes differently but reading the following will give you a feel for what to expect.

Once you have arrived someone will advise you of what happens next. Most likely this will be to direct you to a lecture theatre big enough to seat students from all the nursing branches and possibly from other courses as well (e.g. midwifery, physiotherapy or social work). As all students need to be given the same basic information on the first day, and during the first week, it is practical to get everyone together for this purpose.

Fact box: Where to go on the first morning

At some point *before* your first day, the university will have sent information to tell you where to go on your first morning, where to park (if relevant) and how much it will cost. Do not forget to take this information with you when you leave home.

Nurse teacher comment

"As CFP lead I organize the induction week and the welcome. My message always is to enjoy their first day. I stress the need to read everything we hand out. Many of the answers to questions new students have are in the programme handbook we give them. In a subtle way, I give the message right from day one, that they are adult learners, that this is a partnership."

Student comment

"For me the big lecture theatres and the number of students were the scariest things, when I was in sixth form we only had about 15 students in each class. The way I got over that at first was by making a small group of friends and sticking with them when in big lecture theatres."

Induction (introductory) activities

It is common practice to start the pre-registration nursing programme with an induction and your first day at university is the first day of this. This will be designed to ensure you have all the necessary basic information required for your time on the course and to help you settle, explore the campus and locate key places, such as classrooms. Some universities run extended induction periods, from 2 weeks up to 1 month. These give your teachers time to cover basics, such as study skills (numeracy, literacy, note taking and essay writing) to help prepare you for the course. They may also arrange a visit to the partner NHS Trust in which you will be doing your placements. A 1-week induction will just have time to cover the essentials you need to know, leaving topics (e.g. study skills) to be taught later.

A word about: What to take with you on your first day

You are advised to take with you all the information you have been sent so far plus a few pens, a diary, note book and file paper. A note book is handy for jotting down room numbers and names of people you meet, and a diary for any appointments not on your timetable (e.g. to meet your personal tutor). File paper is good for any important information that you may need to refer to in the future, as it can easily be filed later. Different coloured pens can be helpful to differentiate sessions on your timetable.

Fact box: Induction

Expect to be sitting listening to people talking, for what may feel like long periods of time. If you are usually active, this can be surprisingly hard at first; but you must get used to it for the weeks ahead sitting in lectures.

The first welcome may be quite formal and from someone you may not see a lot of in the future, such as the head of the faculty. Later, talks will be from the people who are directly involved in your programme.

At some time during induction, expect to listen to presentations about fire, health and safety matters and security. If you are resident on campus or elsewhere in university accommodation, it is likely there will be advice particularly directed to you. The well-being of you and your fellow students is obviously a priority for the university and listening to the advice given makes sense.

Representatives from occupational health, the university counselling service, the library and IT support may also speak during the induction programme. Other talks may be from an NHS Trust representative, from 'professional bodies', such as the Royal College of Nursing (RCN) and possibly from the students' union. Just sit back and listen and later read any information handed out.

Fact box: Paper

It is stating the obvious to say that paper is expensive, photocopying in large numbers costly. It follows that if you are given paper copies, the university believes it justifies the expense. It suggests they want you to read, file it and refer back to it when necessary. At some point you will also be directed to access information through virtual learning environments (such as Blackboard, Web CT, Moodle and so on).

Other likely induction-period activities

Registering with the university

This may be done online or involve filling in paper forms. This activity is important as it puts you on to the central university database, gives you your student number and makes you 'officially' a student of the university. You cannot start the course, logon to the computers, get your university email address, access the library, get your campus card or other ID, parking permit and so on, until you have done it. Expect to be asked for the name of someone who can be contacted in case of an emergency. Make sure you have the person's agreement, telephone number and address to hand. It is essential that you do not miss registration. If you have to for any reason, you must let a member of staff know so that alternative arrangements can be made.

Criminal Record Bureau (CRB) check

Note that this may happen during induction for some, for others before starting the course. Universities vary in their procedures.

All student nurses must declare any criminal conviction and, prior to interview, you will have agreed to a police check. Before you can start in practice you must be cleared by the CRB. You must provide evidence to confirm that you are who you say you are, and you will need, for example, to show a birth certificate or passport and to give details of your previous addresses. Your university will advise about this and how to complete the form.

Do not worry and assume that if you had a minor conviction some years ago this will prevent you from continuing on the programme. This is not necessarily the case. There will be a 'CRB counter signatory' or similar role title who will be able to advise you. The report back from the CRB is confidential. If you have had a minor conviction in the past, this should not become common knowledge to all your teachers, but only to the CRB counter signatory. If the CRB reveals a student with a record of certain serious convictions, they may be asked to leave the course or, if the CRB check was done in advance, they will not have been permitted to start.

Occupational health clearance

You are considered fit to go into practice following consultation with an occupational health department/health centre for screening. Like the CRB checks, this may happen either before you start your programme or soon afterwards. Failure to attend could mean a delay in going out to placements and later problems if you then run out of time to complete your placement hours. You could try to change your appointment if it clashes with a lecture or other session, but if you cannot do so, you must attend when asked. Occupational health nurses are there to support and help you, not to judge you.

Fact box: How to recognize which group or cohort you are in

For organizational purposes all groups must have a name, and it is customary to use the month and year the course started for this, e.g. 'September 2010'. A further means of splitting up the group is by future branch choice (e.g. child nursing) and programme followed, e.g. 'Jimmy Singh' Child Branch Degree, September 2010.

Uniforms

All universities manage the obtaining of uniforms differently. You will be advised of the arrangements for your university.

Brief overview of subjects covered during the CFP

Wherever you are studying, certain key areas will be taught in the CFP. Nurses must have an understanding of anatomy, physiology and biological science, and psychology and sociology, as applied to nursing and healthcare. You will need to understand theories of communication and how health and social services are organized, as well as the roles of professionals who make up the multi-disciplinary/multi-agency. Health promotion is another important area. Planning the care of your patients and clients will be taught, as well as the skills necessary to practise within professional codes and guidelines. Ethics, law and social policy are all subjects likely to be taught in the first year. Chapter 9 says more about the teaching and learning methods used in practice.

Other useful information

Students with a disability or special need

Most universities operate a philosophy of 'self-definition' of any disabilities and special needs of their students. In other words, it is your responsibility to draw to their attention to any particular needs you may have in order that the correct support systems can be put in place. The Disability Discrimination Act (2005), exists to protect people with disabilities and health conditions from unfair discrimination. The university has a duty in law to ensure its procedures are fair and to ensure that all disabled students can access all the areas that other students can.

For a pre-registration nursing student, the issue is whether once registered you would be capable of safe and effective practice, and it will be for your university and the commissioning NHS Trusts to consider individual circumstances. See the Equality and Human Rights Commission website http://www.equalityhumanrights.com or Equality Commission for Northern Ireland website http://www.equalityni.org for further information.

Students with dyslexia

If you know that you have dyslexia or other difficulties in learning, make this known to someone. Your programme handbook will explain what you need to do. Otherwise search your university website or ask to speak to the special needs representative in your department.

You must make your needs known in order to qualify for special examination arrangements or the Disabled Students Allowance (DSA) in order to receive any equipment for which you may eligible.

Mature students with dyslexia

Some very able students come to university having managed through school with their difficulties with writing without having been assessed for dyslexia. If it is suggested that you are assessed, it is in your best interests to do so in order that the necessary support systems can be put in place.

Evaluation of taught sessions

Nurse teachers always work to improve their programme and receiving feedback from the 'customers' is important. Sometimes evaluations are done in groups, with notes made as you respond to questions about what you have been doing. At other times you will be asked to complete an evaluation form. If you want your comments to be considered, it is important to fill these in carefully following the instructions given.

Student representation and participation on the course

Your group will be asked to nominate one or more student representatives. Most courses have staff/student meetings, where students talk about any difficulties or make other comments they have about the course. Student representatives also attend more formal meetings such as boards of study. These are rewarding roles, as you help shape how your course is developed and learn more about your programme from the teachers' perspective. It also looks good on your future curriculum vitae (CV) as well!

Summary

This chapter has explained a lot of what you need to know to make good start and to feel confident at the beginning of your programme. The next chapter is going to give you some advice about settling in.

Top tips

- At a minimum it is a 3-year course you are on. Take time to settle in.
- The first days can be nerve-racking: do not let it put you off your chosen career.
- Keep calm; deep, steady breathing helps.
- Remember, you are all newcomers in the same boat.
- Read all the paper work you are given.
- If, having done this (and looked at the department website), you still do not know the answer to your query—ask for help.
- The course is not a competition, everyone can do well.
- Make friends and support each other.

More advice

- You can find out much more advice to help you succeed in first year in *Nursing: Study and Placement Learning Skills* by Sue Hart from which this chapter has been taken.

Online resource centre

To make the most of the advice in this chapter, and to develop you knowledge and skills further, now go online to **www.oxfordtextbooks. co.uk/orc/hart/** to read important updates on nursing education and to explore useful websites, such as the Nursing and Midwifery Council, the Royal College of Nursing and more.

References

Disability Discrimination Act (2005) The Stationery Office, Norwich.

NMC (2004) *Standards of proficiency for pre-registration nursing education.* Nursing and Midwifery Council, London.

Further reading

Your programme handbook (read through electronically if you do not have a hard copy).

Start reading texts from your first unit reading list—they may include books such as:

Garrett L, Clarke A and Shihab P (2007) *Get ready for a&p for nursing & healthcare.* Pearson Education, UK.

Hinchliff S, Norman S and Schober J (eds) (2008) *Nursing practice and healthcare: a foundation text* 3rd end. Hodder Arnold: London.

Websites

Equality and Human Rights Commission: www.equalityhumanrights.com
Equality Commission for Northern Ireland: www.equalityni.org
NHS Student Bursaries Home Page: www.nhsbsa.nhs.uk
NMC website at: www.nmc-uk.org

Settling in

Settling in 38
Healthy you 40
Healthy finances 42
Who will support me to succeed? 46
How to find out what you need to know 50
Communicate, communicate! 52
Tips for success 56
Summary 60

Settling in

The aims of this chapter are:
- To provide tips for healthy living and healthy finances
- To understand how you will be supported
- To understand why good communication is very important
- To consider what you bring to the course

This chapter starts with a focus on you. If you want to care for other people, you must think about your own health, so that you are fit and well enough to do this. This chapter also explores how your attitude to the course and your behaviour can impact on your success (or otherwise). It stresses why communication with your teachers and mentors, who are there to support you, is so important. Whether you have just left home to start this course or you are a mature student with lots of life experience to draw on, some of the following may help. Take from it what you need.

Healthy you

The message is simple: if you are going to look after other people you need to look after yourself. Taking care of yourself will improve your chance of success on the course. What follows are some healthy living suggestions. If you feel you would benefit from reading these please continue. If not, go straight to "Healthy finances".

Eating

Breakfast is a must, plus least two more meals a day. If you are working on a busy unit or out in the community, looking after other people, you will need energy (which comes from your calorie intake). Aiming to eat five portions of fruit or vegetables every day is good. If you enjoy it, then eat fast food/junk food as a treat, not a lifestyle. Good for you, and inexpensive, are jacket potatoes, raw carrots, watercress, apples, bananas, eggs, wholemeal bread, yoghurt, nuts and tinned fish.

Watch your weight

Both being too slim or too heavy can be problematic. If you are failing to give yourself the necessary nutrients, you may lack the energy to perform well in practice and to concentrate in class. Conversely, if you carry a lot of extra weight, your body has to work harder to be active and you may be too weary to complete all your tasks. Occupational health will advise. See more information at the online resource.

Drinking

Try to drink at least six glasses of water a day. (If you do not like water, then dilute fresh fruit juice with water as a second-best option.) Enjoy alcohol, caffeine and sugar-rich carbonated drinks *in moderation only*. Some non-alcohol days are good for your liver. Restricting your use of caffeine as a stimulant is wise; use herb/fruit teas and decaffeinated coffee as alternatives.

Smoking

You do not need this book to tell you it is best not to; just read the packet. If you must do it, then do so in moderation only, and plan to stop. Seeing **www.nhs.uk/gosmokefree** will be helpful.

> ### Stop and think
>
> If you are on a hospital ward and you smoke during your break in practice, then you must use a breath freshener and wash your hands thoroughly to remove any smell before going near patients. If they are unwell, the smell of smoke from you could be difficult for them to cope with and may cause nausea.

Illegal drugs

The use of illegal drugs of any type can be dangerous for your health and, if discovered, put your future as a registered nurse in jeopardy.

Rest

Getting enough sleep and quiet time is essential. Before lectures, or going into clinical practice, aim to get as many hours sleep as you know is good for you. However busy you are, try to have at least 10 minutes every day doing nothing. Just stop, relax, recharge your batteries.

Stress

This is better dealt with using healthy, rather than unhealthy, techniques. Stress happens for a reason; getting help to work out why you are stressed is the best way to approach it. Avoidance, increased alcohol consumption or smoking to try to combat stress are not helpful, and may make matters worse (Davis *et al.* 2008).

Nurse teacher comment

"If you are upset by an incident in practice, talk to your mentor. It may also help to talk it through with friends (remembering confidentiality). If you are still worried, then talk to your personal (or liaison) tutor. See more about these roles below. If your difficulty is of a personal nature, then see a counsellor. Most universities offer free or reduced rate counselling services for students. Remember, it is not just having the problem but how you *deal with the problem* that is the issue."

Exercise

Exercise is good for your body and mind. If you are physically tired after a day in practice, a short walk in the fresh air, swimming, cycling or yoga would be good. Try to develop good habits and keep them.

Have fun

You are on a tough course, which at times will stretch you physically, intellectually and emotionally. Plan your time out as you plan your work. See a movie, spend time with friends and talk about things other than the course. Give yourself a break, and be surprised how much better you feel afterwards.

As a registered nurse you have a professional responsibility to deliver care based on the best available evidence (NMC 2008). You will be more credible when giving health-promotion messages to patients and clients if you look like you care for yourself.

Fact box: Sick leave

If you are unwell, you must take the time you need to recover. It is your responsibility to do so. But do note that your sick days on the course are recorded and will be asked for by a future employer as a matter of course. If you *abuse* sick days and take them here, there and everywhere, this is not going to give a good impression. In the worst case scenario the employer may give the staff nurse job to someone else with a better record. Nurses have got to be reliable. You may look like you are not!

Healthy finances

> **Student comment**
>
> "When the loan comes through at the beginning of term it's easy to feel like you have a lot of money. Try to resist the temptation to spend it all, as you will find you really need it in the last few weeks of every term!"

Many students struggle with their finances when on the pre-registration programme. Difficulties can result from taking a drop in income, a lack of experience in budgeting or, for some, from sending money overseas to support their family. A National Union of Students (NUS 2008) survey found that students underestimate the costs of university life by up to £500 per year, and that the majority have to do additional paid work.

Important note

Be alert that too much extra paid work can detract from your studies: *do not do so much that you risk failing the course.*

> **Student comment**
>
> "When out shopping I have a think about whether I *want* it or need it, and if the answer is *want*, then I don't buy it. It gets quite boring after a while but does the job. You can cut corners by taking a packed lunch everywhere you go."
>
> "I have a mortgage and two small children. The big thing is the child care, which you can claim for on the diploma programme. Although means-tested it helps massively and is in fact the difference between being able to do the course or not. It's important to budget and live within it. Make sure you get all the discounts, such as the council tax. Parking is a big issue with me. It was £160 per year at uni and then another £50 at hospital and then out in the community I had to pay to park in car parks. This takes a big wedge out of your money, so it's worth looking for places to park before practice. Car-sharing is a good way to save on petrol and sometimes the car park."
>
> "Doing some bank shifts for a hospital and a nursing home as a health-care assistant has helped me. You can apply for a student loan, which is paid back once you are working again. If you Google 'student loan' or go to your local council there is plenty of advice to be had. A bit of advice though is to make sure you do not encroach on uni time and work ... it's better to go without rather than not complete work or, worse still, fail something."

What help is available?

Many nursing students are eligible for an NHS bursary. Contact the NHS Grants Unit (**www.nhsbsa.nhs.uk/**) for information. You do not have to repay a bursary. If you are an older student with dependants, make sure that you are getting all the available allowances for which you are eligible from the NHS Grants Unit (such as tax credits or child care). Note the rules are different in the four countries, so you will need to check this.

Otherwise a student loan is one of the cheapest ways to support you through university. At the time of writing, these only have to be repaid once you are earning £15,000 at 3.8% interest. The current maximum is £4625, increasing to £6475 for London-based students. Anyone on an eligible course can get 75% of the maximum loan, the remainder being means-tested. It is possible to apply for a top-up from your local authority or the Student Loans Company (**www.slc.co.uk**).

Dependent on your household income and personal circumstances, it may be possible to get a maintenance grant (currently worth between £50 and £2835). Special support grants of up to £2835 are also available to fund child care, travel and equipment for the course. If you have a spouse or children, the child care grant, adult dependants' grant, the parents' learning allowance and the lone parents' grant are all means-tested grants available through the Student Loans Company or your local authority. You can also claim back essential travel costs, such as getting to placements (beyond £290). The disabled students allowance exists to cover additional costs you may have.

Most universities will have a hardship fund to which students with serious financial difficulties could apply for a loan. Some offer bursaries for students struggling financially, see 'student finance' at the **direct.gov. uk** website.

Nurse teacher comment

"If you are receiving an NHS bursary, you will be eligible to claim travel costs to and from your placements over certain miles (normally miles exceeding your home-to-uni-distance), either using your car or public transport."

See the money doctors!

This term refers to a training course sponsored by the Financial Services Authority to support university students to become 'financially capable'. Several universities have money doctors' courses. Your student services office or student union will advise.

Exercise 3.1

Find out if 'money doctors' are running courses at your university. If so, the best time to attend is early on, in the first year. Then you have more time, and also it helps to learn about good money management sooner rather than later.

Other money tips

Surfing the net looking for ways to save money will repay in saving the time you spend doing it.

Price-comparison websites are helpful for getting good deals for your mobile 'phone, computer, etc. (e.g. Gocompare.com, Uswitch or Compare and Buy at **www.guardian.co.uk**). Supermarket price-comparison sites (e.g. Mysupermarket.com) can guide you to the cheapest outlet for your basic foodstuffs. Money-saving expert websites (**www. moneysavingexpert.com**) also can be helpful. Always explore whether what you need is available through an online auction (such as eBay), rather than buying it new. Pick up discount vouchers when you see them and use the '20p off your next purchase' type offers. Even if you do not need them at the moment, buy non-perishable products when they are in a 2-for-the-price-of-1 offer. Look at **Raileasy.co.uk** or **Megabus.com** for good public transport deals. **Freebiesbank.co.uk** has free goods!

There is a lot you can do for yourself to settle on to the programme, but you will need the help and guidance of many people if you are going to be successful. What follows explains who's who and how this will happen.

Links to these can be found at the online resource.

Who will support me to succeed?

Some of the following you will get to know well, such as teachers and mentors. With others, such as support staff, placement officers and so on, your dealings will be mainly via email and telephone. The following explains the roles of people who will support you through the course.

Be aware that some of the following role titles may be slightly different where you are.

University-based support

Programme lead

Whatever their title, it is usual for one person to be responsible for the *entire* pre-registration programme. Find out the name of this person in case you need to contact them in the future.

Meet 12 busy nurse teachers

Special needs representative   Chair of the Examination Board

Module team member and library representative

CRB counter signatory

Department head

Field of practice lead

Director of studies

Professor of nursing

Personal tutor

Recruitment lead

Liaison teacher

Module leader

Figure 3.1 Nurse teachers' additional roles. Artist: Emma Heaton

University-based nurse teachers

Teachers have various job titles (tutor, lecturer, senior lecturer, principal or clinical lecturer). Ask at your university about the differences, as there is no standard definition. Nurse teachers will all be on the nursing register, will usually have higher education qualifications (such as a Masters degree) and normally will have done a course to qualify them to be a teacher. Some may have studied for a PhD (doctor of philosophy). Professors are experts in their own field and, along with senior nurse practitioners, lead the development of nursing. You may be taught some subjects by non-nurse teachers, such as sociologists, psychologists or biological scientists.

In many ways the term 'nurse teacher' does not do justice to the variety of the role these individuals perform. Many are involved in practice development, research and writing articles for journals and books. See below and Figure 3.1 to understand why they always seem so busy.

Personal tutor

It is usual for all students to have a named personal tutor (PT) who supports and advises a group of personal tutees. In some universities, a PT may offer support with regard to personal, as well as course-related, difficulties, if these are affecting your studies. Your PT will direct you to sources of advice. Personal tutors generally like to see their tutees by prior arrangement for an occasional one-to-one meeting, and at other times in a group. It is very important to have the contact details of your PT easily available; you never know when you may need to contact them. *You must contact your PT if you are having problems.*

Exercise 3.2

Find out all the important telephone numbers you will need to know: your personal tutor, the number to ring if you need to report sick, the library to renew books and put these in your 'phone or in a notebook. Today!

Do the same with email addresses on your computer.

Module or unit leaders

The programme will be organized into blocks of learning called modules or units. Module or unit leaders have personal responsibility for planning the content, organizing the timetable, devising the assessments, and **marking and moderating** written work. Also, they will liaise with external examiners and the examination office staff. Once the teaching is completed, they will evaluate the module and, based on the feedback, recommend developments to the module, to the programme management team, board of study or other group who oversee the course.

Module or unit teams

These teachers work with module leaders to deliver the module. All teachers will be members of one or more module or unit teams.

Field-of-practice leaders

These teachers must ensure that the branch for which they are responsible is represented in the first year, as well as in the second year and beyond. They must ensure there are sufficient learning opportunities to enable all the outcomes for year one to be met.

Link or liaison teachers (both terms used)

Most nurse teachers are also link tutors to designated clinical placement areas. Wherever you go in practice there should be a named 'link tutor'. Part of their role is to support students in situations where they may be experiencing difficulties.

Special needs representatives

These people ensure that students with disabilities and dyslexia or other additional learning needs are directed to get the extra support they need.

Lecturer practitioners

Some universities and NHS Trusts jointly appoint nurses to work some proportion of their time (often half) in practice and the remainder in nurse education. For example, a registered mental health nurse may work 2.5 days per week as a community psychiatric nurse (CPN) and 2.5 days as a mental health nurse teacher. If your personal tutor has such a post, you will need to know the hours they work.

University-based support staff

Nursing programmes could not be delivered without these people, who perform a range of duties. They prepare programme and module handbooks and ensure that they are available (hard copy or electronically, whichever system your uni is using). Other support staff will keep the department website up-to-date and prepare the timetables. You may have already been given a uniform and a badge and it is likely that members of the support staff were involved in organizing this to happen.

Placement departments

These people may be called 'placement officers' or something similar. In collaboration with nurse teachers they determine where you need to go in practice, make contact with the placement and prepare the list of allocations. These lists are sometimes referred to as 'change lists'.

Exams office staff

Yet another team of support staff run the examination office and, with the teachers, oversee all aspects of your programme assessments, the schedule of submission dates and organize the exam boards and ensure you get the result of your work on time.

Clinical practice-based support

Mentors

Mentors are often, but not always, nurses who have undertaken a mentor preparation course; they will guide, support, teach and assess you in your placements. As a student nurse, whenever you are out in a placement your named mentor is accountable for everything you do, although this does not stop the need for you to be personally accountable and responsible for your actions.

Exercise 3.3

You may also meet other staff with titles such as 'practice placement managers' or 'practice placement facilitators'. Find out what they do and how they can help you.

How to find out what you need to know

You will not succeed on the programme, and be where you need to be, unless you understand what information is essential and *where to locate* it. All universities manage information sharing differently. Most now have a student website, which will have pages for your group, your timetable, copies of lecture notes for pre-reading and so on. Sometimes essential information may be handed out in hard copy in lectures. For instance, you will *probably* be given a paper copy of a programme handbook early in the course and reading this will be a source of valuable information and advice.

Notice boards or plasma screens are used to display important information (e.g your class timetable) and alert you to any unexpected changes on the day, such as a cancelled lecture. It is a good habit always to check these on the days you are in the university.

Later in the course you will need to find out where you are going to for your placements, also where to look for the results of your examinations and assignments. Your teachers will explain where you can find this information (possibly on notice boards and/or the student website).

Communicate, communicate!

Keeping in touch with the university: some guidelines

Sometimes the uni may need to write to you at home with important information. It is *essential* that you notify the department of any change in your home address. *In the long run failure to do so may disadvantage you.*

Other information may come to you personally, or to the entire group by email. So make it your habit to check your university email inbox whenever you logon. Also, look at the student website for any 'news'.

If your university is using a virtual learning environment (such as Blackboard), also get used to logging-on there regularly.

There may be 'pigeon holes' where alphabetically by surname you can pick up correspondence addressed to you. If you are given one, check your pigeon hole regularly.

There will be times when you will need to contact the university, e.g. if you are unwell and need to miss a lecture. You may have to miss lectures for other reasons, such as a family illness or bereavement. How you need to manage these situations varies according to the circumstances. The following may be helpful:

- If you are unwell on the day of an examination *speak to someone in person before the start time of the exam*. If you are very unwell, ask someone to telephone on your behalf. If you do, and later provide a medical certificate, there is a chance that your non-attendance will be discounted (which is to your advantage). Failure to communicate your absence in good time may mean you are awarded zero. This means you would have to sit the examination as if you were doing it as a second attempt (you lose your first attempt).

- If you are unwell on a Monday, and know you will be away for a week at least, and are due to see your personal tutor on Friday, an email to explain the situation and apologize for not attending would be acceptable. You are allowing enough time to expect your PT to have read the email.

- If you are ill on a Monday morning and had been due to see your PT that afternoon, a telephone message (to their voicemail or via a member of the support staff) would be better.

We asked a nurse teacher to talk to us about communication with some (by no means all) nursing students. Although it is stating the obvious, you are more likely to get a response if, when leaving a voicemail message, you speak slowly and clearly, saying your first name, surname and cohort and explaining briefly why you are calling. If you want a reply, then give the number where you can be contacted by speaking slowly enough for it to be heard.

Nurse teacher comment

"As a teacher, it is difficult to hear a voicemail that says 'Hello, it is Jo. It's urgent. Please ring me back on 020?XX?342?'. Jo who? What was that number? I have listened three times and more sometimes and still cannot catch it. On the student database I go through everyone called Jo (Josephine? Joe?). Then I try the numbers, and work out who it might be and discover the student moved house a month ago and has not told us. I do not want to sound grumpy, but please do say to your readers how important communicating with us is!"

Communication in clinical practice

During the course you will need to be able to speak with patients, clients and their families, fellow students and your mentors. Ideally you need to be able to write clearly as well, so that essays and reports, etc. are unambiguous. You will need to listen well in order to understand what is being said and, where necessary, pass messages accurately. You need to be succinct (i.e. keeping to the point and not rambling) and have a good understanding of 'professional' and nursing terminology. Chapter 11 explains more about this.

Learn to be aware of the tone, rhythm, pronunciation and speed of your speech. You will need to use professional language in exchanges with mentors and teachers. Later you may be required to *interpret* (i.e. to re-word) messages into everyday language to help your patient understand what is being said. When nursing people who do not have English as a first language, or others who have learning or sensory disability, non-verbal language, sign language and other alternative means of communication are helpful.

Basic tips to aid all communication

Communication is enhanced by facing the person you are speaking to, this can be seen in Figure 3.2. If they are sitting down you do the same; if they stand, so do you. If the person is hard of hearing, be aware of this. They may ask you to stand to one side (e.g. their best ear). Some eye contact is good, but not staring. Try always to wait for the other person to finish speaking without interruption. You can show you have listened by summarizing what they said to you, e.g. 'Ok, I will come back in an hour with a hot drink for you'.

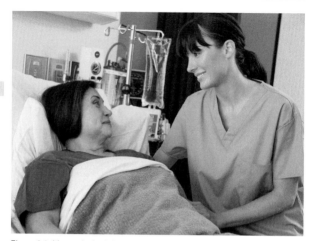

Figure 3.2 Notice the body language used by the nurse. ® iStockphoto

Emails

Never write anything in an email that you would not say to a person's face. Keep emails brief. Note that capitalized text CAN LOOK AS THOUGH YOU ARE SHOUTING. A similar effect can be given by writing in red.

Be professional

Although it is not unpleasant to receive an email from a student that says 'love Di, xxx' (yes, it does happen!), it is not the language that should be used between students and nurse teachers or mentors. Always use your university email address when on the course. If for some reason you need to use a home email, make sure the address is acceptable; keep 'sexygirl' or 'cuteguy' to your private life emails. (Again, yes, it does happen!)

Texts

Text messaging is not a useful way of communicating anything other than short messages. Not everyone knows what cul8r means, or I will b l8. Speaking to the person is better.

Mobiles

NEVER ring a mentor or nurse teacher from a mobile 'phone when you are driving, or speak to them unless you are 'hands free'. Remember the law and the safety of other road users, as well as yourself.

Telephones in practice placements

Chapter 10 has advice about how to manage this element of communication.

Tips for success

Your success (or otherwise) on the first year of the pre-registration nursing programme, is down to you. When you do well, the achievement is yours. If you do less well, blame others if you must, but 99.9% of the time, if you are honest, you will recognize your role in the situation. There is often a fine line between success and failure and often *it is an individual's own strengths that make the difference.* It helps to recognize what you bring to the course.

Determination

Your determination, ambition and the amount of energy you give to your studies will influence your results. How hard you are prepared to work to overcome obstacles you face will be influenced by how determined you are to succeed.

Attitude

According to Eiser and van der Pligt (1988) our 'attitude' is primarily evaluative (i.e. we assign a value to it). What will be your attitude toward the programme? If criticized, will you bear a grudge? Will you sometimes be 'closed' to learning? Or will you be willing to learn, enthusiastic and open to new ideas? If so, you will get more out of the course. Decide now that you will accept constructive criticism, and then grow from it and move on. Stay positive.

> ### Student comment
>
> "Some advice I was given was, when in a difficult situation, name at least one positive aspect of it. At the time I thought the tutor was barmy but having done it I can see a reason for it."

Assertiveness

If you are going to be successful, you will have to get what you need to succeed. If you are shy or lacking in confidence, then learning some assertiveness skills could help. Back and Back (1991) say that when a person behaves assertively they express their needs in a direct and honest way. But, importantly, it is done in a manner that does not violate (disregard) the rights of others. By contrast, when a person behaves *aggressively* they ignore or dismiss the needs of others. Non-assertive people fail to stand up for their own rights and can be disregarded by others. Consider learning more about assertiveness if you feel it would help you.

Please read the following exercise imagining you are in this predicament.

Exercise 3.4

You are on a hectic SCBU (special care baby unit) that is short-staffed. Your mentor Jon is busy nursing a sick baby girl and also supporting her understandably anxious family. You are feeling worried because you need Jon to sign your practice assessment paperwork as soon as possible or you risk submitting it late at the university, at the end of the week. How can you possibly ask Jon to put your needs before the needs of others?

Please stop reading for a moment and think about how you might approach this difficult situation. Now read the following advice. How does it compare with what you had thought to say?

Your aim is to ask Jon for what you need in a clear and direct way.

It is not a good idea to open the conversation apologizing, e.g. 'Jon I am very sorry to bother you, I see you are busy, I hope you don't mind?'; this is not a good opening line.

Find time when you can get Jon's attention. Speaking steadily and calmly be direct: 'Jon, I need to speak with you sometime today, please. It is about agreeing a time when we can meet so you can sign my assessment of practice document.'

Jon may agree a time with you at this point. If he does not, go on to give a reason for your request: 'Jon, it is very important that we plan a date to meet as my assessment is due in on Friday.'

Student comment

"Ask for help if you need it. I have found all university lecturers to be really helpful when I have needed advice. Also, when out in placement, other students (who are further ahead) have also pointed me in the right direction, showing me how to present my portfolio or answering questions about bits of work that I was not sure about. I know there is a danger in asking other students but most of the people I have asked have been really good at telling me what I needed to know. When one student started to tell me what I should and should not put in a reflection, after I had spent hours completing it, I just smiled sweetly and ignored her. Learn how to use the advice given."

Saying 'no'

You may find yourself in a situation where you feel you are being asked to do something you would do not wish to. Saying 'no' can be hard. We worry people will not like us, or that they may be angry or hurt, or feel that we are unkind.

> ### Exercise 3.5
> Marion, a fellow student, keeps suggesting you go with her for lunch, when really you would prefer to use the time in the library. Think of ways you could say 'no', and not hurt her feelings.

It would help here to keep your reply fairly short, but not abrupt. Avoid long explanations as to why you are saying no. It is important to be kind as you acknowledge the request made:

'Thank you for asking me Marion, but I need to go to the library now', is a direct, honest and clear response.

If she persists with the request, a sensitive and clear way to respond would be to say something like: 'It is thoughtful of you to ask me to join you, but I prefer to use my free time when I am here studying, so I can spend time with my family in the evenings.'

Negotiation

Skills in negotiation are needed when two or more people have conflicting needs. Sometimes you may need to negotiate with classmates or your mentor. The best negotiations end with a 'win/win' situation; where both parties feel that they obtained a satisfactory outcome. Important stages in negotiation are:

- Clarifying needs: be clear, direct and honest about what you need and why.
- Accepting needs: listen carefully, and value what the other person has to say: 'Ok, I accept that matters to you.' 'I see your need to do X'.
- Resolving needs: can be done by offering or asking for alternative suggestions—making agreements.

Values and beliefs: your own moral compass

The values and beliefs you have are important in your development as a nurse. If you value honesty, caring and kindness, and believe you should always do the best for patients and clients, and support your colleagues, by being a good team player, then you have a positive foundation on which to build. Know your weak spots and leave them at home!

Student comment

"I found it hard when I was splitting up with my partner and feeling upset a lot of the time. Some days I just had to take a deep breath and push myself to go into my placement. It would have been so easy to stay in bed. But now I know it was the best thing to push myself. It was a hard lesson, but you have to put other people first. When you are on duty, that's what this job is about. (I am with a gorgeous new man now, so it all worked out in any case!)"

Summary

You must look after yourself if you are going to be effective in your caring for other people and find the energy to do all that is expected of you on what is a demanding course. Support is available at all times and this chapter has introduced you to the main ways that this happens. Your success ultimately is down to you. Knowing and practicing the skills you need to succeed is important.

Top tips

- You and no one else is responsible for how well (or otherwise) you do on the programme.
- Who you are, and what you bring to the course, are important in determining your success.
- Being positive helps success.
- Communicate clearly—practice helps.
- Be assertive and clear in your interactions.
- Avoid compromising your success on the programme by doing too much additional paid work; budgeting helps.
- Make time to enjoy leisure pursuits and breaks.

More advice

- You can find out much more advice to help you succeed in first year in *Nursing: Study and Placement Learning Skills* by Sue Hart from which this chapter has been taken.

Online resource centre

You can find further advice and practical tips to assure your time on the course goes well by going online to **www.oxfordtextbooks.co.uk/orc/hart/** where you can find useful checklists, exercises and online tools for financial and personal well being.

References

Back K and Back K (1991) *Assertiveness at work: a practical guide to handling awkward situations*, 2nd edn. McGraw Hill International, Maidenhead, Berkshire.

Davis M, Robbins Eshelman E and McKay M (2008) *The relaxation and stress reduction workbook*. New Harbinger publications, Oakland, California.

Eiser RJ and van der Pligt J (1988) *Attitudes and decisions*. Routledge, London.

National Union of Students (2008)
http://www.nus.org.uk/en/Advice/Money-and-Funding/Higher-Education/The-true-cost-of-university

Nursing and Midwifery Council (2008) The code: standards of conduct, performance and ethics for nurses and midwives.
http://www.nmc-uk.org/Nurses-and-midwives/The-code/

Further reading

enworthy N, Snowley G and Gilling C (2001) *Common foundation studies in nursing*, 3rd edn. Churchill Livingstone, Edinburgh.

Lewis M (2005) *The money diet: the ultimate guide to shedding pounds off your bills and saving money on everything*, 2nd edn. Vermilion, London.

Websites

Martin Lewis, Money-saving expert: www.moneysavingexpert.com

NHS Choices website to support people who want to stop smoking cigarettes: http://smokefree. nhs.uk/

NHS Student Bursaries Home Page: www.nhsbsa.nhs.uk

Student Loans Company: www.slc.co.uk

Chapters 2–3 from
Clinical Nursing Skills: Core and Advanced

Edited by

Ruth Endacott

Professor of Critical Care Nursing,
Plymouth University and La Trobe University,
Melbourne, Australia

Phil Jevon

Clinical Skills Lead, Manor Hospital,
Walsall, UK

Simon Cooper

Associate Professor, Monash University,
Australia

OXFORD
UNIVERSITY PRESS

Communication skills

Definition 66
It is important to remember 67
Prior knowledge 67
Background 68
Context 74
Procedure 78

Definition

Communication is the two-way process of giving and receiving information, both verbally and non-verbally. It is a key and essential aspect of nursing care. Communication is a core dimension in the *NHS Knowledge and Skills Framework* (Department of Health 2004) and within the Nursing and Midwifery Council (NMC) *Code of Standards* (Nursing and Midwifery Council 2008). Both refer to the requirements for communication with a range of people (colleagues, external agencies, and patients) on a variety of simple and complex matters. The Quality Assurance Agency (2006: 6) also lists communication as a key subject benchmark, stating that health and social care staff should be able to:

- 'Make active, effective and purposeful contact with individuals and organizations, utilizing appropriate means such as verbal, paper-based and electronic communication.
- Build and sustain relationships with individuals, groups and organizations.
- Work with others to effect positive change and deliver professional and service accountability.'

Nurses must be able to assess, identify, and prioritize patients' needs, facilitate the expression of feelings, and build a relationship for effective care (Dougherty and Lister 2008).

It is important to remember:

- Communication requirements vary dependent on the situation.
  The nurse must be prepared to adapt to the needs of the situation.
  Examples include breaking bad news, cultural differences in
  communication, communicating with children or the elderly, or the
  specific requirements of those with physical or learning disabilities.
- Communication competence varies depending on an individual's
  character and background. It is central to the patient's experience
  and therefore essential that all nurses throughout their career reflect
  on and (where appropriate) develop their communication skills as an
  integral part of professional development.

Prior knowledge

Prior to reading the following sections, consider your communication
experiences to date, how these have influenced your development, and
the skills you will need to develop in your nursing career. For example:
- How do children communicate?
- Do nurses need to adapt their communication skills for the working
  environment?
- What influences the development of communication styles?
- What forms of communication are there?
- Who are nurses required to communicate with?
- What are the communication barriers?

Background

Effective communication in the health care setting improves recovery rates and reduces pain and complications rates (Wilkinson et al. 2003). However, poor communication is cited in many NHS complaints (Bayer 2003). Catherine McCabe (2004) found that patients felt that nurses' communication skills needed to be improved, as they concentrated more on clinical tasks than talking to patients. She emphasizes the importance of 'patient centred communication' and its central role in delivering quality patient care.

Models of communication

A number of communication models have been proposed, with descriptions of the processes and templates for best practice. Ellis et al. (2003: 5) describe the basic components of communication (shown in Figure 2.1) as being context specific, i.e. they should change depending on the situation. The sender (patient, nurse, doctor) aims to convey a message to a receiver who may or may not interpret it as intended. The message may have been misread due to contradictory body language, misheard or not heard at all, or generally 'lost in translation'.

Effective communicators rely on feedback from the receiver (two-way communication) requiring understanding or additional messages from the sender. Good communicators tend therefore to send messages in a consistent and clear way, their non-verbal and verbal language conveying the same message. For example, 'How are you feeling today Mrs Jones?' is said with empathy and concern, while waiting patiently at the bed for a reply, and then responding appropriately.

Ley (1988) developed a useful evidence-based model for improving patient communication and for improving medication compliance rates. Compliance rates can be quite low, for example Haynes et al. (2005) suggest that those prescribed self-administered medication may take less than half their prescribed medication. Ley found that where understanding and memory were enhanced, patients were more satisfied with their care and more likely to comply with treatment.

Understanding and memory can be improved by avoiding jargon, simplifying language, and highlighting key issues at the start of the consultation, at the end, and where they are important, a process known as primacy, recency, and importance. Written explanations in the form of patient information or mail and e-mail reminders are also important, as well as telephone texting (texting4health 2008). Finally, satisfaction can also be improved by reducing waiting times, maintaining a friendly attitude, and allowing patients to tell their story in their own words and to express their worries and expectations.

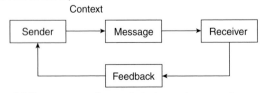

Figure 2.1 The components of communication in a nursing context; the nurse may act as the 'sender', e.g. explaining to the patient what a procedure will involve, or as the 'receiver', e.g. listening to a patient's description of their pain symptoms.

A key model and set of skills for managing a patient consultation have been produced in the form of the Calgary–Cambridge Guides (Silverman et al. 2005). This model has been well researched and evaluated. The general principles can be used for nurse assessments with patients. Stages of consultation/assessment are listed as:

- Initiating the session' – where a rapport is built and the reasons for the meeting established.
- Gathering information' – for an exploration of the patient's problems, using skills such as listening to the patient's own story and identifying concerns and expectations.
- 'Building a relationship' – through appropriate verbal and non-verbal behaviour.
- 'Explanation and planning' – through the provision of information and shared decision-making.
- 'Closing the session' – with reference to further action and planning for unexpected outcomes (safety netting).

In the following sections we break down the stages of communication into three phases: the set, dialogue, and closure (Mackway-Jones and Walker 1998).

- 'Set' is the preparation phase – reading the patient's notes, introductions, ensuring that the patient and/or family are comfortable, etc.
- 'Dialogue' is the active communication stage, involving, for example, listening skills, verbal and non-verbal skills, and open and closed questioning.
- 'Closure' is the summary phase, with checks on understanding and safety netting.

Set

Where possible the nurse should become familiar with the patient's history prior to any meeting and should be updated on their condition as long as they remain in the nurse's care. An applicable amount of time should be allocated to each meeting to ensure that it is not rushed.

However, where unavoidable interruptions occur, the patient should be reassured of the nurse's return. Special consideration should be given to assessing communication needs, which are categorized by Hilton (2004) as:

- Physical aspects such as hearing, talking, and writing skills.
- Psychological issues such as anxiety, intelligence, and anger.
- Sociocultural aspects in relation to dialect, first language, and cultural and religious issues.
- Environmental constraints such as temperature, noise, safety, and physical barriers to communication such as beds and desks.

In establishing an initial relationship, the nurse should greet the patient (and family if applicable), introduce themselves, and explain their role. Where required, informed consent should be gained for treatment (Dougherty and Lister 2008). Appropriate dress should be worn and the nurse should use a friendly and professional approach, aiming to make patients feel welcomed and supported (Pendleton et al. 2003). Particular attention should be paid to the environment, ensuring that the patient is comfortable, warm, and safe, and that privacy and confidentiality are maintained, especially in busy wards where curtains are the only dividers.

The reason for the meeting should be identified and the consultation developed through open questions, e.g. 'What is the problem today?' or 'How can I help you?' and, where appropriate, through closed questions such as 'How old are you?' and 'Where does it hurt?' (Hilton 2004, Silverman et al. 2005). The nurse should encourage the patient to discuss their problems/issues openly while listening closely, maintaining an awareness of their emotional state, and 'showing empathy, concern and optimism' (Kruijver et al. 2001).

Dialogue

Once the ice is broken and the initial introductions are completed there are a number of communication elements that the nurse should be aware of. The ability to develop rapport is important; treatment goals are more likely to be achieved when the patient is comfortable and relaxed, and where the nurse is non-judgemental, values opinions, and acknowledges individuals' views.

This 'accepting response' is described by Silverman et al. (2005) as a process of acknowledgement. It is achieved through the reiteration and clarification of patients' concerns (using comments such as 'So, you're concerned that the tablets have given you an ulcer') and by acknowledging their rights ('I can see that you may want to get a second opinion on that') or by giving them the 'space' to say more, through appropriate pauses and non-verbal behaviour.

This 'acceptance' does not imply agreement but places a value on patients' beliefs. For example, it would be inappropriate to dismiss patients' concerns with a comment such as 'There is nothing to worry about,' and more appropriate to acknowledge their concerns by stating 'I can understand why you are worried; we will make sure we check it out and let you know as soon as possible.'

A second and essential element is the ability to listen actively and demonstrate or clarify that we have 'heard' our patients correctly. In diabetes research, patients claimed that their knowledge about their condition and its management was not heard by health care professionals (Pooley et al. 2001). Hawkins and Lindsay (2006) highlight the significance of listening to patients' stories to enhance health professionals' understanding and to improve patients' 'physical and psychological healing'.

Gask and Usherwood (2002) describe a number of communication and active listening skills that should be used during a consultation. These include:

- Open and closed questions. Questions that encourage patients to expand on their answer but give 'yes' or 'no' responses where applicable.
- Checking. Repeat back patient responses to ensure joint understanding.
- Demonstrating empathy. For example, 'I am so sorry, this is clearly a concern to you.'
- Facilitation. Encouraging patient responses by non-verbal responses, e.g. nodding, or by verbal responses, e.g. 'Yes – and then what?'
- Offering support. Questions such as 'How can I support you with this condition?'
- Legitimizing feelings. Expressing your concern and understanding about the problem.

- Negotiating priorities. Decide, with the patient, the key priorities for their care.
- Summarizing. Clarify and summarize your agreement with the patient prior to closing the consultation.

A key element of communication is the non-verbal component (Ellis *et al.* 2003, Dougherty and Lister 2008), which includes your own and the patient's non-verbal behaviour. When working with patients, think about how they respond to you, bearing in mind cultural differences. Consider the following:

- Their body language and personal distance – do they move their chair away from you, or are they reluctant to sit down?
- Level of eye contact (Ruusuvuori 2001). Do they avoid your gaze? Do they constantly look around?
- What is their facial expression/gaze like?
- What are their voice, tone, inflection, and volume like?
- Do they have an open or closed posture – for example do they look relaxed and casual or do they have tightly folded arms and face away from you? Do they avoid your touch?
- Are they well dressed and groomed or do they look dishevelled and unclean?
- How are they moving? Are they slow and lethargic or is their gait awkward or shuffling?

As a nurse, consider how you may need to adapt your behaviour for specific situations. For example, nurses in elderly care have been found to display more non-verbal behaviours, such as touch, smiling, and patient-directed gaze, than community nurses (Caris-Verhallen *et al.* 1999).

Barriers to effective communication skills

Environmental factors can have major influences on the way we communicate. In hospitals and nursing homes, nurses who care for the elderly have been found to use communication as a means of maintaining power over vulnerable patients (Brown and Draper 2003). Chant *et al.* (2002) found that nursing work and high stress levels can act as 'barriers to empathy and communication skills implementation', while Yam and Rossiter (2000) refer to the hierarchical nature of health care and how this may have negative impacts on communication and patient care. Environmental influences and interruptions, e.g. phones, children, and door bells, may also hinder effective communication.

Throughout all phases, but particularly during the dialogue, consider how communication can be hindered. Think about privacy issues and the patient's level of anxiety, for example are they tachycardic, hypertensive, or perspiring (Grandis *et al.* 2003)? Are there physical restrictions to communication, for example a tracheostomy, or perhaps the patient has had a laryngectomy? Request a translator if the patient or family are non-English speakers (many health providers maintain a list of foreign language speakers for this purpose).

Avoid the use of medical jargon and think about your speech rhythm, pace, emphasis, intonation, pitch, and tone. These are known as paralinguistic features ('features of the spoken message that are not contained in the message alone,' Ellis *et al.* 2003) and care must be taken to ensure that the patient does not misinterpret your meaning. For example, depending on the word emphasis, 'I will see you in the ward at 10 o'clock' may be considered a command to be in the ward at 10 o'clock, or alternatively a friendly and reassuring promise of your return.

It is important to remember that there may be a number of patient-related communication barriers, which Park and Song (2004) list as:

- Tiredness.
- Pre-health conditions (physical disability, poor hearing or sight, impaired levels of understanding).
- Life stresses related and unrelated to the illness.
- A short attention span.
- Low education levels.
- Differing social norms.
- Lack of trust.
- Accent issues.
- The withholding of information.
- Generation gaps.

In summary, Silverman et al. (2005) describe the key elements of the 'dialogue' as building a relationship and exploring of the patient's problems, including encouraging them to tell their own story, using open and closed questions, listening, picking up on verbal and non-verbal clues, and clarifying and checking on the story. Explanations should be clear and provided in small 'chunks', with appropriate use of repetition and checks on patient understanding, aiming for a shared decision by the end of the consultation.

Closure

Appropriate summing up, emphasis, checks on understanding, and future plans are the final essential elements of any patient communication episode. It is important that this phase is relatively short and sharp to ensure that the key elements of the communication remain salient.

Silverman et al. (2005) have again produced a very useful template for closing a consultation, suggesting that the 'next steps' should be discussed and safety issues should be raised, covering what to do if the plan is not working and how to seek help (safety nets). Sessions should be summarized with final checks on agreement, plans, and questions.

Where applicable, documentation should be completed, ideally in a multidisciplinary format (Dougherty and Lister 2008) to ensure that all health professionals are kept up to date. Finally, again where applicable, close attention should be given to handover procedures; for example, in the Accident and Emergency setting, Jenkin et al. (2007) found that listening skills, repetition, and a phased approach to handover are important.

A British Medical Association (2004) report also concludes that multidisciplinary handovers are an important element of good communication and that effective handovers are vital for patient safety – safe handovers = safe patients.

As Information Communication Technology (ICT) develops, the traditional models of communication will need to be reviewed. Health care providers are rapidly investigating how ICT can be utilized in improving health care. Wahlberg et al. (2003) discuss the development of 'telephone nurses' and the prospect of e-mail and virtual nurses. This study highlights the importance of supporting nurses who are delivering health care without direct visual contact and the impact this has on telephone nurses' ability to make informed decisions.

These ICT developments bring with them different communication cultures and a requirement for training and development. For example, nurses will need to adapt their approach on the phone to draw out information and to focus on the problem, while being reassuring and confident. In fact, Wahlberg et al. (2003) found that 'nurses seemed to lack confidence in their competence' when delivering telephone-based health care, which may be due to the lack of visual contact and communication feedback issues.

Context

In the communication setting there are a number of special considerations that the nurse should be aware of. Below an outline of these is all that is possible, as in all of the following situations there will be individual and context-specific requirements.

Learning disabilities

Key considerations for patients with learning disabilities are their mode of communication and level of understanding (Grandis *et al.* 2003). Their mode of communication includes their likes and dislikes, ways of expressing discomfort and pain, sign language, and level of self-help. The level of understanding and comprehension will influence how the nurse structures information for the patient, and the degree of professional support required.

It may, for example, be necessary to refer the patient for speech therapy or request guidance from a learning disability nurse. As Grandis *et al.* (2003: 213) suggest, 'the responsibility here lies with the nurse to find a suitable and appropriate means of communication in order to establish a mutual frame of reference.'

Workplace violence

Communication is a two-way process, and patients and colleagues have an equal responsibility to communicate with you in an appropriate manner. However, violence in the workplace is increasingly common (Department of Health 2001, International Labour Organization *et al.* 2005), especially in the A & E setting. Hilton (2004: 168) lists four 'A's for managing aggression, with the objective of awareness and avoidance wherever possible:

- *Awareness* of the likelihood of aggression. For example, patients who have taken drink or drugs, or those who portray unusual or threatening body language.
- *Alertness* to situations and changing moods.
- *Avoidance* if at all possible; being aware of the patient history or the presenting case.
- *Appropriate* and prompt responses. For example, carrying of personal attack alarms and ensuring that there is an escape route and police support.

Braithwaite (2001) also discusses ways of managing aggression, including body language, assertiveness, and diffusion techniques, which Bibby (1995) describes as the calming, reaching, and controlling stages. These stages consist of: 'calming' by talking and listening in an unthreatening posture; 'reaching' the aggressor by encouraging them to explain their grievances; and 'controlling' by working together, setting joint, realistic agreements, and admitting mistakes where applicable.

Breaking bad news

Breaking bad news is one of the most difficult and emotional experiences in the nurse's role and is often poorly managed by health professionals (Dias et al. 2003). Faulkner and Maguire (1994) suggest that health professionals tend to 'block' the emotional flow by, for example, ignoring cues, selective attention, inappropriate encouragement, giving premature and false reassurance, and switching topics.

The Resuscitation Council (UK) (2006) provides comprehensive guidance suggesting that wherever possible, bad news should be delivered face to face in a private, quiet, and homely setting without fear of interruption. Key issues for consideration are:

- Where possible, take time to prepare yourself before going into the meeting and, if available, take a colleague with you.
- Allocate a suitable amount of time, so that the exchange is not rushed.
- Check that you are talking to the correct relatives and exchange introductions.
- Maintain eye contact and be direct, honest, and sensitive throughout.
- Give accurate and clear explanations, avoiding the use of terminology, e.g. 'Her heart has stopped', instead of 'She has had a cardiac arrest.' Say '. . . he has died', instead of euphemisms such as '. . . he has gone to a better place.'
- Be prepared for questions and a wide variety of emotions and use touch if it feels right.
- Avoid platitudes such as 'I know what it feels like.'
- Explain and discuss with the family what will happen next and identify any culturally specific requirements, for example the management of the body after death.

Cultural considerations

Nurses deliver health care to a wide range of patients/clients from a wide range of cultural backgrounds. Nurses need to be aware of and respect cultural differences and recognize potential weaknesses in traditional communication methods. Rhodes and Nocon (2003) outline the differences in communication in ethnic minority communities and report that there are gaps in communication when interpreters are used. For example, the interpreter may not speak the dialect, may miss critical information, may lack rapport, or may not pass on information using caring and applicable language. For interpreters to be effective, they need to be integrated within the health care service and gain an understanding of the concerns of patients/clients. However, such integration may prove difficult in rural areas with small ethnic minority communities. It is therefore important to be aware of the services available in each area, for example refugee centres or relevant ethnic community groups.

The elderly

Communicating with the elderly may take time and patience. As with all patients, but especially with the elderly, you should check their previous health care records to determine if their condition will affect their ability to understand and respond to you, for example, if they have had a stroke, or have diabetes or dementia. It is then important to establish if the elderly person can hear, see, and understand you.

At all times, avoid behaviour that may be interpreted as patronizing, for example speaking to the individual as if they were a child or carrying out procedures without explanation or permission. Brown and Draper (2003) demonstrated that it is common within elderly health care for nurses to use 'accommodation speech', defined as being simplified, projected in a high pitched tone, and involving increased use of questions, imperatives, and repetition. La Tourette and Meeks (2001) emphasized the need to listen to the elderly and found that nurses were rated more highly when they used non-patronizing speech.

Finally, there is some evidence that technology may help the elderly. For example, Savenstedt et al. (2005) found that video conferencing had a positive effect on elderly patients suffering from dementia.

Interdisciplinary/interprofessional working and teamwork

Key to team building and communication within health care is communication between the professions (Molyneux 2001), a process known as interprofessional working. Interprofessional working is described by the Centre for the Advancement of Interprofessional Education (CAIPE 2002) as 'occasions when two or more professions learn with, from and about each other to improve collaboration and the quality of care'.

Of course an interprofessional approach should be adopted even where the individual is not a formal member of a 'team'. The need to communicate well with your colleagues, as well as your patient, is critical to the continued development of and improvement in patient care (Ginsbury and Tregunno 2005). For example, poor communication between midwives and medical staff can lead to an increase in mortality rates (Revill 2004). Good communication practices between professionals, on the other hand, improve discharge planning (Pethybridge 2004), and in multidisciplinary teams where trained supervisors are allocated to each team, there are improvements in cohesion, joint decision-making, and communication (Hyrkas and Appelqvist-Schmidlechner 2003). Training also makes a difference to communication skills; for example, leadership training improves workplace performance (Cooper 2003).

It is important to remember that the communication skills used with colleagues may differ from the skills used with patients. However, there are core competencies for interprofessional working that are relevant to any communication episodes (CAIPE 2002):

- Equity – all contributions are valued.
- Respect differences.
- Confidentiality.
- Avoid or explain jargon.
- Check understanding.
- Identify mutual goals and where there are differences.
- Discuss the challenges of collaborative working.
- Identify a strategy to deal with disagreements.

Procedure

Box 2.1 lists the key requirements for effective communication. Note that the stages and emphasis may change depending on the situation.

Reflection and evaluation

Reflect on each communication episode you've been involved in and think about the following issues.

- Did you make the patient feel welcome and supported?
- Were you aware of the patient's emotional state?
- Did you encourage the patient to 'open up' and raise any problems and issues?
- Did you recognize and value cultural diversity?
- Did you consider treatment options and agree a plan?
- Did you identify a multiprofessional patient care pathway, where applicable?
- Did you develop a rapport by:
  - Being non-judgemental?
  - Acknowledging that the patient is an individual and has a right to their view?
  - Valuing the patient?

Further learning opportunities

Communication is improved with practice so develop your skills in role play scenario situations with your colleagues. Where communication is likely to be challenging, for example breaking bad news, observe an experienced colleague first and ask for their support on later occasions to develop your competence and confidence.

Reminders

As you practise talking to patients/staff and build your communication skills, remember the following points:

- Communication is critical to the patient experience.
- Adopt a patient-centred communication approach.
- Be culturally aware in your approach and acknowledge that in 'translation' your empathetic approach may be lost. It is important therefore to use your non-verbal communication skills to demonstrate concern and openness.
- Actively listen to your patients, 'hearing' what they say and 'seeing' how they feel.
- Ensure excellent communication skills are adopted with your colleagues.
- Make sure you value communication exchanges and seek support where there are difficulties.

Box 2.1 The key elements of each phase of communication

Set

Preparation

Consider the context of the forthcoming communication by:
- Reading the patient's notes and records.
- Communicating with the multidisciplinary team.
  Will it involve patients who have:
- Learning disabilities?
- Understanding or memory problems?
- Specific language requirements?
- Cultural differences?

Or patients who are:
- Elderly or infirm?
- Angry or violent?

Anticipate and rapidly assess communication issues:
- Hearing.
- Verbal communication.
- Anxiety levels.

Lead in

Prepare the environment:
- Personal dress/uniform.
- Temperature.
- Seating.
- Privacy.
- Comfort.

Initiate the session:
- Greet – introductions and preferred names.
- Consent to treatment (where applicable).
- Identify the key issues.
- Jointly plan the agenda.

Dialogue (active communication)

Build a rapport by:
- Being non-judgemental.
- Valuing opinions.
- Acknowledging views.
- Accepting and acknowledging concerns.
- Active listening (maintaining an open posture, eye contact, attention, and waiting and pausing).
- Using open and closed questions.
- Being sensitive and supportive.

Consider your own and the patient's verbal and non-verbal behaviour:
• Personal space.
• Eye contact.
• Posture (open or closed?).
• Movement.
• Dress and grooming.
• Voice, tone, inflection, and volume.

Maintain a structured approach by:
• Considering the sequence of the discussion.
• Exploring problems and issues through the patient's story, using listening skills and open and closed questions.
• Restricting the use of medical terminology.
• Supplying applicable information.
• Repeating information.
• Explanation and feedback.
• Reinforcing information with written and illustrative feedback (e.g. using an anatomical model or showing an X-ray).
• Emphasizing and highlighting key issues at the start and end of the conversation.

▶**Patient scenario**
Consider what you should do in the following situations, then turn to the end of this section to check your answers.

1. Patient care advice
Miss Kosovich has recently been diagnosed as diabetic. You are responsible for advising her on her diet. However, Miss Kosovich is very outgoing, loves drinking and smoking, and is extremely depressed that her lifestyle may change. You notice from her records that she has been given health promotion advice but that she appears to be ignoring it. She has collapsed four times during the past month after not taking her insulin and drinking alcohol in excess. How are you going to deal with Miss Kosovich?

2. Patient referral
Mr Dorrington has missed three appointments but managed to turn up today. However, he appears disorientated and his behaviour concerns you. He keeps jumping up and down saying that people are following him. You are a nurse who is advising him on his back pain. What should you do?

3. Communication with colleagues
You are a nurse attending a meeting to discuss one of the patients on the rehabilitation ward where you work. The senior registrar is at the meeting, together with the physiotherapist. The senior registrar and the physiotherapist are discussing the patient's health care and use terms you are not familiar with. You are the lead nurse for this patient's care. How would you approach this situation to ensure maximization of patient care?

4. Patient assessment

Miranda, a frequent attendee, arrives in Alison's (a nurse practitioner) office concerned about numbness in her left hand. Alison ascertains that she has had the symptoms for a week. After a full examination she refers Miranda to her GP for further investigations. She is concerned that Miranda may have the early signs of multiple sclerosis.

Miranda does not keep the GP appointment but returns to Alison's office a few months later complaining of fatigue and feeling more emotional than usual, crying over the smallest issues. Alison focuses on these issues and suggests a number of stress management techniques.

A few days later, while at work, Miranda suddenly finds the numbness in her hand has returned but now also includes her face, and she is unable to focus due to blurred vision. She immediately arranges an appointment with her GP. Her GP is concerned that Alison has not mentioned Miranda and her previous visits. He immediately refers her for further investigations to a colleague who specializes in conditions that affect the nervous system.

Website

🖳 **http://www.oxfordtextbooks.co.uk/orc/endacott**
You may find it helpful to work through our short online quiz and additional scenarios intended to help you to develop and apply the skills in this chapter.

More skills

You can find clear explanations and step by step instructions for more clinical skills in *Clinical Nursing Skills: Core and Advanced* edited by Endacott, R., Jevon, P., and Cooper, S., from which this chapter has been taken.

References

Bayer A (2003). Telling older patients and their families what they want to know. *Reviews in Clinical Gerontology*, **13**(4), 269–72.

Bibby P (1995). *Personal safety for health care workers*. Ashgate, Aldershot.

Braithwaite R (2001). *Managing aggression*. Routledge, London.

British Medical Association (2004). *Safe handover: safe patients. Guidance on clinical handover for clinicians and managers*. British Medical Association, London.

Brown A and Draper P (2003). Accommodative speech and terms of endearment: elements of a language mode often experienced by older adults. *Journal of Advanced Nursing*, **41**(1), 15–21.

Caris-Verhallen WMCN, Kerkstra A, and Bensing JM (1999). Non-verbal behaviour in nurse–elderly patient communication. *Journal of Advanced Nursing*, **29**(4), 808–18.

Centre for the Advancement of Interprofessional Education (2002). [online] http://www.caipe.org.uk/ accessed 27/02/07.

Chant S, Jenkinson T, Randle J, and Russell G (2002). Communication skills: some problems in nursing education and practice. *Journal of Clinical Nursing*, **11**(1), 12–21.

Cooper SJR (2003). Does LEO roar: an evaluation of the Leading Empowered Organisations leadership development programme. *Nursing Standard*, 14 Feb, 33–9.

Department of Health (2001). National Task Force on Violence Against Social Care Staff – Report and National Action Plan [online] http://www.dh.gov.uk/en/Publicationsandstatistics/Publications/PublicationsPolicyAndGuidance/DH_4010625 accessed 18/08/08.

Department of Health (2004). *The NHS Knowledge and Skills Framework (NHS KSF) and the development review process. Appendix 2: core dimension 1: communication*. Department of Health Publications, London.

Dias L, Chabner BA, Lynch TJ, and Penson RT (2003). Breaking bad news: a patient's perspective. *The Oncologist*, **8**, 587–96.

Dougherty L and Lister S (2008). *The Royal Marsden Hospital manual of clinical nursing procedures*, 7th edition. Blackwell Publishing, Oxford.

Ellis RB, Gates B, and Kenworthy N (2003). *Interpersonal communication in nursing. Theory and practice*, 2nd edition. Churchill Livingstone, London.

Faulkner A and Maguire P (1994). *Talking to cancer patients and their relatives*. Oxford University Press, Oxford.

Gask L and Usherwood T (2002). ABC of psychological medicine. *BMJ*, **324**(7353), 1567–9.

Ginsbury L and Tregunno D (2005). New approaches to interprofessional education and collaborative practice: lessons from the organisational change literature. *Journal of Interprofessional Care*, **1**, 177–87.

Grandis S, Long G, Glasper A, and Jackson P (2003). *Foundation studies in nursing. Using enquiry-based learning*. Palgrave Macmillan, Basingstoke.

Hawkins J and Lindsay L (2006). We listen but do we hear? The importance of patient stories. *British Journal of Community Nursing*, **11**(9), 6–14.

Haynes RB, Ackloo E, Sahota N, McDonald HP, Yao X. *Interventions for enhancing medication adherence*. Cochrane Database of Systematic Reviews 2008, Issue 2. Art No.: CD000011. DOI:10.1002/14651858.CD000011.pub3

Hilton PA (2004). *Fundamental nursing skills*. Whurr Publishers, London.

Hyrkas K and Appelqvist-Schmidlechner K (2003). Team supervision in multi-professional teams: team members' descriptions of the effects as highlighted by group interviews. *Journal of Clinical Nursing*, **12**(2), 188–97.

International Labour Organization, International Council of Nurses, World Health Organization, and Public Services International (2005). *Framework guidelines for addressing workplace violence in the health sector. The training manual*. International Labour Office, Geneva.

Jenkin A, Cooper S, and Abelson-Mitchell N (2007). Patient handover: time for a change? *Journal of Accident and Emergency Nursing*, **15**, 141–7.

Kruijver IPM, Kerkstra A, Bensing JM, and Van der Weil HBM (2001). Communication skills of nurses during interactions with simulated cancer patients. *Journal of Advanced Nursing*, **34**(6), 772–9.

La Tourette R and Meeks S (2000). Perceptions of patronizing speech by older women in nursing homes and in the community. *Journal of Language and Social Psychology*, **19**(4), 463–73.

Ley P (1988). *Communicating with patients. Improving communication, satisfaction and compliance*. Croom Helm, London.

Mackway-Jones K and Walker M (1998). *Pocket guide to teaching for medical instructors*. BMJ Books, London.

McCabe C (2004). Nurse–patient communication: an exploration of patients' experiences. *Journal of Clinical Nursing*, **13**, 41–9.

Molyneux J (2001). Interprofessional team working: what makes teams work well? *Journal of Interprofessional Care*, **15**(1), 29–35.

Nursing and Midwifery Council (2008). *The Code: standards of conduct, performance and ethics for nurses and midwives*. Nursing and Midwifery Council, London.

Park EK and Song M (2004). Communication barriers perceived by older patients and nurses. *International Journal of Nursing Studies*, **42**, 159–66.

Pendleton D, Schofield T, Tate P, and Havelock P (2003). *The new consultation*. Oxford University Press, Oxford.

Pethybridge J (2004). How team working influences discharge planning from hospital: a study of four multi-disciplinary teams in an acute hospital in England. *Journal of Interprofessional Care*, **18**(1), 29–41.

Pooley C, Gerrard C, Hollis S, Morton S, and Astbury J (2001). Oh it's a wonderful practice . . . you can talk to them: a qualitative study of patients' and health professionals' views on the management of type 2 diabetes. *Health and Social Care in the Community*, **9**(5), 318–26.

Quality Assurance Agency (2006). *Statement of common purpose for subject benchmark statements for the health and social care professions* [online] http://www.qaa.ac.uk/academicinfrastructure/benchmark/health/StatementofCommonPurpose06.pdf accessed 18/08/08.

Resuscitation Council (UK) (2006). *Advanced life support*, 5th edition. Resuscitation Council (UK), London.

Revill J (2004). *When the baby is forgotten*, March 7 [online] http://www.guardian.co.uk/medicine/story/0,,1164082,00.html accessed 18/08/08.

Rhodes P and Nocon A (2003). A problem of communication? Diabetes care among Bangladeshi people in Bradford. *Health and Social Care in the Community*, **11**(5), 45–54.

Ruusuvuori J (2001). Looking means listening: co-ordinating displays of engagement in doctor–patient interaction. *Social Science and Medicine*, **52**, 1093–108.

Savenstedt S, Zingmark K, Hyden LC, and Brulin C (2005). Establishing joint attention in remote talks with the elderly about health: a study of nurses' conversations with elderly persons in teleconsultations. *Scandinavian Journal of Caring Sciences*, **19**, 317–24.

Silverman J, Kurtz S, and Draper J (2005). *Skills for communicating with patients*. Radcliffe Publishing, Oxford.

Texting4health (2004). [online] http://www.texting4health.org accessed 18/08/08.

Wahlberg AC, Cedersand E, and Wredling R (2003). Telephone nurses' experiences of problems with telephone advice in Sweden. *Journal of Clinical Nursing*, **12**(1), 37–45.

Wilkinson SM, Leliopoulou C, Gambles M, and Roberts A (2003). Can intensive three-day programmes improve nurses' communication skills in cancer care. *Psychooncology*, **12**(8), 747–59.

Yam B and Rossiter JR (2000). Caring in nursing: perceptions of Hong Kong nurses. *Journal Of Clinical Nursing*, **9**(2), 293–302.

Useful further reading and websites

Check **http://www.oxfordtextbooks.co.uk/orc/endacott** for updated research and guidelines.

http://www.healthline.com – general communication information.

http://www.skillscascade.com – good resources website.

http://www.bmj.com – free articles on medical communication.

http://www.cisco.com/uk/humannetwork – virtual networking.

http://www.cardiff.ac.uk/– health communications research centre.

Guly HR (1996). *History taking, examination and record keeping in emergency medicine*. Oxford University Press, Oxford.

▶Answers to patient scenarios

1 Miss Kosovich has concerns regarding her diagnosis, and fears that being diabetic means her life will dramatically change. You need to adopt a communication approach that recognizes Miss Kosovich's dilemma and values her views, even if they conflict with your own. You both need to discuss relevant role models and management of diabetes within her lifestyle. She needs to know that life can still be exciting and that her character does not need to change, but that her view on diabetes may need to be integrated into her social activities so she can enjoy her life long term.

2 As a general nurse, mental health issues are outside your professional expertise, but you may have colleagues within your multiprofessional team who have the necessary experience. If you don't, you can make an appropriate referral, but you need to identify the most effective way to proceed. Referral and support is the key in the long term. If it is possible to continue the current appointment then adopt a reassuring communication method, acknowledge his anxiety, but focus on his back pain. If this fails, the most appropriate step would be to stop the appointment and arrange another date. In the interim contact other health care professionals for advice.

3 It is important that you do not feel devalued or undermined as this may lead to defensive behaviour, which will limit communication. Ask your colleagues to explain terms that you are not familiar with and describe your experience of the patient in full.

4 Emphasis on the importance of keeping referral appointments is essential and it is good practice to check that appointments have been kept. Communicating with other health care professionals is also essential.

The patient pathway

Principles of good record keeping

Definition 86
It is important to remember 87
Prior knowledge 87
Background 88

Definition

A health record is defined as 'any electronic or paper information recorded about a person for the purpose of managing their health care' (**Data Protection Act 1998**) and includes 'medical records, patient records and notes, case notes and obstetric records' (National Health Service Litigation Authority (NHSLA) 2005).

Health records provide evidence of health professionals' involvement with patients (Griffith 2004) and demonstrate the delivery of 'safe and effective care based on current evidence, best practice and, where applicable, validated research' (Nursing and Midwifery Council (NMC) 2007a). This section includes: completing an entry in a health care record; use of diaries for clinical information; using computer-based records; standardizing patient wristbands; and writing an incident report.

It is important to remember:

- The purpose of health records is to provide a current picture of the patient's problems, management, and response to treatment.
- Health records hold the key to identifying changes in the patient's condition, from physiological parameters to progress with rehabilitation. To fulfil this purpose, records must be complete, accurate, and timely.
- An ultimate outcome of poor record keeping is poor quality care and inappropriate patient management.
- The best health care record is the product of communication between members of the health care team and the patient/client (NMC 2007a).
- Information about patients must be treated as confidential and used only for the purposes for which it was given. NMC guidance about confidentiality applies to verbal and written (paper and computer-based) patient information.

Prior knowledge

Before completing an entry in a health care record, make sure you are familiar with:

1 NMC (2008) *The Code: standards of conduct, performance and ethics for nurses and midwives.*

2 NMC (2007c) *Standards for medicines management.*

3 NMC advice sheets on: confidentiality, delegation, and accountability (see the Further reading section at the end of this skill).

4 NMC (2005b) *An NMC guide for students of nursing and midwifery.*

5 Your employer's policy for record keeping.

Background

In order to understand why good record keeping is central to delivering good quality patient care, it's helpful to examine circumstances in which records have been found to be inadequate. The NMC (2005a) identified that 39% of charges brought before the professional conduct committee concerned clinical practice, with 6% related to poor record keeping. In addition, much of the research concerning poor management of patients who deteriorate emphasizes incomplete recording of vital signs (e.g. National Confidential Enquiry into Patient Outcome and Death 2005, Endacott *et al.* 2007). Factors that contribute to effective record keeping are summarized in Box 3.1.

The content of health records should meet the following requirements:
1 Be recorded, wherever possible, with the involvement of the patient/client or their carer.
2 Be recorded in terms that the patient/client can understand.
3 Be consecutive.
4 Identify risk and/or problems that have arisen and the action taken to rectify them.
5 Provide clear evidence of the care planned, the decisions made, the care delivered, and the information shared.

NMC (2007a)

These requirements and the factors identified by the NMC in Box 3.1 should be applied to both paper and electronic health records.

When discussing health records with the patient, it is important to explain what is being recorded and why, and to identify goals that are important to the patient.

Box 3.1 Effective record keeping

Patient/client records should:
- Be factual, consistent, and accurate, recorded so that the meaning is clear.
- Be recorded as soon as possible after an event has occurred, providing current information on the care and condition of the patient/client.
- Be recorded clearly and in such a manner that the text cannot be erased or deleted without a record of the change.
- Be recorded in such a manner that any justifiable alterations or additions are dated, timed, and signed or clearly attributed to a named person in an identifiable role, and so that the original entry can still be read clearly.
- Be accurately dated, timed, and signed, with the signature printed alongside the first entry where this is a written record, and attributed to a named person in an identifiable role for electronic records.
- Not include abbreviations, jargon, meaningless phrases, irrelevant speculation, or offensive or subjective statements.
- Be readable when photocopied or scanned.

NMC (2007a)

Completing an entry in a health care record

When completing a health care record, the principles in Table 3.1 must be followed.

Retention of records

The period for which health records are required to be kept will depend on local and government health department policies. Such policies and protocols usually state that records should be kept for a minimum period of 8 years and, in the case of a child, at least to the date of the child's 21st birthday (NMC 2007a). The recording of patient information in diaries is a controversial area; advice from the NMC is provided in Box 3.2.

Terminology used in patient records

Consistency in terminology is crucial; Zeleznik *et al.* (2003) found that language used by doctors and nurses to describe skin ulcers in patient records varied considerably. They found a total of 66 different terms (including 38 non-medical, non-specific, or ambiguous terms) used to describe skin ulcers; the most frequently omitted component was the size of the ulcer. Ambiguity in terminology was also highlighted in a legal case where different interpretations of a term used in ophthalmology led a surgeon to conclude that a patient had deteriorated. The surgeon consequently undertook surgery that resulted in severe complications and was held to be negligent (*Scheck v. Dart High Court,* 22/10/04, cited in NHSLA 2006). Particular care should be taken to avoid communication-related errors when using terms that sound or look similar, for example prefixes such as anti and ante, ab(duction) and ad(duction) (Lyons 2008).

Box 3.2 Advice from the NMC (2007a) regarding use of diaries for clinical information

Diaries containing clinical information are considered part of a patient or client's clinical record and should be kept for the minimum period of eight years or to a child's 21st birthday in the case of children's records.

The NMC recommends that clinical information should not be recorded in diaries. Where it is, then the information must be transcribed into the patient or client's records within 48 hours. Registrants should, however, be aware of local policies, as many state that diaries should only be used as a tool enabling registrants to log appointments. Providing the diary contains no clinical information or that this has been transcribed into the patient/client's own records, they should be retained for one year from the date of their completion.

Table 3.1 Principles of record keeping

Principle	Rationale
Write legibly	In order to meet the stated purpose of managing [patient's] health care (Data Protection Act 1998), records need to be read accurately by others.
Include date and time	The sequence of events is important when reviewing patient progress and, more importantly, patient deterioration, as well as providing evidence of chronology in legal cases.
Sign all entries and print name	The person providing care has accountability for that care. (See also guidance on delegated accountability and record keeping in Box 3.5.)
Use only approved, unambiguous abbreviations	Abbreviations may be clear to one group of professionals but ambiguous to others. Abbreviations can also become outdated; records may be reviewed many years after they are written, either for legal reasons or, more usually, in an attempt to understand more about treatment the patient received in the past.
Do not alter entries or disguise additions made at a later stage	It is essential that any changes to records are legible and dated.
Do not use offensive, personal, or humorous language	Such language is easily misinterpreted, even if intended as a reflection of the patient's situation.
Check everything you've written/typed before adding your signature	Some programmes used for electronic health records do not include spell-checkers; it is easy to miss errors.
Ensure reports (e.g. investigations) are seen, evaluated, and initialled before being filed in the patient's records (follow your local Trust policy)	Overdiligent filing of reports can result in abnormal results being overlooked.
Do not destroy patient records	Incomplete records can result in unsafe patient care. Trusts have local policies for storing of health records, for example some Trusts keep fluid balance charts while others do not.

Adapted from Norwell's Ten Commandments of record keeping (1997).

Using computer-based records

Major drawbacks with paper-based health records include difficulty in retrieving vital information about the patient and different document designs, even within the same organization (Taylor 2003). Computer-based records (or electronic health records, EHRs) may be one solution to these problems; however, they are themselves not without difficulties. Researchers in the USA found that patient attitudes to EHRs (including web messaging and online access to their EHR) were more positive than those of clinicians (Hassol *et al.* 2004). A review of 26 studies by Delpierre *et al.* (2004) found that user and patient satisfaction were improved with the use of computer-based records, although the impact of EHRs on patient outcomes was inconclusive.

In a survey of 225 primary care nurses and doctors, Linder *et al.* (2006) found a number of barriers to using the EHR during a patient visit, the most common reported as: loss of eye contact with patients (62%); falling behind (52%); computers too slow (49%); inability to type quickly enough (32%); feeling that using the computer in front of the patient is rude (31%); and preferring to write long prose notes (28%). However, the electronic health care record is a cornerstone of future developments in patient documentation (see NHS Connecting for Health, http://www.connectingforhealth.nhs.uk) and hence it is important that these barriers are overcome. The NHS Code of Practice for Confidentiality guidance on electronic data storage provides helpful guidance (see Box 3.3).

In order to maintain patient confidentiality, care records should only be accessed by those involved in the patient's care. Under the NHS Care Record Scheme, an audit trail will be kept of all staff who access an individual patient record (BMA/NHS Connecting for Health 2008) and patients will be able to request a copy of their audit trail.

Box 3.3 NHS Code of Practice for Confidentiality: specific guidance for electronic record keeping

- Always log out of any computer system or application when work on it is finished.
- Do not leave a terminal unattended and logged in.
- Do not share logins with other people. If other staff need to access records, then appropriate access should be organized for them – this must not be by using others' access identities.
- Do not reveal passwords to others.
- Change passwords at regular intervals to prevent anyone else using them.
- Avoid using short passwords, or using names or words that are known to be associated with them (e.g. children's or pets' names or birthdays).
- Always clear the screen of a previous patient's information before seeing another.
- Use a password-protected screensaver to prevent casual viewing of patient information by others.

(http://www.connectingforhealth.nhs.uk/systemsandservices/infogov/codes/confcode.pdf)

The move to electronic records opens up a number of different ways of sharing patient information, for example:

1 Access to records by clinicians in different settings. This is particularly useful when patients may access more than one health care provider, for example a number of different walk-in centres in the same area (Colucci 2007).

2 Electronic transfer of vital signs data. In an attempt to improve recognition and timely management of patients with abnormal vital signs, some hospitals are using PDAs to record vital signs, linked to a central monitoring system (Smith et al. 2006).

Further initiatives such as drugs trolleys accessed/secured by thumbprint are currently being piloted by some hospitals.

Standardizing wristbands

Complete, legible, and up-to-date health records are crucial to provide safe and timely patient care. Safe care is also dependent on correct patient identification; the National Patient Safety Agency (NPSA) reported 2900 instances of incorrect patient identification due to inadequate documentation on patient wristbands in England and Wales in 2006. As a result, new guidelines were issued in 2007 (http://www.npsa.nhs.uk/display?contentId=6076); the requirements from July 2008 are listed in Box 3.4.

Box 3.4 NPSA requirements for wristband use

- Wristbands will have to meet NPSA requirements.
- Wristbands must only include the patient's last name, first name, date of birth, and NHS number (or a temporary identification number).
- Organizations must develop clear and consistent processes specifying who can produce, apply, and check wristbands.
- Wristbands must be white with black text.
- Patients with known risks such as allergies, or patients who do not wish to receive blood products, should be given a red wristband with text in black.
- Wristbands should be generated and printed from the hospital patient information system, at the bedside wherever possible.
- In Wales the first line of the patient's address must be included.

Writing incident reports

If you are asked to write a report about a clinical incident, it is important to remember the following:
- Identify what happened, to whom, and how.
- Identify where the incident happened.
- Report facts only – do not be tempted to provide an opinion about why the incident might have happened.
- Include, in a factual manner, any unusual circumstances (e.g. unexpected staff sickness/absence) or unusual workload issues (e.g. an emergency with another patient).

One of the goals of clinical governance, in the light of the Bristol Inquiry (Kennedy 2001), is that a more 'open' culture should be evident when clinical incidents occur, for example:

- Focusing not on who went wrong but on what went wrong.
- Talking through the incident rather than instigating an investigation.
- Treating the incident as a training point rather than a disciplinary matter.
- Learning lessons and changing systems as appropriate.

The processes used by most NHS Trusts follow the root cause analysis method (see http://www.nrls.npsa.nhs.uk/report-a-patient-safety-incident/).

Reviewing health records

Health records should be regularly audited as part of NHS Trust risk management processes. Records may, however, also be reviewed some time after they were written to ascertain whether safe and appropriate care was provided. This type of review may be part of a legal case or a professional misconduct hearing. Tables 3.2 and 3.3 identify lessons to be learnt about health care records from both types of case.

Other aspects of documentation

Delegation

As a Registered Nurse or midwife, you are responsible for any activity you have decided to delegate to others. The NMC Code (2008) states:

You must establish that anyone you delegate to is able to carry out your instructions. You must confirm that the outcome of any delegated task meets required standards. You must make sure that everyone you are responsible for is supervised and supported.

Delegation to others must also be documented appropriately (NMC 2007b); see Box 3.5.

Documentation of care, including any discussions with the patient or relatives about care management, is the responsibility of the person who has undertaken the care. This will include those to whom care has been delegated, e.g. unregistered staff and students. The Registered Nurse/midwife who has delegated the activity may be required to countersign the record, according to local Trust policy. All entries in patient records made by students must be countersigned by a Registered Nurse or midwife (NMC 2005b). Don't forget that documenting care should only be delegated to others if the Registered Nurse/midwife has evidence of their competence in this skill.

Box 3.5 NMC advice regarding documentation of delegation

- The registrant has a responsibility to ensure that any aspect of care delegated has been documented appropriately.
- Documentation should clearly outline any decision making processes and must be patient/client specific.
- The most appropriate place to record this information should be decided based on the working environment, i.e. patient held records/ care plans.
- At each delegation, the names of those being delegated to must be clearly stated.

NMC (2007b)

Table 3.2 Lessons to be learnt from legal case

Detail	Key lessons
Saunders v. Leeds Western HA [1993] Healthy 4-year-old child suffered cardiac arrest and brain damage during an arthroplasty operation. Operating department team claimed that the child's heart had simply stopped abruptly. There was no evidence in the records of a sequence of events leading to the heart stopping. The Health Authority was found to be negligent.	Records need to be sufficiently detailed to demonstrate an appropriate standard of care.
McLennan v. Newcastle HA [1992] A patient claimed she had not been told of the relatively high risk associated with her operation. The surgeon had written in the notes that the risks were explained and understood by the patient. The court found in favour of the Health Authority.	It is essential to record details of conversations with patients at the time they occur (a contemporaneous record). If the procedure for which the patient is giving consent is particularly rare or complex, a written patient information sheet is also helpful.
Prendergast v. Sam Dee [1989] An illegible prescription from a GP resulted in the patient being given the wrong drug by a pharmacist. The patient suffered harm as a result. The pharmacist was held to be 75% liable for the harm and the GP 25% liable due to his poor handwriting.	Illegible writing can result in harm to patients and liability for those responsible.

Table 3.3 Cases reviewed by the Nursing and Midwifery Council Fitness to Practise Committee (reported in the NMC Annual Report 2004-05)

Proven charges	Implications
An adult nurse (RN) working as an emergency nurse practitioner based in a hospital: • failed to triage patients properly • failed to complete triage documentation • falsely represented that she had completed triage documentation • failed to deal properly with a complaint relating to a patient in the triage process. Similar issues had been raised in the past concerning the quality of the nurse's triage and record keeping.	Appropriate treatment was delayed with potentially serious consequences; this was compounded by false recording. The nurse's actions clearly demonstrated unsafe practice and had been repeated on previous occasions. **NMC decision:** **Removed from the register**
An adult nurse (RN) was employed as a staff nurse at a nursing home and admitted the following charges: • failed to update the notes of a diabetic patient whose condition was poor • failed to give drugs at the correct time • signed for medication when there was doubt whether it was given • signed for medication when it had not been given • on 14 occasions failed to record the pulse of a patient on digoxin.	The nurse failed in her obligations to keep proper and accurate records. The nurse's actions demonstrated a lack of understanding regarding the administration of medicines and the essential requirements of good record keeping. **NMC decision:** **Removed from the register**

Reflection and evaluation

When you have completed an entry in the patient's records, think about the following questions:

1 Is my entry clear, unambiguous, legible, dated, timed, and signed? Review the entries made by others; do these also meet these requirements?

2 Have I used available opportunities to discuss the health record entry with the patient? Is the patient aware of the goals that have been set and the actions planned?

3 Would I be able to provide safe care for the patient based on the information in the health record?

Further learning outcomes

Look at the records written by experienced colleagues. How do their entries differ from yours? As electronic health records become more commonplace, look at the steps taken in your workplace (or placement venues) to protect patient confidentiality.

Reminders

Don't forget to:

- Check all entries you make in health records to ensure they meet the requirements of Table 3.1.
- Ensure that you maintain the confidentiality of patient information held in health records.

▶Patient scenarios

Consider what you should do in the following situations, then turn to the end of this section to check your answers.

1 Mr Jones has chronic obstructive pulmonary disease and asked to see his health records. He is alarmed that the GP has written that he might need to be considered for 'LTOT', and the practice nurse has reported that on attending the practice respiratory clinic, he is increasingly 'SOB'. He assumes that the nurse is calling him a 'son of a bitch' and the GP is making some detrimental reference to his occasional drinking habit. How can this situation be avoided?

2 You are a student working on a medical ward. A doctor from the Emergency Department requests to see the notes of his sister-in-law, who has been admitted for investigations. What action should you take?

Website

🖥 http://www.oxfordtextbooks.co.uk/orc/endacott

You may find it helpful to work through our short online quiz and additional scenarios intended to help you to develop and apply the skills in this chapter.

More skills

You can find clear explanations and step by step instructions for more clinical skills in *Clinical Nursing Skills: Core and Advanced* edited by Endacott, R., Jevon, P., and Cooper, S., from which this chapter has been taken.

References

British Medical Association/NHS Connecting for Health (2008). *Joint Guidance on Protecting Electronic Patient Information* [online] http://www.connectingforhealth.nhs.uk/systemsandservices/nhscrs/publications/staff/jointguidance.pdf accessed 12/08/08.

Colucci M (2007). Moving to a paperless walk-in centre. *British Journal of Healthcare Computing and Information Management*, **24**(4), 14–16.

The Data Protection Act (1998). [online] http://www.hmso.gov.uk accessed 12/08/08.

Delpierre C, Cuzin L, Fillaux J, Alvarez M, Massip P, and Lang T (2004). A systematic review of computer-based patient record systems and quality of care: more randomized trials or a broader approach? *International Journal for Quality in Health Care*, **16**(5), 407–16.

Endacott R, Kidd T, Chaboyer W, and Edington J (2007). Recognition and communication of patient deterioration in a regional hospital: a multi-methods study. *Australian Critical Care* **20**(3), 100–5.

Griffith R (2004). Putting the record straight: the importance of documentation. *British Journal of Community Nursing*, **9**(3), 122–5.

Hassol A, Walker JM, Kidder D, *et al.* (2004). Patient experiences and attitudes about access to a patient electronic health care record and linked web messaging. *Journal of American Informatics Association*, **11**(6), 505–13.

Kennedy I (2001). *The report of the public inquiry into children's heart surgery at the Bristol Royal Infirmary 1984–1995: Learning from Bristol.* The Stationery Office, London.

Linder JA, Schnipper JL, Tsurikova R, Meinikas AJ, Volk LA, and Middleton B (2006). Barriers to electronic health record use during patient visits. *AMIA Annual Symposium Proceedings*, 499–503.

Lyons M (2008). Do classical origins of medical terms endanger patients? *The Lancet*, **371**, 1321–2.

National Confidential Enquiry into Patient Outcome and Death (NCEPOD) (2005). *An acute problem?* NCEPOD, London. [online] http://www.ncepod.org.uk accessed 20/08/07.

National Health Service Litigation Authority (2005). *CNST general clinical risk management standards.* NHSLA, London.

National Health Service Litigation Authority (2006). Clinical cases. *NHSLA Journal*, **5**, 8–9.

Norwell N (1997). The ten commandments of record keeping. *Journal of the MDU*, **13**(1), 8–9.

Nursing and Midwifery Council (2005a). *Fitness to practice annual report 2004–2005.* NMC, London.

Nursing and Midwifery Council (2005b). *An NMC Guide for Students of Nursing and Midwifery* [online] http://www.science.ulster.ac.uk/nursing/mentorship/docs/updates/An%20NMC%20guide%20for%20students%20of%20nursing%20and%20midwifery.pdf

Nursing and Midwifery Council (2007a). *Advice sheet on record keeping.* NMC, London.

Nursing and Midwifery Council (2007b). *Advice sheet on delegation.* NMC, London.

Nursing and Midwifery Council (2007c). *Standards for medicines management* [online] http://www.nmc-uk.org/Documents/Standards/nmcStandardsForMedicinesManagementBooklet.pdf accessed 12/07/2011.

Nursing and Midwifery Council (2008). *The Code: standards of conduct, performance and ethics for nurses and midwives.* NMC, London.

Smith GB, Prytherch DR, Schmidt P, *et al.* (2006). Hospital-wide physiological surveillance – a new approach to the early identification and management of the sick patient. *Resuscitation*, **71**, 19–28.

Taylor H (2003). An exploration of the factors that affect nurses' record keeping. *British Journal of Nursing*, **12**, 751–8.

Zeleznik J, Agard-Henriques B, Schnebel B, and Smith DL (2003). Terminology used by different health care providers to document skin ulcers: the blind men and the elephant. *Journal of Wound, Ostomy and Continence Nursing*, **30**(6), 324–33.

Useful further reading and websites

Department of Health (2004). The NHS Knowledge and Skills Framework (NHS KSF) and the development review process. DH, London. [online] http://www.dh.gov.uk.

Nursing and Midwifery Council (NMC) advice sheets:
Confidentiality (http://www.nmc-uk.org/Nurses-and-midwives/Advice-by-topic/A/Advice/Confidentiality/)
Delegation (http://www.nmc-uk.org/Nurses-and-midwives/Advice-by-topic/A/Advice/Delegation/)
Accountability (http://www.nmc-uk.org/Nurses-and-midwives/Advice-by-topic/A/Advice/Accountability/)
Royal College of Nursing (2006). *Competencies: an integrated career and competency framework for information sharing in nursing practice.* RCN, London. [online] http://www.rcn.org.uk/__data/assets/pdf_file/0003/192468/003264.pdf

Electronic health record websites for England, Scotland, Wales, and Northern Ireland:
Connecting for Health (England) – http://www.connectingforhealth.nhs.uk
The e-health programme (Scotland) – http://www.ehealth.scot.nhs.uk
Informing health care (Wales) – http://www.wales.nhs.uk
HPSS ICT programme (Northern Ireland) – http://www.dhsspsni.gov.uk

See http://www.hmso.gov.uk for details of Acts relating to information and health care.

►Answers to patient scenarios

1 All records should be written with the assumption that they will be read by the patient and/or relatives. All abbreviations should be fully explained with the full version (e.g. LTOT – long-term oxygen therapy) written in the narrative. When a patient requests their notes, the records should be scanned to identify abbreviations that are acceptable across health professions but ambiguous to the patient. If time allows, a health professional should be available to answer any queries the patient may have.

2 The ED doctor has no right to view the records of his sister-in-law. The only circumstance in which the doctor would be allowed to view the notes is with the express permission of the patient. Local Trust policy may require this to be given in writing. It is the responsibility of Registered Nurses and midwives to protect confidential information (NMC 2008). The management of this scenario is beyond the expected competence of a student, so you should refer the doctor to a Registered Nurse.

The patient pathway

Completing an effective patient admission assessment

Definition *100*
It is important to remember *101*
Prior knowledge *101*
Background *102*
Context *105*
Procedure *106*

Definition

Patient assessment on admission can be defined as the act of evaluation of a patient's condition and welfare, in order to plan and implement appropriate care on admission to a health care setting.

It is important to remember:

- An effective admission assessment is essential to ensure that the patient's needs are identified and met as fully as possible, and that the patient is fully and appropriately prepared for discharge.
- Good record keeping within the patient assessment will also allow for effective continuity of care and promotes communication and sharing of information between members of the interprofessional health care team (NMC 2007).
- Nursing records are subject to audit as part of the clinical governance cycle. Therefore, any patient assessment you undertake may be subject to review. The level of detail you include may assist in the development of health care when the quality review cycle takes place.
- As part of the *Access to Health Records Act* (1990), any nursing assessment made after 1 November 1991 may also be viewed by the patients you have cared for, at any time.
- *Any* patient record can be used as evidence to investigate potential discrepancies either at the local level or in a court of law. Keep in mind that the detail you record today may reliably assist you in remembering the care you delivered to your patient in many years to come.

Prior knowledge

Before undertaking a patient admission assessment, make sure you are familiar with:

1 Section 3.1 of this book, *Principles of good record keeping*.
2 The NMC guidelines for records and record keeping (NMC 2007).
3 *Going lean in the NHS* (NHS Institute for Innovation and Improvement 2007).
4 Local policies and guidelines relating to record keeping.

Background

There is currently no single model or template for a quality admission assessment; however, in England the NHS is seeking to standardize and improve communication and record keeping by implementing a new integrated information technology system. 'NHS Connecting for Health' is providing the delivery of these systems and services, enabling information to be shared between NHS organizations across England and Northern Ireland. Similar projects are taking place across Scotland, Wales, and Ireland.

Assessment models

Across health care settings, different modes of assessment may be used dependent on anticipated patient needs. An acute NHS medical inpatient unit will initially want to focus on managing the patient's presenting condition and the assessment will reflect this. However, a Stroke Rehabilitation Unit may need to address the development needs of the patient in order for them to maintain their own care; the format of the assessment will reflect this.

Most assessment tools are based on a cyclical process that enables appropriate assessment, planning, implementation, and evaluation of care; in nursing this has been referred to as the nursing process, first described in the 1960s (Orlando 1961). The frameworks developed to tailor the assessment to patient needs are usually referred to as nursing models and became popular in nursing practice in the 1980s. These models tend to be tailored according to the eventual goal for the patient – for example the self-care model first described by Orem (1971) or the adaptation model described by Roy (1976). In the twenty-first century these have been described as outdated and remote theories, full of 'pretentious jargon' (Salvage 2006).

One of the most widely used nursing models in the UK was developed in 1980 by three nursing leaders who were significantly disenchanted with the existing **'biomedical'** approach to nursing care (Salvage 2006). The Roper, Logan, and Tierney (RLT) model of nursing (Roper et al. 1983) started out as a nursing education tool but was rapidly adopted as a framework for planning patient care. The model uses 12 activities of living as the basis for assessing the patient and planning/evaluating care (see Figure 3.1).

In 2000 the authors wrote their final account of The Roper-Logan-Tierney model of nursing (Roper et al. 2000) but suggested that others may choose to develop it as the face of nursing develops and progresses. Re-evaluation of the processes used to plan care is vital and, as a student or newly Registered Nurse, your fresh eyes may note areas of weakness where improvements could be made.

Whichever mode of assessment your department uses, the principles remain the same. The aim is to achieve the best possible account of the patient's needs on admission and, through effective record keeping, to provide optimum care throughout the hospital stay and the best possible outcome on discharge. Best practice promoted by the NMC (2007) requires assessment of the patient's immediate needs within 4 hours of the patient's arrival, followed by full documentation within 24 hours.

There may be variations in the detailed requirements for admission assessment in public and private hospitals, nursing homes, and community settings. However, the principles of admission assessment remain the same throughout different care settings. For the purpose of this chapter, the example of a patient arriving for care within the NHS acute sector via an 'Admissions Unit' is used.

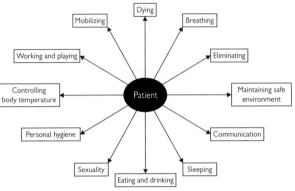

Figure 3.1 The Roper, Logan, and Tierney activities of living model.

Clinical observations

If the patient is acutely ill, your admission assessment is likely to include the following clinical measurements:

- Blood pressure
- Temperature
- Respirations
- Pulse
- Oxygen saturation
- Neurological status

The purpose of this chapter is to prepare you to undertake a **baseline** admission assessment. More details of specific physiological assessments are provided in the following sections: 6.1 *Visual assessment of the cardiac patient*; 6.2 *Measuring and recording the pulse*; 6.3 *Measuring and recording blood pressure*; 7.1 *Visual respiratory assessment*; and 10.1 *Nutritional assessment*.

The quality of the written patient assessment is dependent on the care taken by the person making the record. It therefore has the potential to fall foul of human error. Remember that all documentation you complete is a 'window' of your practice, so give thought to the detail you include in your assessment. Some examples of legal cases and cases of misconduct reported to the NMC that related to patient documentation are provided in Section 3.1. The **mandatory** standard for nursing documentation is also made explicit in the guidelines from the NMC (2007) shown in Box 3.1 on page 88.

Context

When to undertake an admission assessment

All patients should be assessed when they first enter a different health care setting. For example, a patient transferred from hospital to a nursing home will require an assessment to identify needs specific to that setting. The detail of the assessment will be tailored according to circumstances, for example a patient admitted to the resuscitation area of an Emergency Department will require rapid assessment and prioritizing of their life-threatening condition.

Do not undertake this task until you have observed others undertaking it and feel suitably prepared for your first time. You are not letting anybody down by taking your time and learning the skill. Better to take your time and ensure accuracy than to rush and miss a vital part of the admission assessment.

Alternative interventions

Use all sources of information available to you; this may include family members and paramedic/ambulance staff. This should not be considered 'alternative' but should be a normal dimension of admission assessment. However, most of the admission assessment detail depends on communication with the patient. Where this is not possible, for example if the patient is unconscious, as much detail as possible should be gleaned from family and other professionals.

Procedure

Preparation

Prepare yourself

Ensure you have all relevant information about the patient to hand. As far as possible, plan your workload in order to undertake the admission assessment with the minimum of interruptions.

Prepare the patient

Undoubtedly, wherever you work, your area will be busy and high expectations will have been placed upon you. When the patient arrives on the ward, take the opportunity to take a step back and put yourself in their position. Consider how the patient is possibly feeling at that moment:
- Unwell
- Unclean
- In discomfort
- Vulnerable
- Anxious

With this in mind, consider your response. A welcoming smile and an indication that you are prepared for them could put the patient at ease. If the patient's arrival is unexpected or there are going to be any delays in facilitating their admission, then try not to look blank or too busy to be concerned. Take sufficient time to reassure the patient and assist them into a bed space as expediently as possible, ensuring that you provide appropriate care and consideration for relatives as required.

Prepare the equipment/environment

Prior to the patient's arrival on the ward, think about the materials and information you will need and prepare your area.

Be aware that some of the equipment used to record clinical observations is electronic and will require charging. Therefore, before you use any equipment, check that it is sufficiently charged and in full working order. After use, check that it is clean, in good working order, and returned to its designated area for charging. If your clinical area is likely to receive these admissions, hopefully it will have adopted the NHS '5S' approach (NHS Institute for Innovation and Improvement 2007) to the preparation of its environment (see Figure 3.2). You will then find that an allocated area will have been designated for this purpose.

With equipment available and ready for use, your patient should experience minimal delay in the assessment process and you as a nurse will endure less frustration in delivering your practice.

Documentation

Once again, if the '5S' principle is used, this would allow for the unit to have admission packs ready prepared and easily to hand. This achieves two possible benefits when the patient arrives into your care: firstly, it ensures maximum nursing time is available for direct patient care and, secondly, it demonstrates a professional approach to the patient.

Ensure that the documentation is relevant to the patient you are admitting. It may include items from the following list:

- Admission pack
- Medical notes
- X-ray/Blood/Culture/Investigation request forms
- Manual handling score chart
- Dietary assessment tool
- Observation record sheets
- Physio/OT/Social services referral forms
- Pressure area record sheet (e.g. Waterlow Scoring Tool)

It may be advantageous throughout the admission process for your area to consider the development of a checklist approach. This would ensure that you had everything to hand and also ready to operate at the right time.

Bed space

Prior to the patient's arrival (preferably at the start of your shift), assess your patient bed space and ensure that it is clean, tidy, and fit for purpose, e.g. oxygen port and mask. Finally check that the patient name board has been completed, together with locally required additional information, e.g. admitting physician.

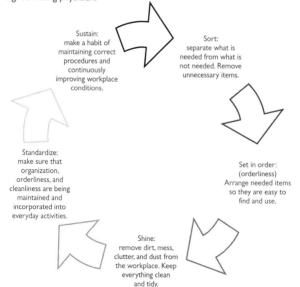

Figure 3.2 The 5S approach to preparation of the environment. NHS (2007).

Step-by-step guide to undertaking an admission assessment	
Step	**Rationale**
1 Introduce yourself, confirm the patient's identity, explain the procedure, and obtain consent.	To identify the patient correctly and gain informed consent.
2 For each of the activities of living, consider how your patient normally coped at home prior to the onset of the admission and also how they are at the time of assessment.	This will provide a baseline and allow early planning for discharge
3 Assess each of the activites of living using the questions in the following sections.	To ensure a systematic approach is followed. The patient may have a set of symptoms (e.g. respiratory difficulties) that take priority, but may also have problems with other activities of living.
4 Confirm contact details regarding next of kin; check that they are aware of the patient's admission.	To ensure that next of kin can be contacted quickly should an emergency arise.
5 When the assessment is complete, ensure the patient is as comfortable as possible and aware of the next stages in their care.	To alleviate patient anxiety as far as possible.

Assessment framework

1. Breathing

As you speak with the patient, consider how the patient is breathing on arrival. There are a variety of signs to look for and each of these may indicate a particular illness. Points to consider include:

- Is it laboured?
- Is it shallow?
- Is the patient mouth breathing?
- Is the patient using diaphragmatic breathing?
- If oxygen is required, is the patient distressed? Would a mouthpiece be more effective than a mask?
- Does the patient have chronic obstructive pulmonary disease (COPD)? If so, remember that patients with advanced COPD may be dependent on low oxygen saturation to maintain their respiratory drive, and high levels of oxygen should only be used under written medical advice.
- Would the patient prefer to be sitting up? How many pillows are required?

Ask questions that establish answers to the above or use your observation skills to decide for yourself. Careful documentation and reporting of findings could prevent serious patient deterioration (Smith 2003) or potential fatality.

2. Elimination

Think about what you are asking. This is not just about ascertaining bowel movements. When at home, how does your patient manage with the passing of urine and faeces? Consider:

- How often does the patient pass urine?
- What volume?
- Does the patient experience nocturnal micturition?
- Does the patient require diuretics?
- How often does the patient open their bowels?
- How formed are bowel motions?
- Does the patient suffer from an irritable bowel?
- Does the patient take iron medication?
- Does the patient require laxatives/aperients?
- Does the patient require assistance?
- Are any aids required to ease elimination?

These questions are not exhaustive but will allow you to delve deeper into the patient's normal elimination habits and provide assistance when normal habits change. Remember that reduced mobility and changes to fluid intake and diet will have effects on your patient. Daily assessment will demonstrate changes early and therefore aid you in preventing complications. This will also include the need to undertake urinalysis on a regular basis, dependent on the needs of the patient. This will assist in indicating issues such as infection or potential diabetes.

3. Maintaining a safe environment

Throughout your patient's stay, they will have to negotiate a period of their life through illness. This may be a short- or long-term event but your care will hopefully allow this period to be as comfortable as possible. On admission, consider the needs of the patient during their hospital stay and what their needs may be on discharge.

Assess the patient for any factors that may make them unsafe in a different environment. For example, if the patient suffers from any loss of sight, how can you best promote their care? Can you place them near the nurses' station and within easy reach of the toilet with uninterrupted passage? The patient's safety is particularly dependent on their ability to communicate their needs; specific assessment questions for this are detailed in the next section.

4. Communication

The ability of the patient to communicate is dependent on a number of interrelated factors (e.g. intact speech, sight, and hearing). It is important to assess these when you first meet the patient to ensure they are as involved in planning their care as possible. The following questions are helpful:

- How does your patient appear on arrival to the ward?
- Is the patient alert and orientated?
- Is the patient relaxed and communicating well or anxious and only able to provide closed answers?
- Does the patient have any speech or hearing difficulty?

Don't judge the patient as being 'awkward' if their answers are clipped. There may be predisposing factors that are leading to this, such as respiratory illness causing breathlessness. All sorts of external factors could potentially influence your patient's response and you as a professional need to identify these. For a patient who is giving restricted responses but their partner is speaking for them, ensure you take time to assess their communication when their partner has left.

In order to review and improve your own communication skills, please refer to Chapter 2 for further information.

5. Sleeping

At home, what is the patient's usual routine? Do we meet this when we are providing care? Reflect on your own night-time routines: how do you settle to sleep at night? Do you have a milky drink at 8.30 p.m. with lights out at 11.30 p.m.? Do you fall asleep and then have someone wake you at 12.30 a.m. to give you your night sedation?

As nurses we cannot totally break with ward routine and our routine will be different from the patient's usual experience. Therefore, what can we do to ensure they obtain a good night's sleep? Firstly, your admission assessment should obtain usual habits and ascertain if any night sedation is required. Are they awoken by the need for nocturnal micturition? Once this information has been collated, we can be aware of and prepared for any difficulties the patient may experience. We can also establish if there has been a change in the patient's normal habits.

6. Eating and drinking

So often, meaningless phrases are used, e.g. 'Patient maintains a normal diet'. What is normal? Each of us has different needs and there is much to be questioned here.

- How many meals does the patient have per day?
- Are these cooked independently or provided by a service such as 'meals on wheels'?
- Does the patient have any special dietary needs, e.g. gluten free, vegetarian?
- How many litres of fluid does the patient drink a day and in what capacity? (The patient is likely to answer this question in terms of numbers of cups of tea, etc., with no knowledge of fluid volume.)

7. Personal hygiene

Each patient admitted to hospital will have their own standards of personal hygiene, and as health care professionals we should endeavour to meet these. Patient hygiene may not appear particularly 'high tech' but the provision of this to a high standard can improve the patient experience considerably.

Throughout the assessment process, we need to ascertain what the patient's normal standard is so this can be met. Points to consider include:

- How often does the patient wish to be washed?
- Does the patient prefer to bath or shower?
- Has the patient brought provisions to hospital to maintain hygiene needs?
- How often does the patient wash their hair? Will this be achievable in hospital?

- Does the patient wish to use soap on their face?
- Does the patient like the use of flannels? If so, how many? (Some people use four flannels for different parts of the body.)
- How much assistance is usually required to meet hygiene needs?
- On return home, is it likely they will need assistance/equipment provided in order to maintain hygiene?

8. Controlling body temperature

This is not necessarily an area of concern for many patients, but for some patients, temperature control can be problematic. There are a variety of methods that can be used to assist patients to warm up or cool down; however, it is important also to consider how your actions may influence other patients. For those patients who feel the cold, it would be considerate to move them away from draughty doorways.

9. Working and playing

Patients who have been admitted may experience considerable anxiety in relation to their condition. Preparing for returning home and to work can add to this stress and therefore we need to consider how this will impact on their progress.

Consider the 52-year-old gentleman working as a sales representative who is trying to achieve targets and needs to be on the road, meeting customers. How is the news that he has had a myocardial infarction going to impact on his life? How likely is it that he will heed your advice to take it easy? Consider his need for counselling and support to facilitate this.

For most patients, admission to hospital removes them from their social life. It is useful to ask about their usual social habits when the patient is admitted, as these can provide useful goals for rehabilitation.

10. Mobilizing

On admission, health professionals tend to restrict the movement of patients to reduce any worsening of their presenting condition. Therefore, we may subconsciously view them in a different light to how they 'normally' mobilize.

The 74-year-old lady presenting with a fractured scaphoid, following a trip at home, may be admitted and nursed in a bed. Unable to bear weight on the affected wrist, she may require assistance to move up the bed. Yet at home, the same lady may be fully able to drive long distances and maintain a household independently.

It is vital we are aware of patients' 'normal' ability in relation to mobility, so that we may be able to return them as closely as possible to this position.

11. Sexuality

In this present era of the NHS, mixed wards are a necessity for most NHS Trusts. However, in keeping with government policy (Department of Health 2007), mixed bays are kept to a minimum. Yet patients do hold this as important to their own values. Therefore, as health care professionals, where possible we need to promote and uphold patients' needs in relation to sexuality.

This equally applies to patients who may be preparing for gender reassignment, etc., and these views need to be considered. Considering a person's view of their sexuality pre-admission is vital in ensuring the same standard is provided throughout the hospital stay and in preparation for discharge.

Throughout the patient's stay, it is also of high importance that we as practitioners consider the needs of patients in the same way that we may consider our own. Being in hospital does not stop the need for an individual to feel at their best where possible, and the use of make-up or relevant prosthetics may enhance the patient experience.

12. Dying

While death is part of everyone's life, it will always remain a difficult area to be faced by our patients and colleagues. Alterations to our normal way of life through illness will often present a question of our own mortality and dealing with this can be difficult.

As health professionals, we need to be prepared and trained for this in order to identify fear and be able to act upon it. It will be a difficult question to ask on admission and it is unlikely that it will be appropriate to ask in a direct manner. However, the topic can be approached indirectly by asking about religious needs and ascertaining if the patient would wish to see any representative of the hospital or local spiritual community.

This may lead to further statements or questions that we need to pick up on and question, leading to provision of relevant service advice or support.

Following the admission assessment

1 Ensure the patient has a call bell and (if appropriate) a drink within reach.

2 Ensure that documentation is complete; alert colleagues if you have uncovered any patient needs that require immediate attention.

3 Refer the patient to other professionals (e.g. physiotherapist or occupational therapist) as appropriate and according to local policy.

The information offered within this chapter is not exhaustive. It is intended to provoke thought and encourage you to reflect on your own practice. The hospital admission will undoubtedly be time-consuming and cause pressure on your working time. However, the detail you obtain at this important stage of the patient's illness will inform the wider health care community as to the needs of your patient, as illustrated in Figure 3.3.

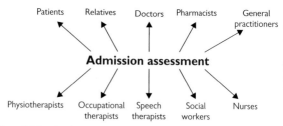

Figure 3.3 People who may access the admission assessment.

Reflection and evaluation

When you have completed an admission assessment, consider the following questions:

Did you find it easy to ask the patient about their normal daily activities?

Did any of the patient's answers surprise you?

Did the documentation help or hinder you in your conduct of the assessment?

What aspects of the documentation might you change?

In what circumstances might the admission assessment be less straightforward?

Further learning opportunities

Observe an experienced nurse undertaking an admission assessment. Take particular note of any steps taken to put the patient at ease.

Review admission assessments for other patients, particularly the language used to document the clinical assessment.

Consider liaison with family/next of kin to confirm patient perspective is shared. This holistic approach may alleviate discharge difficulties where family and patient have different views on the patient's needs.

Reminders

Don't forget that:

- The admission assessment can determine how quickly the patient's needs are addressed.
- The admission assessment should not be viewed in isolation but as the first stage of a cyclical process of assessment, planning, implementing, and evaluating care.
- Preparation is key – ensure you have the bed space ready for the patient's arrival, with documentation to hand.
- First impressions are important – make the patient feel welcome and in competent hands!

►Patient scenarios

Consider what you should do in the following situations, then turn to the end of this section to check your answers.

1 A patient is admitted to your surgical ward from a nursing home. His family live some distance away and he has to have surgery in the next 4 hours. What steps can you take during the admission assessment to reduce his anxiety?

2 You are asked to prepare a bed space for a patient waiting in the Emergency Department. The patient has chronic obstructive pulmonary disease and is thought to have an acute infection. How would you prepare the bed area?

Website

🔲 **http://www.oxfordtextbooks.co.uk/orc/endacott**

You may find it helpful to work through our short online quiz and additional scenarios intended to help you to develop and apply the skills in this chapter.

More skills

You can find clear explanations and step by step instructions for mo clinical skills in *Clinical Nursing Skills: Core and Advanced* edited by Endaco R., Jevon, P., and Cooper, S., from which this chapter has been taken.

References

Access to Health Records Act (1990). HMSO, London.

Department of Health (2007). *Privacy and dignity – A report by the Chief Nursing Officer into mixed* sex accommodation in hospitals [online] http://www.dh.gov.uk/en/Publicationsandstatistics/ Publications/PublicationsPolicyAndGuidance/DH_074543 accessed 20/08/08.

NHS Institute for Innovation and Improvement (2007). *Going lean in the NHS: how lean thinking w enable the NHS to get more out of the same resources.* University of Warwick.

Nursing and Midwifery Council (2007). *Advice sheet on record keeping.* NMC, London.

Orem DE (1971). *Nursing: concepts of practice.* McGraw-Hill, New York.

Orlando J (1961). *The dynamic nurse/patient relationship: function, process and principles.* GP Putnams and Sons, New York.

Roper N, Logan W, and Tierney A (1983). Nursing process, a nursing model. *Nursing Mirror*, May 25, 17–19.

Roper N, Logan W, and Tierney A (2000). *The Roper-Logan-Tierney model of nursing based on acti ties of living (Monograph).* Churchill Livingstone, Edinburgh.

Roy C (1976). *Introduction to nursing: an adaptational model.* Prentice Hall, Englewood Cliffs, NJ.

Salvage J (2006). Model thinking. *Nursing Standard*, **20**(17), 24–5.

Smith GB (2003). *ALERTTM Acute Life-threatening Events Recognition and Treatment: a multiprofes-sional course in the care of the acutely ill patient.* University of Portsmouth.

►Answers to patient scenarios

1 Introduce yourself and the patients in the immediate bed area. Ensur you take next of kin contact details from the nursing home staff or th ambulance crew and ascertain what they have been told. If the patient able to understand, have this conversation in his presence. Orientate th patient to the ward layout and ensure he is as comfortable as possibl before starting the assessment. If the nursing home has provided patien information, check the accuracy of the information with the patient an transfer relevant details onto the admission documentation.

2 Check that all relevant documentation is at the bed space. This shoul include: an admission pack, manual handling assessment, pressure are record sheet, observation record sheet. Ensure the bed space is clean an tidy. Attach a clean oxygen mask to the oxygen port. Check whether a intravenous infusion has been inserted in the ED; if so, put a drip stand i the bed space. Complete the patient name board.

The patient pathway

Planning the effective patient discharge

Definition *116*
It is important to remember *117*
Prior knowledge *117*
Background *118*

Definition

Patient discharge planning can be defined as the act of facilitating the movement of a patient from one area of health care to another based on accurate assessment of their needs and subsequent implementation of an effective plan.

It is important to remember:

- Good record keeping throughout the patient discharge will also allow for effective continuity of information between members of the interprofessional health care team (NMC 2007).
- Nursing records are subject to audit as part of the clinical governance cycle. Therefore, any discharge planning that you undertake may be subject to review. The level of detail you include may assist in the development of health care when the quality review cycle takes place.
- Planning for patient discharge should begin as soon as possible after admission; it is therefore important to engage other members of the multidisciplinary team as soon as a patient need becomes apparent.

Prior knowledge

Before undertaking a patient admission assessment, make sure you are familiar with:

- Guidelines for records and record keeping (NMC 2007).
- Local policies and guidelines relating to record keeping.
- The range of services available in the local community.
- Chapter 3a (pp. 85–98) of this book, *Principles of good record keeping*.
- *Achieving timely 'simple' discharge from hospital: a toolkit for the multidisciplinary team* (Department of Health 2004).
- *Discharge from hospital: pathway, process and practice* (Department of Health 2003).
- Principles of informed consent.
- The Community Care Act *(synopsis)*.

Background

As with patient admission, there is currently no single model or template for a quality discharge plan; however, in England the NHS is seeking to standardize and improve communication and record keeping by implementing a new integrated IT system. 'NHS Connecting for Health' is providing the delivery of these systems and services, enabling information to be shared between NHS organizations across England. Similar projects are taking place across Scotland, Wales, and Ireland. This is a particularly important development when patients are discharged from a health care setting.

The patient's discharge process commences on their admission to your area. When you are questioning your patient and their carers about their present status, you need to be preparing for what will be required on discharge and putting this in place at the earliest opportunity. Patients are encouraged to expect this level of planning (see *Your guide to the NHS*, NHSE 2001) with assurance that any requirements at home will be provided as promptly as possible.

If structural changes to the home are needed, consider the amount of notice needed to facilitate this. By planning effectively, this will potentially allow the patient to maintain an optimum level of independence. For some patients, this means returning home.

If the patient has received input from social services, the service provider will need to be made aware of the patient's admission in order to suspend any support provided at home. Ensure that patient documentation prompts the person responsible for discharge planning to reinstate these resources quickly and effectively.

An effective discharge planning process enables the following to occur:
- Effective communication between health care professionals and with social services.
- The patient is able to move in a timely and safe manner to an area relevant to their needs.
- The patient is able to achieve a level of independence with support of family and social care facilities, where appropriate.

Improving discharge processes has distinct benefits for patients, the service, and health professionals (see Boxes 3.6–3.8).

Carer involvement in the discharge process

It is essential that informal carers are engaged as early as possible and their anxieties/needs addressed throughout the hospital stay. Two decades ago, the UK Department of Health (DH) acknowledged that the majority of care is provided by informal carers and that they require sufficient help to fulfil this role (DH 1989). A more recent report identified that one in six over 65s were providing some form of informal care (Wanless 2006).

Taking on the role of carer can be viewed as a duty or obligation, and health care professionals need to assess the support that carers themselves may require. Engaging the carers from admission will allow you to identify where increased input or support is required.

Box 3.6 Benefits for patients

- Identifying expected date of discharge can help patients to plan for when they go home.
- Patients' own responsibility for elements such as transport and arrangements at home can be clarified, discussed, and agreed in advance.
- Patients' experiences can be improved when they have more information about their care and they feel included in the decisions.
- Patients have more realistic expectations of the care they will receive.
- Patients only stay in hospital for the optimum amount of time for their recovery and are less likely to pick up a health care-associated infection (HCAI). (Department of Health 2004).

Box 3.7 Benefits for the service

- Health and social care can work as a whole system, supported by a managed care approach, resulting in improved quality, better match between demand and capacity, and better use of resources such as staffed hospital beds.
- Improved discharge processes contribute to improving patient flow and the effectiveness and efficiency of the system: right patient, right place, right time.
- Increased bed days will be available for the organization, reducing queues and cancellations.
- More effective communication between hospital and community will mean more streamlined services for all.
- Consistency in approach to single assessment and services based on need – joint assessment processes mean an integrated approach and less time wasted on duplicating the assessment process by different teams (Department of Health 2004).

Box 3.8 Benefits for health professionals

- Improved discharge processes make professionals' working lives easier and clearer, seeing their role as part of the whole system with each part impacting on the effectiveness of every other part.
- The development of proactive processes and a more managed care approach to their work, potentially leading to greater job satisfaction.
- Professionals have an increased sense of responsibility, recognition, and support for the work they contribute.
- Clinical team members will be directly contributing to improving the patient's experience.

Patient involvement in the discharge process

In the UK, the Department of Health promotes a partnership approach to patient discharge, with the patient taking an active role in discharge planning. A sample discharge proforma is suggested in Figure 3.4.

Detailed discharge planning

The 12 activities of living (Roper *et al.* 1983, 2000), used as a template for admission assessment, provide a useful framework for detailed discharge planning. For full details on these, please refer to the admission assessment skill (Chapter 3b, pp. 99–114). It is essential that these questions are addressed well in advance of the time of discharge.

Consider these suggestions as prompts – they are not intended to be exhaustive:

- **Breathing** – Is any respiratory support needed? For example, oxygen at home, COPD specialist nurse?
- **Elimination** – Has the patient returned to normal bowel habit on day of discharge? Is further advice or support needed? Do they have access to a toilet on either level of home? Has a risk assessment been completed?
- **Maintaining a safe environment** – Have relevant agencies been involved in ensuring safe place of residence on discharge?
- **Communication** – Are family and external agencies aware of pending discharge? Has relevant patient and family education been provided?
- **Sleeping** – Has relevant medication been dispensed with patient, including night sedation? Has this been explained to patient and/or carers?
- **Eating and drinking** – Is patient able to maintain their own dietary needs? If not, has Meals on Wheels been contacted or have dieticians provided sufficient gastrointestinal feeds for patient prior to review by GP?
- **Personal hygiene** – Has district nurse team been contacted in order to assist patient at home on discharge? Are resources required to facilitate this? Is there provision/availability of bath chair and shower for patient at home? Can this be provided?
- **Controlling body temperature** – Has the home been prepared so patient will be warm and comfortable on arrival? Does the patient have access to hot fluids and sufficient layering of clothing at home to maintain a comfortable body temperature?
- **Working and playing** – Is patient able to return to work? If so, do they require sickness authorization for work?
- **Mobilizing** – Has the physiotherapy team been required during the hospital stay? Are they aware of discharge plan? Is transport home appropriate and has the ambulance service been contacted if required?
- **Sexuality** – Does the planned discharge environment allow for the patient to be cared for in single sex accommodation, if they wish?
- **Dying** – If relevant, has an appropriate care environment been provided to allow the patient to die with dignity or to allow them to discuss this as a concern? Has the palliative care team been contacted?

Clinical observations

Patients are increasingly discharged from health settings with a chronic condition. In general these patients fall into one of two categories: firstly, those who were living with the disease prior to their current admission and, secondly, those for whom this admission has resulted in a diagnosis of a condition that requires considerable adaptation to their previous lifestyle.

For patients with a new diagnosis, one of the goals of discharge planning is to equip them with the knowledge and skills needed to take on self-care. For some patients this will mean ensuring they have information about how to access support services. Age becomes a factor when considering communication strategies proposed for increasing self-care; sources of information are increasingly internet-based but in 2006 less than 30% of older people (over 65) had access to the Internet and only 9% had Internet access via broadband (according to an Ofcom Consumer Panel).

Accountability and responsibility

Overall legal responsibility for a patient's care remains with the named consultant during admission, hospital stay, and discharge. However, the consultant can delegate responsibility to an appropriately qualified health professional. When a task is delegated, the consultant/lead clinician assumes responsibility for delegating appropriately. The person to whom the responsibility is delegated takes on commitment and responsibility for carrying out the task in a responsible, accountable, reasonable, and logical manner in keeping with their own professional code of conduct (DH 2004).

The person to whom responsibility is delegated should be aware that they are accountable for all their actions. There should be clear lines of communication between the consultant/lead clinician and the health professional discharging the patient so that they are accessible for advice when necessary.

It is recommended that the parameters of clinical/medical stability for each individual patient are agreed with the consultant or lead clinician and recorded on a locally developed form or documented in the patient's health care record.

Reflection and evaluation

When you have completed a patient discharge, consider the following questions:

1 Did you find it easy to liaise and organize the discharge with your patient?

2 Did any events surprise you?

3 Did the documentation gained on admission help or hinder you in your conduct of the discharge?

4 What aspects of the documentation might you change?

5 In what circumstances might the discharge be less straightforward?

Patient section Please complete these questions and the nurse will collect the form from you.	
Your name:	
Date:	
Is this the first time you have attended the department?	▢ Yes ▢ No
Do you understand your diagnosis?	▢ Yes ▢ No
Has a clinic appointment been made for you?	▢ Yes ▢ No ▢ Not sure
Have further investigations been arranged for you?	▢ Yes ▢ No ▢ Not sure
Have you been prescribed any medications?	▢ Yes ▢ No
Do you understand your medications?	▢ Yes ▢ No ▢ Not sure
Do you require a sick cerificate?	▢ Yes ▢ No ▢ Not sure
Thank you for completing this, please hand to the nurse looking after you.	
Nurses to complete	
Clinically stable and medically fit for discharge (in notes)	▢
Venflon removed	▢
Discharge discussed with patient	▢
GP discharge letter given to patient	▢
Drugs to take home supplied and explained	▢
Patient's own drugs returned	▢
Dressings and equipment supplied	▢
Information provided about self-care and who to contact if symptoms return	▢
District nurses contacted	▢
Follow-up call indicated	▢ Yes ▢ No
Notified patient about follow-up call	▢ (time)...............................
Clothes for discharge and keys on ward area	▢
Clerical staff	
Transport arranged	▢ (time)..........(how)............
Appointments and relevant documentation	▢ (with)...................................
Other follow-up arranged	▢..
Discharging signature .... (time)...............................	

Figure 3.4 Discharge planning proforma for completion by patient, nurse, and ward clerk. Amended from Department of Health (2004).

Further learning opportunities

1 Observe an experienced nurse planning a patient's discharge. Take particular note of any steps taken to put the patient at ease.
2 Review discharge plans for other patients, taking note of the range of professionals involved in ensuring a safe and timely discharge.

Reminders

Don't forget to:
• Initiate planning for discharge as soon as possible after admission.
• Provide appropriate support and education to enable the family to be involved as much as possible.
• Ensure communication with the multidisciplinary team is maintained.

►**Patient scenarios**

Consider what you should do in the following situations, then turn to the end of this section to check your answers.

1 Mr Kershaw is adamant that he should return to his own home following major abdominal surgery. What factors should you consider when planning his discharge?

2 Mrs Jitesh is being discharged tomorrow to a residential home following surgery for breast cancer. Her wound has not yet healed and requires regular dressings. What do you need to include in your discharge planning for this patient?

Website

📰 **http://www.oxfordtextbooks.co.uk/orc/endacott**

You may find it helpful to work through our short online quiz and additional scenarios intended to help you to develop and apply the skills in this chapter.

More skills

You can find clear explanations and step by step instructions for more clinical skills in *Clinical Nursing Skills: Core and Advanced* edited by Endacott, R., Jevon, P., and Cooper, S., from which this chapter has been taken.

References

Department of Health (1989). *Caring for people*. DH, London.

Department of Health (2003). *Discharge from hospital: pathway, process and practice*. DH, London.

Department of Health (2004). *Achieving timely 'simple' discharge from hospital: a toolkit for the multi-disciplinary team*. DH, London.

NHS Executive (2001). *Your guide to the NHS*. HMSO, London.

Nursing and Midwifery Council (2007). *Advice sheet on record keeping*. NMC, London.

Roper N, Logan W, and Tierney A (1983). Nursing process, a nursing model. *Nursing Mirror*, May 25, 17–19.

Roper N, Logan W, and Tierney A (2000). *The Roper-Logan-Tierney model of nursing based on activities of living* (Monograph). Churchill Livingstone, Edinburgh.

Wanless D (2006). *Securing good care for older people; taking a long term view*. London, King's Fund.

►**Answers to patient scenarios**

1 It is important to establish the patient's wishes as early as possible during the hospital admission; this provides as much time as possible for planning. The feasibility of Mr Kershaw's return home will depend largely on his level of independence prior to hospital admission. If he was receiving health or social services support prior to admission, these may need to be reviewed and extended. A number of other health care professionals, for example physiotherapist and occupational therapist, are likely to be involved in assessing Mr Kershaw's fitness for discharge home. This may include assessment of his home. Specific advice will be provided depending on the type of surgery, but may include avoiding stairs unless absolutely necessary; this will be difficult if he lives alone with the bathroom upstairs and kitchen downstairs. In addition, dietician advice may be required if he has to adapt his diet following surgery. If wound dressings are required, liaison with the community nursing service at an early stage is essential.

2 Ensure that community nursing services are alerted to the requirement for dressing changes and that the residential home is aware of Mrs Jitesh's needs. By their nature, residential homes do not provide nursing care; ensure Mrs Jitesh is sufficiently prepared for discharge to recognize any symptoms that may require review of the wound site. Follow your local policy for supply of wound dressings on discharge.

The patient pathway

Last offices

Definition 126
It is important to remember 127
Prior knowledge 127
Background 128
Procedure 134

Definition

Last offices are the last moments of care that we provide as health care professionals for patients who have recently died. It is a time in which full dignity should be provided and all religious and cultural beliefs fully met, ensuring that the health and safety of staff, other patients, and the deceased patient's relatives is protected.

It is important to remember:

- The deceased is your patient and you are responsible for them and their relatives/friends until they leave your care.
- As health professionals, we need to be considerate of the patient's religious and cultural needs. Local demographics will highlight changes in ethnicity; as care providers we need to be prepared to meet a wide range of needs relevant to the patient population.
- *Any* patient record can be used in evidence to investigate potential discrepancies either at local level or in a court of law. Keep in mind that the detail you record today may reliably assist you in remembering the care you delivered to your patients in many years to come. Documentation is particularly important if the patient has specific religious or cultural requirements that will affect last offices.

Prior knowledge

Before undertaking a patient admission assessment, make sure you are familiar with:
1 Guidelines for records and record keeping (NMC 2007).
2 Local policies and guidelines relating to record keeping.
3 Local polices and guidelines relating to the provision of last offices.
4 Local guidelines and support on spiritual care.
5 Patient/family wishes.
6 Local infection control policies

Background

Nursing care does not cease when a patient dies (Quested and Rudge 2003) and preparation for last offices often starts through discussion with the patient and family to ascertain their wishes.

The death of a patient can be one of the most traumatic events in your nursing career; Neuberger (2003) emphasizes the enormous demands placed on the nurse to make a difference for the dying and the bereaved when death is imminent. However, care of the dying patient can provide one of the most fulfilling periods of nursing care when carried out in a planned and organized way.

The final moment cannot be truly determined until the last breath is taken; therefore, any prior consideration to a potential death can alleviate distress for all involved. The actions included in last offices, for example washing the body, can also mark a point of closure in the relationship between the nurse and the patient (Cooke 2000).

Nurses working in specialist environments will become aware of particular conditions that are likely to result in death and can mentally prepare for this eventuality. For those nurses working in a respiratory role, for example caring for patients with cystic fibrosis, this can result in a close therapeutic relationship. However, the patient's eventual death, sometimes at a young age, can be distressing. Therefore, any planning for this likely outcome can help assure relatives and nurses that the patient's wishes are addressed.

The circumstances leading up to a patient's death vary widely, from a sudden, unexpected, traumatic death to a prolonged death surrounded by technology in an intensive care unit or a peaceful anticipated death in which symptoms are controlled.

The relationship between the nurse undertaking last offices and the deceased patient may also vary widely and you may experience a range of reactions to the death, some of which may seem out of proportion to your relationship with the patient and family. The support of colleagues is important at these times (Wilkin and Slevin 2004) and supervised reflective practice can be a useful strategy (O'Connell 2008). It is important to remember that the bereavement and counselling services offered by health services can play a useful role in supporting staff.

Verifying and certifying death

Death should be verified by a health care professional, most commonly a doctor, by checking for an apical heartbeat; some employers provide training for senior nursing staff to undertake this under agreed criteria (e.g. the expected death of a palliative care patient). An unexpected death must be verified by a doctor. **Verification of death**, including time and the name of the practitioner verifying death, must be recorded in the medical and nursing records.

The death must also be certified, a separate process that may occur after the body has been moved to the mortuary or funeral home; in hospital, this commonly occurs while the body is still on the ward. A death certificate must be provided by a registered medical practitioner who managed the patient during their last illness.

Rigor mortis occurs 2–6 hours after death, with full intensity within 48 hours, then disappears within another 48 hours (Robbins 1995). There are no specific requirements regarding when last offices must be completed; however, it is generally accepted practice for last offices to be undertaken as soon as possible after death, taking account of family wishes, potential infection control risks, and, in a hospital or institutional setting, the needs of other patients. It is easier to prepare the body before full rigor mortis is established.

Religious requirements

Neuberger (1999) makes it clear that it is impossible to provide last offices without knowing the patient's religious background. Therefore, it is vital that the admitting nurse establishes a full history of the patient on admission and establishes the wishes of the patient in relation to meeting religious and dying needs (Roper *et al.* 2000) – for further detail, see Chapter 3b.

Having obtained this information, the nurse should take the time to understand what relevant procedures will be needed in the event of the death of the patient. This may involve some research on a particular culture or faith; health services will have prepared for this through their 'Spiritual Department' or designated representative. There should be supportive literature or a direct contact to provide advice on what will be required.

The following guidelines are provided in order to support your study (see also the Further reading section). However, these are not exhaustive, and subtle changes may exist between individuals who practise the same faith. Therefore, if in doubt, seek advice from family or an appropriate faith leader. If the patient expresses any deviation from the accepted 'norms' for their faith, ensure this is documented.

Baha'ism

- Normal last offices procedure is appropriate, but relatives may wish to pay their own respects prior to this.
- Patients of this faith must not be cremated, embalmed, or transported more than 60 minutes away from the place of death.
- A special ring may be placed on the patient's finger and under no circumstances must this be removed.
- Post-mortems or donation of bodies to medical science is perfectly acceptable should patients wish it.

Buddhism

- Nurses should be aware that there are a variety of versions of this faith so specialist advice should be sought.
- Normal last offices procedure is appropriate, but a religious representative may wish to be present.
- If prayers are required, the body should not be moved for at least 1 hour.

Christianity

- Normal last offices procedure is normally appropriate. However, there are many denominations so specialist advice should be sought.

Hinduism

- Certain readings may be required throughout the last offices so contact of the local temple may assist.
- Family, in particular the eldest son, may wish to be involved with the procedure and at times this may involve a large number of people. Preparation for this may be advisable. Patient should be dressed in their own clothes.
- If no relatives are present then staff of the same sex should carry out the procedure wearing gloves and an apron.
- No washing of body should be undertaken. Nurses should straighten the body, close the eyes, and support the jaw before wrapping in a sheet. No removal of jewellery should be undertaken.
- Bodies should be cremated as soon as possible and generally post-mortems are considered inappropriate.

Islam

- It is desirable in the event of death that the patient's head is facing Mecca. If this is not possible then the patient should be turned on their right side so that their face faces Mecca.
- Owing to the faith objecting to the body being touched by a non-Muslim or person of the opposite sex, the nurse should ensure they wear gloves and an apron at all times. The eyes should be closed, the jaw supported, and the body straightened. The head should be turned to the right shoulder and the body covered in a white sheet.
- Toenails and fingernails should not be cut or the patient's body washed.
- The patient's body is normally taken home or to a mosque to be washed by another Muslim of the same sex. Cremation is forbidden and burial normally takes place within 24 hours.

Jehovah's Witness

- Relatives may wish to be present during last offices, either to pray or to read from the Bible. The family will inform staff should there be any special requirements, which may vary according to the patient's country of origin. Normal routine is appropriate.
- Jehovah's Witnesses usually refuse post-mortem unless absolutely necessary. Organ donation may be acceptable.

Judaism

- The family will contact their own Rabbi if they have one. If not, the hospital chaplaincy will advise. Prayers are recited by those present.
- Traditionally the body is left for about 8 minutes before being moved while a feather is placed across the lips and nose to detect any signs of breath.
- Usually close relatives will straighten the body, but nursing staff are permitted to perform any procedure for preserving dignity and honour. The body should be handled as little as possible but nurses may, while wearing gloves:
  - Close the eyes.
  - Tie up the jaw.
  - Put the arms parallel and close to the sides of the body, leaving the hands open. Straighten the patient's legs.
  - Remove tubes unless contraindicated.

- Watchers stay with the body until burial (normally completed within 24 hours of death). In the period before burial a separate non-denominational room is appreciated, where the body can be placed with its feet towards the door.
- It is not possible for funerals to take place on the Sabbath (between sunset on Friday and sunset on Saturday). If death occurs during the Sabbath, the body will remain with the watchers until the end of the Sabbath. Advice should be sought from the relatives. In some areas, the Registrar's office will arrange to open on Sundays and Bank Holidays to allow for the registration of death where speedy burial is required for religious reasons. The Jewish Burial Society will know whether this service is offered in the local area.
- Post-mortems are permitted only if required by law. Organ donation is sometimes permitted.
- Cremation is unlikely but some non-Orthodox Jews are now accepting this in preference to burial.

Sikhism

- Family members (especially the eldest son) and friends will be present if they are able.
- Usually the family takes responsibility for the last offices, but nursing staff may be asked to close the patient's eyes, support the jaw, straighten the body, and wrap it in a plain white sheet.
- The family will wash and dress the deceased person's body. Note the 5 Ks in Box 3.10.
- Post-mortems are only permitted if required by law. Sikhs are always cremated.
- Organ donation is permitted but some Sikhs refuse this as they do not wish the body to be mutilated.

Box 3.10 The 5 Ks in Sikhism

Do not remove the '5 Ks', which are personal objects sacred to Sikhs:
- *Kesh*: do not cut hair or beard or remove turban.
- *Kanga*: do not remove the semi-circular comb, which fixes the uncut hair.
- *Kara*: do not remove bracelet worn on the wrist.
- *Kaccha*: do not remove the special shorts worn as underwear.
- *Kirpan*: do not remove the sword: usually a miniature sword is worn.

Zoroastrianism

- Customary last offices are often acceptable to Zoroastrian patients.
- The family may wish to be present during, or participate in, the preparation of the body.
- Orthodox Parsees require a priest to be present, if possible.
- After washing, the body is dressed in the *Sadra* (white cotton or muslin shirt symbolizing purity) and *Kusti* (girdle woven of 72 strands of lambs' wool symbolizing the 72 chapters of the *Yasna* (Liturgy))).
- Relatives may cover the patient's head with a white cap or scarf.
- It is important that the funeral takes place as soon as possible after death.

- Burial and cremation are acceptable. Post-mortems are forbidden unless required by law.
- Organ donation is forbidden by religious law.

Further advice is provided in *A guide to cultural and spiritual awareness* published by Nursing Standard (2005).

Special considerations

Legal requirements

There are a number of circumstances in which the procedure for last offices has to be adjusted (see Table 3.4).

Death of an infected patient

Infection Control Services (2006) state four key points that must be attended to when an infected patient dies:

1 Place the patient in a waterproof body bag.
2 An infected body should be handled using the same precautions that were in place when the patient was alive.
3 According to local policy, complete a risk/hazard form to accompany the patient to the mortuary.
4 No religious procedure that carries the risk of spread of infection should be carried out on an infected body.

Check your local policy to clarify what categories of infected patient would be handled in this way.

Personal interpretations of death

A patient's death will affect each member of staff differently, depending on the relationship that they have developed with the patient, together with their own cultural and religious beliefs. Be aware that the way in which you present yourself to those around you will affect their expression of grief. If you are a student assisting with last offices for the first time, look at how your colleagues handle the situation.

Nurses may add their own personal touch to the formal last offices procedure. Examples of how this may occur could include the following, observed in colleagues who displayed sensitivity and a caring approach, despite the pressure of a busy ward. Some of these may appear quirky but highlight practices that you may witness:

- After the moment of death, place the body in a relaxed position and cover with sheet.
- Where possible, leave the body in privacy for a few minutes' rest, before undertaking the last offices procedure.
- When the patient has been wrapped and labelled, place a flower on top of the sheet and tape into place before requesting porters to transport the deceased patient to the mortuary.

Although these are not required practices, they demonstrate an intrinsic disposition to care rather than perform a task. However, regardless of the personal style of individual nurses, it is important to ensure that any special considerations, either for religious or legal reasons, are adhered to.

Table 3.4 Legal requirements associated with circumstances of death

Circumstance	Requirement
Death occurring within 24 hours of an operation.	All tubes, drains, catheters, and cannulae must be left in position. Post-mortem examination will be required to establish the cause of death. Any tubes, drains, etc. may have been a major contributing factor to the death (e.g. sepsis arising from infected central venous catheter).
Unexpected death or unknown cause of death.	As above. Post-mortem examination of the body will be required to establish the cause of death.
Patient brought into hospital who is already deceased.	As above, unless patient seen by a medical practitioner within 14 days before death. In this instance the attending medical officer may complete the death certificate if they are clear as to the cause of death.
Patient who dies after insertion of radioactive material.	Wards caring for patients with radioactive implants should have procedures in place for last offices. These are likely to include: **1** Informing the medical physics department. **2** Removal of radioactive sources after death is confirmed but before last offices are undertaken. **3** Use of a Geiger counter to check that all sources have been removed. The time and date of removal of the sources should be recorded.
Patient and/or relative wishes to donate organs/tissues for transplantation.	Contact local transplant coordinator as soon as decision is made to donate organs/tissue and before last offices is attempted. Obtain verbal and written consent from next of kin, as per local policy. Prepare body as per transplant coordinator's instructions (Travis 2002).

Procedure

Preparation

Prepare yourself

If this is the first time you have performed last offices, ask a more experienced nurse to assist. Check the patient's records for any specific wishes to be followed after death. If the patient's religious or cultural beliefs require certain procedures that you are unfamiliar with, seek advice from an appropriate faith leader.

Prepare the family

Ensure family are informed as soon as possible after death is confirmed. Provide verbal and written information regarding sources of support. If possible, provide a private room for family. Ascertain whether relatives wish to view the body; this should happen before last offices are completed. If relatives or next of kin are not contactable by telephone or via the GP, the police will attempt to locate them.

Family members may wish to undertake or assist with last offices; for some people, this provides a degree of comfort (Wong and Chan 2007, Marie Curie 2008). This option should be available whether the patient dies in hospital, in a residential setting, or at home.

Prepare the equipment/environment

Ensure you have equipment for washing the patient, shaving, combing hair, mouth care, and covering wounds or cannula sites. In addition, gather the documentation you need, according to local policy. This will include identification labels, notification of death cards, and the hospital property record book. Ascertain whether the patient is to be dressed in a shroud or their own clothes. Check the bed for any 'sharps' that may have been left on the bed during the urgency of resuscitation and dispose of them appropriately.

Step-by-step guide to last offices

Step	Rationale
1 Put on gloves and apron.	To reduce risk of cross-infection.
2 Lay the patient on their back with the assistance of two nurses (according to your employer's manual handling policy).	
3 Remove all but one pillow. Support the jaw by placing a pillow or rolled-up towel on the chest underneath the jaw.	To maintain the patient's dignity and to assist with future management of the body.
4 Straighten the limbs. Remove any mechanical aids such as pressure-relieving pads, patient-controlled analgesia pumps, etc., subject to the advice in Table 3.4.	
5 Document actions in patient records.	
6 Close the patient's eyes by applying light pressure to the eyelids for 30 seconds.	To maintain the patient's dignity and for aesthetic reasons. Closure of eyes will also provide tissue protection in case of corneal donation (Green and Green 1992).
7 Drain the bladder by pressing on the lower abdomen.	To prevent leakage that may pose a health hazard to staff.
8 Depending on local policy, pack orifices with gauze if fluid secretion continues or is anticipated. If excessive leaking of bodily fluids occurs, consider suctioning.	To prevent leakage that may pose a health hazard to staff. In some settings, this will be undertaken by mortuary staff – check your local policy.
9 Exuding wounds should be covered with a clean absorbent dressing and secured with an occlusive dressing. If a post-mortem is required, existing dressings should be left in situ and covered.	To prevent leakage that may pose a health hazard to staff.
10 Remove drainage tubes, etc. unless otherwise stated and document actions and any tubes remaining, e.g. CVP lines. Cover open drainage sites and seal any tubes with a spigot or cannula. If a post-mortem is required drainage tubes, etc. should be left in situ.	To prevent leakage that may pose a health hazard to staff.
11 Wash the patient, unless requested not to do so for religious/cultural reasons. If necessary, shave a male patient.	For hygienic and aesthetic reasons.
12 Clean the patient's mouth using a foam stick to remove any debris and secretions. Clean dentures and replace them in the mouth if possible. If this is not possible, place dentures in a clean, labelled denture pot and send to the mortuary with the body.	For hygienic and aesthetic reasons.

Step	Rationale
13 Remove all jewellery (in the presence of another nurse) unless requested by the patient's family to do otherwise. Jewellery remaining on the patient should be documented on the 'notification of death' form. Record the jewellery and other valuables in the patient's property book and store the items according to local policy.	To address legal requirements, local policy, and relatives' wishes.
14 Dress the patient in night clothes, other personal clothing, or a shroud, depending on hospital policy or relatives' wishes.	To meet the wishes of the deceased patient and the family.
15 Label one wrist and one ankle with an identification label. In the hospital setting, include the name of the ward on which the patient died, according to local policy. Complete any documents such as notification of death cards. Tape appropriate documentation securely to clothing or shroud.	To ensure correct and easy identification of the body in the mortuary.
16 Wrap the body in a mortuary sheet, ensuring that the face and feet are covered and that all limbs are held securely in position.	To avoid possible damage to the body during transfer and to prevent distress to colleagues, e.g. portering staff.
17 Secure the sheet with tape.	To avoid health and safety hazards associated with using pins.
18 Place the body in a sheet and then a body bag if leakage of body fluids is a problem or is anticipated, or if the patient has an infectious disease.	To prevent leakage that may pose a health hazard to staff.
19 Tape the second notification of death card to the outside of the sheet (or body bag).	For ease of identification of the body in the mortuary.
20 Screen off the area where removal of the body will occur.	To avoid causing unnecessary distress to other patients, relatives, and staff.
21 Remove gloves and apron. Dispose of equipment according to local policy and wash hands.	To minimize risk of cross-infection.
22 Record all details and actions in the patient records. Include time of death, names of those present, and names of those informed.	To ensure optimal communication.
23 Transfer property and patient records to the appropriate administrative department	To facilitate timely production of death certificate and the collection of property by the next of kin.

Following the procedure

1 Ensure the patient is moved to the chapel of rest/mortuary as soon as possible. Decomposition of the body may pose a health and safety hazard for those handling the body (Cooke 2000).

2 Other patients are often aware that a death is expected or has occurred. Be prepared to answer their questions honestly. It is also important to offer support and reassurance and to allay any misconceptions and fears.

3 If the patient is to be moved straight from the ward to the undertakers, contact the senior nurse for the hospital. There are a number of additional legal procedures to be followed including obtaining a Certificate for Burial or Cremation from the local registry office and obtaining written authority from the next of kin for removal of the body. Your employer should have policies (and a named person) in place to manage this situation.

4 If the relatives want to view the body after it has been removed from the ward, contact the mortuary staff. The hospital chaplaincy or bereavement support officer may accompany relatives to the mortuary viewing room, according to local policy.

Reflection and evaluation

When you have completed last offices, consider the following questions:
1 Did you find it easy asking what a patient's wishes were in relation to religious and dying needs?
2 Did any events surprise you?
3 Did the documentation gained on admission help or hinder you in your conduct of last offices?
4 In what circumstances might last offices be less straightforward?

Further learning opportunities

1 Observe an experienced nurse breaking the news of a patient's death to next of kin. Take particular note of how the experienced nurse responds to difficult questions.
2 Observe an experienced nurse break the news of a patient's death to fellow patients.

Reminders

Don't forget:
- That you are responsible for the deceased person and their family until they leave your care.
- That you too may need help and support after participating in last offices.

►Patient scenarios

Consider what you should do in the following situations, then turn to the end of this skill to check your answers.

1 A patient dies unexpectedly 6 hours after surgery. What do you need to consider when preparing to undertake last offices?

2 Why is the admission assessment important when preparing to undertake last offices?

Website

🖥 **http://www.oxfordtextbooks.co.uk/orc/endacott**

You may find it helpful to work through our short online quiz and additional scenarios intended to help you to develop and apply the skills in this chapter.

More skills

You can find clear explanations and step by step instructions for more clinical skills in *Clinical Nursing Skills: Core and Advanced* edited by Endacott, R., Jevon, P., and Cooper, S., from which this chapter has been taken.

References

Cooke H (2000). *A practical guide to holistic care at the end of life*. Butterworth-Heinemann, Oxford.

Green J and Green M (1992). *Dealing with death: practices and procedures*. Chapman and Hall, London.

Infection Control Services (2006). Last offices on infected patients [online] http://www.infection-controlservices.co.uk/documents/policies/Last%20Offices%20on%20Infected%20Patients%20Policy%202006.pdf accessed 20/08/08.

Marie Curie Cancer Care (2008). Bereavement: helping you to deal with the death of someone close to you [online] http://www.mariecurie.org.uk/Documents/PATIENTS-CARERS-FAMILIES/Updated-pdf/bereavement.pdf accessed 08/07/11.

Neuberger J (1999). *Caring for dying people of different faiths*. Lisa Sainsbury Foundation, London.

Neuberger J (2003). Commentary: a good death is possible in the NHS. *British Medical Journal*, **326**, 34.

Nursing and Midwifery Council (2007). *Advice sheet on record keeping*. NMC, London.

Nursing Standard (2005). A guide to cultural and spiritual awareness [online] http://nursing-standard.rcnpublishing.co.uk/archive/article-a-guide-to-cultural-and-spiritual-awareness accessed 08/07/11.

O'Connell E (2008). Therapeutic relationships in critical care nursing: a reflection on practice. *Nursing in Critical Care*, **13**, 138–143.

Quested B and Rudge T (2003). Nursing care of dead bodies: a discursive analysis of last offices. *Journal of Advanced Nursing*, **41**, 553–60.

Robbins J, ed. (1995). *Caring for the dying patient and the family*, 3rd edition. Chapman and Hall, London.

Roper N, Logan W, and Tierney A (2000). *The Roper-Logan-Tierney model of nursing based on activities of living* (Monograph). Churchill Livingstone, Edinburgh.

Travis S (2002). *Procedure for the care of patients who die in hospital*. Royal Marsden NHS Trust, London.

Wilkin K and Slevin E (2004). The meaning of caring to nurses: an investigation into the nature of caring work in an intensive care unit. *Journal of Clinical Nursing*, **13**, 50–59.

Wong MS and Chan SWC (2007). The experiences of Chinese family members of terminally ill patients – a qualitative study. *Journal of Clinical Nursing*, **16**, 2359–64.

Useful further reading and websites

Further advice regarding religious practices can be found at the following websites:

Baha'ism – http://www.bahai.org.uk
Buddhism – http://www.nbo.org.uk
Christianity – http://www.ccj.org.uk
Hinduism – http://www.hinducounciluk.org
Islam – http://www.mcb.org.uk
Jehovah's Witness – http://www.watchtower.org/
Judaism – http://www.bod.org.uk
Sikhism – http://www.sikhs.org
Zoroastrianism – http://www.avesta.org

▶Answers to patient scenarios

1 Ensure the relatives are told immediately. It is possible that they haven't visited the patient since before surgery so they may wish to view the body. This should take place before last offices. The patient will undergo a post-mortem to ascertain cause of death, so all drains, cannulae, catheters, and tubes must be left in place. The religion of the patient may mean that post-mortem is unacceptable; the medical staff should be alerted to this as soon as possible in order for appropriate discussions to take place with the family.

2 Essential information is gathered during the admission assessment, including next of kin contact details, the patient's religious preferences, and the storage (or return to relatives) of any valuables that the patient may have brought into hospital. Admission assessment also provides an opportunity to talk with patients and relatives about the possibility of dying.

Chapter 1 from the Oxford Handbook of Mental Health Nursing

Edited by

Patrick Callaghan

Professor of Mental Health Nursing
University of Nottingham & Nottinghamshire
Healthcare NHS Trust

Helen Waldock

Health and Social Care
Advisory Service
London

OXFORD
UNIVERSITY PRESS

Introduction

Concepts of mental health and illness *144*
Explaining mental illness *146*
Understanding mental illness *148*
The stress vulnerability model *150*
The experience of mental illness *152*
Early detection of mental illness *154*
The Capable Practitioner Framework (CPF) *156*
Person-centred mental health nursing *160*
The principles and codes of professional practice *162*
Accountability *164*
Case management skills *166*
Values and attitudes for professional practice *168*
The carer's charter *170*
Guidelines for working with users *172*
Ethics *174*
The essence of care *176*
The Care Programme Approach (CPA) *178*
The Single Assessment Process for older adults (SAP) *180*
The National Service Framework for Mental Health *182*
The National Service Framework for Older People *184*
The biological context of mental health *186*
The socio-cultural context of mental health *188*
Mental health promotion *190*
Transcultural mental health nursing *192*
Models of mental health nursing *194*
Mental health nursing in context *196*
Rehabilitation and recovery *198*

Concepts of mental health and illness

The most common and international definition of health was produced by the World Health Organization (WHO) in 1946. They defined 'health as a state of complete physical, mental and social well-being and not merely the absence of disease or infirmity'.[1] This definition of health relates not only to our minds and our bodies but also to our quality of life – including families, friends, and communities.

Although not without its critics, this definition can also be a starting point for thinking about the concept of mental health – it refers not only to our interior mental well-being but also to the quality of how we live our lives.

A concept can be defined as an abstract thought or idea. There is no one concept of mental health, but several categories of approach that have informed the thinking and delivery of mental health and illness care over the years.

The medical concept

The medical concept was developed by psychiatrists. They perceive the ill person as the problem, and believe that illness stems from a chemical imbalance within the brain. The focus for treatment has been on chemical intervention in the form of medication or psychosurgery. This concept is often criticized for ignoring social or familial links.

The anti-psychiatry concept

This concept stems from the work of T Szasz (1961).[2] He proposed that the experiences and behaviours referred to as mental illness were really problems associated with living, and an individual's inability to adapt to the world around them. Whilst Szasz acknowledged that some behaviour has a physical cause – such as acquired brain injury – he concludes that psychiatrists are oppressors and that there is no such thing as mental illness. He has been criticized for ignoring the genuine suffering of those with mental illness.

The family concept

R Laing (1964) contributed to this debate,[3] believing that the family was the cause of mental illness, particularly schizophrenia. He regarded the family as a pathogenic institution, unable to give a consistent approach to a child. Hence the child grows up unable to please the parents and suffering intolerable emotional stress, leading to mental illness. He proposed that psychiatrists colluded with the family in an attempt to control behaviour that others find a nuisance.

Helen Waldock, Health and Social Care Advisory Service

The labelling concept

Also in the 1960s, it was proposed by T Scheff[4] that labelling was the single most important cause of mental illness, in that you become what you are labelled. He was of the view that certain bizarre or 'deviant' behaviours which did not already fit into a defined category such as 'punk rocker' or 'Goth' (1960s examples being teddy boy or mod), were labelled mental illness. As a consequence, psychiatric symptoms can be seen as instances of residual deviancy which have become part of society's cultural stereotype of mental illness.

This concept helped by drawing attention to the notion of stigmatization of the mentally ill, although Scheff was criticized as the majority of people who become psychiatric patients suffer serious mental disturbances before any label is applied to them.

Psychoanalytical concepts

There are many and varied concepts in this category that understand us from the view of our unconscious and our early childhood experience. Freud's psychodynamic structure of personality suggests that behaviour is influenced by id, ego, and super ego, We are born id and our personality develops in stages during childhood. If there are conflicts associated with a particular phase of personality development (oral, anal, phallic latent, and genital) then fixations can develop that show themselves in personality. Jung and Erikson developed the broader psychodynamic approach believing that it is the social world that influences personality development.

Other concepts include attachment theory which explores the impact of early relationships with the primary carer (typically the mother). The bond between mother and child, or lack of bond, is thought to impact on the child's ability to engage with the world. At the heart of the theory lies a paradox in that children with very close attachments to the mother are also the most able to express their independence. Freudian concepts suggested that failure to break this attachment results in emotional trauma that could lead to later mental illness.

References

1 World Health Organization. Constitution. WHO: Geneva, 1964.
2 Szasz, T. The Myth of Mental Illness. Harper: New York, 1961.
3 Laing, R, Easterton A. Sanity, Madness and the Family. Tavistock: London, 1964.
4 Scheff, T. Being Mentally Ill: A Sociological Theory. Aldine: Chicago, 1966.

Further reading (the classics)

Gabbard, G, Beck, JS, Holmes, J. Oxford Textbook of Psychotherapy. Oxford University Press: Oxford, 2005.
Holmes, J. John Bowlby and Attachment Theory. Routledge: London, 1993.
Pilgrim, D. Key Concepts in Mental Health. Sage Publications: London, 2005.

Explaining mental illness

Recent years have seen many changes in the provision of services and therapies for people suffering from a range of mental health problems. The move away from large-scale institutional care to individual care in the community has been accompanied by a growth in the research and practice of evidence-based psychosocial approaches to care. The pharmaceutical industry has also contributed to current practice with the development of more refined user-friendly medications.

Although the exact cause of mental illness is not known, it is becoming clearer through research that many conditions are precipitated by a combination of biological, psychological, and environmental factors.

Biological Factors

- Abnormal balance of neurotransmitters: nerve cell chemicals enable brain cells to communicate with each other. When neurotransmitters are out of balance or not working properly, symptoms of mental illness can develop.
- Genetics: some mental illness runs in families and is passed on through genes. Rather than one gene causing a mental illness, it is thought that person inherits susceptibility (multiple gene involvement), which when coupled with other factors, can trigger symptoms of mental illness.
- Infections: can be linked to brain damage and the development of mental illness, or the worsening of symptoms e.g. autoimmune neuropsychiatric disorder has been linked to the development of OCD in children.
- Brain injury: cause may be prenatal, birth trauma, exposure to toxins, or acquired brain injury. All may contribute to the development of symptoms as the neurotransmitter pathways are disturbed.

Psychological factors

- Severe psychological trauma as a child e.g. emotional, physical, or sexual abuse.
- A significant early loss e.g. of a parent, sibling.
- Emotional or physical neglect.
- Poor ability to relate to others.

Environmental factors

- A dysfunctional family life.
- Death or divorce.
- Poverty.
- Feelings of inadequacy, low self esteem, anxiety, anger, or loneliness.
- Changing jobs or school.
- Social or cultural expectations.
- Substance misuse by an individual or their parents.

Helen Waldock, Health and Social Care Advisory Service

Although all individuals react in different ways to different events, there are some groups in society that are exposed to more stressors than others. These include migrants, refugees, and asylum seekers, those who live in extreme poverty, and those who have no true sense of self. These people are more vulnerable to developing mental illness, hence the reason for accurate and corroborated history taking.

Further reading

Kuipers, E, Bebbington, P. *Living with Mental Illness: a book for relatives and friends.* Souvenir Press: UK, 2005.

Further viewing (available on DVD)

A Beautiful Mind, Directed by Ron Howard, produced by Brain Grazer and Ron Howard. Distributed by Universal Pictures. Length 134 minutes.
The Snake Pit, Directed by Anatole Litvak, produced by Robert Bassler, Anatole Litvak & Darryl Zanuck. Distributed by 20th Century Fox. Length 108 minutes.

Understanding mental illness

Mental illness refers collectively to all diagnosable mental disorders characterized by alterations in thinking, mood, or behaviour or a combination of these, mediated by the brain and associated with distress and impaired functioning. There have been concerted efforts to develop systems for classifying mental illness that would be relevant for use across cultures. Two classification systems are used:
1) Diagnostic and Statistical Manual of Mental Illness (DSM IV)[5]
2) Diagnostic and Statistical Manual of Mental and Behavioural disorders referred to as ICD 10 (International Classification of Disease version 10)—this is the classification system used primarily in the UK.[6]

Both the above have gone some way to providing uniformity and consistency to the diagnosis and classification of mental illness, however they are not without their critics.

Parker *et al.* (1995) said they 'failed to represent the diversity of the human experiences of distress'.[7] He also argues that these systems fail to take account of race, identity, gender, and social power. They are in themselves social constructs developed by the western world, and based on the medical model.

These classification systems do have their place as they help to determine the severely ill from the moderate or mildly ill. The absence of such systems would hamper the ability to plan services, evaluate treatments or interventions, or evaluate the effectiveness of preventative strategies.[8]

We may all suffer from one or more of the symptoms described in either classification system at some point in our life. It is unhelpful, meaningless, and stigmatizing to have personal distress labelled in such a manner that people respond to the label rather that the individual. This can be demonstrated by the comparison in the table opposite.

It is more important to understand the experience of the person living with mental ill-health rather than attempting to understand mental illness *per se.*

Note:
Co-morbidity – refers to the existence of two or more illnesses in the same individual.

Serious Mental Illness (SMI) refers to people who have an illness that is long lasting and severely interferes with a person's ability to participate in life activities.

Helen Waldock, Health and Social Care Advisory Service

Comparison of the psychosocial and biomedical perspectives

Criteria	Psychosocial	Biomedical
Cause of illness	Behaviour, beliefs, poverty, coping mechanisms, relationships, childhood trauma	Genetics, brain injury, viral or bacterial infection, birth trauma, neurotransmitter imbalance
Responsibility for illness	Individual, social, political, environmental factors, economics	External forces causing internal change
Treatment of illness	Holistic approach: change in beliefs, coping style, economic status, relationships	Medication or other medical intervention, surgery, ECT
Responsibility for treatment	Individual, family, significant other, support networks	The doctor and other professional involved in collaboration with the individual
Relationship between mental health and illness	Both exist on a continuum, with degrees of mental health and mental illness	Dichotomous, the person is either healthy or ill
Relationship between mind and body	The mind and body are mutually interdependent	The mind and body function independently of one another
Role in health and illness	Psychosocial factors contribute to an individual's mental health status	Illness has psychosocial consequences not causes

References

5 American Psychiatric Association. Diagnostic and Statistical Manual of Mental Disorders, 4th revision. American Psychiatric Press U.S.A 1994.

6 World Health Organization. International Classification of Mental and Behavioural Disorders, 10th revision. WHO: Geneva, 1992.

7 Parker, I, Geogarca E, Harper D, McLaughlin T and Stowell-Smith M. Deconstructing Psychopathology. Sage: London, 1995.

8 Newton, J. Preventing Mental Illness. Routledge: London, 1988.

The stress vulnerability model

The stress vulnerability model is of considerable importance in Mental Health Nursing (MHN). It was first described in an article written nearly 30 years ago.[9] This article suggested that a vulnerability to schizophrenia was made up of:

- Variables which could be described as 'inborn', such as genes.
- Variables which could be described as 'acquired', which may include physical events (e.g. perinatal complications and illnesses such as influenza during pregnancy), developmental phenomena, and various life events.

This model has been developed and adapted over the years, and has received some criticism. However, it is of considerable practical use because it embraces a wide range of research demonstrating a wide spectrum of causative factors. It overcomes rather sterile debates about the causation and maintenance of mental illnesses, particularly schizophrenia and other psychoses.

How can the mental health nurse use this model?

This model is particularly useful for the mental health nurse when dealing with people with existing illnesses – particularly schizophrenia and other psychoses – as it recognizes that stress may lead to relapse. The mental health nurse may be very effective in preventing relapse by:

- Helping the person deal with stresses from a range of sources e.g. by anxiety management training, or by teaching the person to cope with hallucinations.
- Providing interventions which deal with the stress itself e.g. family interventions in schizophrenia or interventions for substance abuse.

Relapse is often triggered by a combination of stresses such as boredom, drug use, the stigma attached to the illness and a negative family environment, rather than a single stress.[10] The mental health nurse is ideally placed to deliver a wide range of interventions which can be described as 'psychosocial'; and training in these interventions is now offered to most of these nurses who work in the community.

Although this model is clearly applicable to the practical management of most mental health problems, as noted above, it has been largely applied to schizophrenia. Research now clearly demonstrates that there is an inborn or acquired vulnerability to a range of conditions, including depression, anxiety, and obsessive compulsive disorder. Other disorders may be triggered by the influence of various stressors.

Professor Kevin Gournay Institute of Psychiatry, Kings College, London

References

9 Zubin, J, Spring, B. Vulnerability: A new view of schizophrenia. *Journal of Abnormal Psychology*
86: 260–6, 1977.
10 Warner, R. *Recovery from schizophrenia*, 2nd edn. Routledge: London, 1994.

The experience of mental illness

Mental illness is associated with a significant burden of morbidity and disability. Lifetime rates for any kind of psychological disorder are higher, affecting nearly half the population.[11] Mental disorders are often undiagnosed by doctors, and people are reluctant to seek professional help.

Overall rates of psychiatric disorders are the same for men as they are for women but there are distinctions in the patterns:
- Unipolar depression is twice as common in women.
- Men are three times more likely to be diagnosed with an antisocial personality disorder.
- There are no marked differences in severe mental illnesses between men and women.
- Less than 2% of the population have a severe mental illness.

The experience of mental illness is unique to each individual regardless of the symptoms they are suffering, due to the individual experience of emotion. For example the vast majority of people have felt 'happiness' at some point in their lives, some cried at this time and others laughed.

Common symptoms experienced

Mood changes

- *Anxiety:* this is greater than the tension felt in a stressful situation, such as exams. It is characterized by physical symptoms such as palpitations, sweating, tremor, and the fear that something awful is about to happen.
- *Depression:* this is greater than the accepted response to a sad or tragic life event. It is typical to have disturbed sleep, reduced appetite, little interest in life, feeling hopeless and helpless.
- *Elation:* this is greater than excitement, and is coupled with irritability and impatience. A person's view of themselves may also be altered e.g. by becoming grand and extravagant both materially and personally.

Thought processes

- Delusions; these are greater than just being wrong. It is a belief or impression that is absolute and unshakable, not open to change through experience or discussion. Examples are persecutory delusions, where a person feels they are being 'got at', or delusions of reference, where a person believes that the TV, radio, or newspapers are referring specifically to them.
- Obsessional or compulsive thoughts: these are greater than everyday routines that we all have, or set ways of doing certain tasks. These thoughts are intrusive, unwanted, and beyond a person's control. They may be coupled with repetitive behaviour (ritualistic behaviour) that cannot be interrupted.

Helen Waldock, Health and Social Care Advisory Service

- Odd thoughts: these are greater than the occasional sense of deja-vu experienced by many. It is when a person thinks that others can read/see into their mind (thought broadcast) or are able to put their thoughts into the mind of others (thought insertion).

Perceptual changes

This refers to how an individual experiences the world around them and their unique sense of reality. In mental illness, there are sometimes changes to these experiences that are very real to the individual, but not experienced by anyone else. These experiences are referred to as hallucinations:

- *Auditory:* where voice/voices/conversations/noise that do not belong to the individual are heard within a person's head (most common).
- *Visual:* where a person sees things that are not seen by anyone else.
- *Olfactory:* where a person can smell something that is not smelt by anyone else.
- *Tactile:* where a person can feel something, usually on their skin, that is not connected to any external stimuli.
- *Gustatory:* where a person experiences a particular taste that is not related to anything in their surroundings.

Behaviour changes

These may be marked and varied depending on other symptoms experienced by the person. They sometimes result in poor self-care to the extent of neglect. They are not symptoms in themselves but an indicator that all may not be well.

Speech changes

If thoughts, perception, and mood changes are occurring, then it is logical that a person's speech will change, not only in what they say but in how they say it. They may lose or have exaggerated intonation, or they may struggle to communicate at all. They may keep changing the subject (flight of ideas), or speak so quickly that they are difficult to follow or stop (pressure of speech).

Reference

11 World Health Organization. *The world health statistics annual.* WHO: Geneva, 1995.

Further Reading

Jampolsky, L. *Walking Through the Walls.* Celestial Arts Berkeley, California 2005.
Tessler, RC, Gamache, C. *Family Experiences with Mental Illness.* Auburn House Publishing Company, Westport, CT 2000.
Wahl OF. *Telling is a Risky Business: the experience of mental illness and stigma.* Rutgers University Press: Piscataway NJ, 2000.

Early detection of mental illness

For people of all ages, early detection, assessment, and linkage with treatment and supports can prevent mental health problems from resulting in poor life outcomes. Different behaviours are characteristic for different stages of life. The focus of early detection is on patterns of behaviour. Physical health problems need to be excluded before considering mental illness.

In children and adolescents the onset of illness is usually gradual and it is often difficult to establish if they are going through a temporary phase. The following signs can indicate many things, but if they persist, they may indicate the onset of a mental illness and a thorough assessment by a mental health professional is recommended.

Changes in younger children
- Clear change in school performance.
- Misuse of alcohol and/or drugs.
- Inability to cope with problems and daily activities.
- Marked changes in sleeping and/or eating habits.
- Many complaints of physical ailments e.g. headaches.
- Aggressive or non-aggressive consistent infringement of rights of others.
- Opposition to authority including truancy, thefts, or vandalism.
- Strong fear of becoming obese with no relationship to actual body weight.
- Depression shown by continued, protracted negative mood and attitude, often accompanied by poor appetite, difficulty sleeping, or thoughts of death.
- Recurrent outbursts of anger. Self-injurious behaviour e.g. head-banging, self-biting, cutting.

Changes in pre-adolescents and adolescents
- Clear change in school performance.
- Misuse of alcohol and/or drugs.
- Inability to cope with problems and daily activities.
- Marked changes in sleeping and/or eating habits.
- Many complaints of physical ailments e.g. headaches.
- Aggressive or non-aggressive consistent infringement of rights of others.
- Opposition to authority including truancy, thefts, or vandalism.
- Strong fear of becoming obese with no relationship to actual body weight.
- Depression shown by continued, protracted negative mood and attitude, often accompanied by poor appetite, difficulty sleeping, or thoughts of death.
- Recurrent outbursts of anger.
- Self-injurious behaviour e.g. head-banging, self-biting, cutting.

Helen Waldock, Health and Social Care Advisory Service

Changes in adults

- Withdrawal and loss of interest in usual activities.
- Loss of energy or motivation.
- Problems with memory and concentration.
- Deterioration in work or study.
- Lack of emotional response or inappropriate emotional display.
- Sleep or appetite disturbances.
- Unusual ideas or behaviours.
- Feeling 'changed' in some way.

Changes in the older person (early dementia)

- Recent memory loss that affects employment and social activity e.g. names and people.
- Difficulty performing familiar tasks e.g. cooking, cleaning.
- Problems with language e.g. forgetting simple words.
- Disorientation to time and familiar places e.g. own street.
- Poor or decreased judgements e.g. driving ability.
- Problems with abstract thinking e.g. not recognizing symbols such as £.
- Misplacing things e.g. putting door keys in the fridge.
- Changes in mood or behaviour unrelated to events.
- Changes in personality e.g. stops communicating.
- Loss of initiative e.g. does not get dressed.

Further reading

Cooper, M. Child and Adolescent Mental Health. Hodder Education: 2005. UK
Salovey, PR and Rothman AJ. The Social Psychology of Health. Taylor Francis Ltd. UK. 2003.

The Capable Practitioner Framework (CPF)

Mental health practitioners are facing the greatest and fastest moving set of changes encountered for several decades, courtesy of the Strategy for Mental Health.

The changing arena of service provision is now more varied, dispersed, and complex than ever before. The requirements for effective care now come from numerous agencies such as primary care, housing, social services, the voluntary sector, and the family, as well as specialist mental health services, creating problems of coordination, accountability, and efficiency. Service provision has re-orientated to put the requirements of the service user/family/carer at its centre, and the increasing development of evidence-based interventions has created the need for the capable practitioner.

The capable practitioner is a broad, unifying, theoretical framework which encompasses the set of skills, knowledge, and attitudes required within the work force of mental health practitioners to effectively implement the national service framework. They are not the domain of any one of the professions and are developed as part of pre- and post-registration/qualifying training.

Capability can be defined as:

- A performance component: identifying what people need to possess in the way of knowledge, skills, and attitude, and what they need to achieve in the work place.
- An ethical component: integrating knowledge of culture, values, and social awareness into professional practice.
- An emphasis on reflective practice in action.
- The ability to effectively implement evidence-based interventions in the modern mental health system.
- A commitment to working with new models of professional practice and responsibility for life-long learning.

The capability framework combines the notions of a reflective practitioner with that of an effective practitioner. The process moves from a base where all the workforce must have ethical practice moving through the five domains to increasing specialism that will only apply to some staff.

Five domains for modern mental health practice:

1. Ethical Practice: makes assumptions about the values and attitudes needed for practice.
2. Knowledge: recognized as being the foundation of effective practice.
3. Process of care: describes the capabilities required to work effectively in partnership with users, carers, families, team members, and other agencies.
4. Interventions: these are capabilities specific to a particular evidence base within mental health care.
5. Context specific application e.g. assertive outreach, home treatment, crisis resolution.

Helen Waldock, Health and Social Care Advisory Service

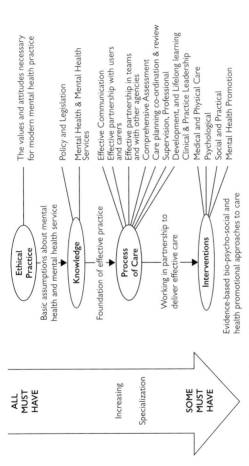

Fig.1.1 A framework for capable practice (SCMM 2001).

Each of these five categories is further subdivided to arrive at specific statements of capability for mental health practice.

Other competency frameworks

Knowledge and skills framework (KSF): NHS-only focus.[13]

National Occupational Standards (NOS): similar to the CPF but designed to provide a measurement of output or performance by detailed descriptions of competence required in providing mental health services.[14]

References

12 National Service Framework Mental Health 1999 Department of Health. The Stationery Office London.

13 Department of Health. Knowledge and Skills Framework. DoH: London, 2004. www.dh.gov.uk

14 National Institute for Mental Health England. National Occupational Standards. NIMHE: London, 2003. www.nihme.org.uk.

Further reading

Sainsbury's Centre for Mental Health. The Capable Practitioner. SCMH London 2001. www.centreformentalhealth.org.uk/.

Person-centred mental health nursing

The National Service Framework for Mental Health (1999) sets out the principles for contemporary mental health care in England. Central to this is the Care Programme Approach (CPA). For the CPA to be effective the service user must be well informed about mental health and mental health services, they must be at the centre of their own care, in partnership with staff and able to exercise informed choice.

The principles of person-centred care are:

The service user

- Should be informed about services and how to access them, in clear language of their choice (including sign language).
- Will have their views and wishes at the forefront throughout assessment, care planning, and service delivery.
- Should be given an assessment that not only identifies what is needed, but takes account of their strengths and abilities.
- Expects processes and services to enable maximum potential for independence.
- Must be involved in decisions about their care and be empowered to determine the level of risk they are prepared to take.
- Should be given realistic options as to how their needs can be met within existing eligibility criteria.
- Consents to information being collected about them and agreeing how this may be shared.
- When somebody lacks the capacity to make decisions to give consent, services must secure their maximum participation whilst safe-guarding their interests.
- Should receive high quality care that is evidence based, efficient, non-discriminatory, tailored to their individual needs, and acceptable to them.

The carers and the family

- Can be involved with the care of the individual if they chose to be, and where the individual has given consent.
- Have their support needs as a carer assessed in their own right.
- Should be supported and educated in the care they give.
- Should be treated with the same respect, consideration and non-discrimination as the service user.

Integrated services (📖 CPA)

- Access to services is via a coordinated and straightforward assessment, with duplication kept to a minimum.
- Effective information sharing, where confidentiality is respected, is crucial for effective person-centred care.

Helen Waldock, Health and Social Care Advisory Service

- Agencies must coordinate services in the best interests of the individual.
- Promoting health and well-being is an integral part of the service to the individual.
- Rehabilitation and recovery should be the models of choice.

Staff

- Should receive proper training and development to adapt to the changing mental health climate.
- Have the right to clinical and professional supervision.
- Receive an annual appraisal and continuing professional development – these are integral to valuing staff (📖 Management supervision).

Further reading

Adams, N. *Treatment Planning for Person-Centred Care: the road to mental health and addiction recovery.* Academic Press: London 2004.

Benson WD, Briscoe L. Jumping the Hurdles of Mental Health Care Wearing Cement Shoes. *Journal of American Psychiatric Nurses Association* **9**: 123–8, 2003.

Bryant-Jeffe, R. *Responding to a Serious Mental Health Problem: person-centred dialogues.* Radcliffe Medical Press: 2005.

The principles and codes of professional practice

All professions provide their own code for professional practice whether they are delivering clinical care or managing services. The purpose of a code of practice is to enable clarity on the basic standards that service users can expect. They ensure that services are provided in a legal and ethical manner by adhering to established protocols, procedures, and guidelines. All codes of practice contain the same fundamental underlying principles:

- To place the needs of service users ahead of the professionals own agenda.
- To promote health and prevent illness.
- To maintain confidentiality in keeping with the law.
- To respect the right to life or death with dignity.
- To respect individuality, regardless of age, race, disability, culture, gender orientation, politics, nationality, or social status.
- To reduce or alleviate suffering with empathy.
- To take personal responsibility and accountability for your practice.
- To act in a manner that promotes the profession.
- To cooperate with other professionals in the delivery of care.

Further detail can be explored by subdividing into key relationships between the profession, the service user, practice, the profession, and colleagues (see table opposite).

Inherent within these principles is the notion of 'Duty of care'.

Duty of care requires that everything possible is done to protect the health and safety of others, whether they are service users or staff.

Individual professions can access their code of practice from the home page of their professional body. For registered nurses in the UK: www.nmc-uk.org.

Key concepts of professional practice include:

Compassion: the humane quality of understanding the suffering of others and wanting to do something about it.

Integrity: the characteristics of honesty and sincerity.

Empowerment: the process of increasing personal, interpersonal, and political power to enable individuals or collectives to improve their life situation. It requires the full participation of people in the formulation, implementation and evaluation of decisions determining the functioning and well-being of society.

Helen Waldock, Health and Social Care Advisory Service

Roles & Responsibilites

Practitioners and service users	Practitioners and practice	Practitioners and the profession	Practitioners and colleagues
Cause of illness	Behaviour, beliefs, poverty, coping mechanisms, relationships, childhood trauma	Genetics, brain injury, viral or bacterial infection, birth trauma, neurotransmitter imbalance	Support workplace systems to promote MD working
Provide adequate information to promote informed choice and consent	Take responsibility for maintaining registration or licence	Support the dissemination of research- and practice-based evidence	Ensure that people and the environment are fit for the purpose
Treat service users with integrity and competence	Strive to improve professional skills of self and other team members	Advance and protect the standards of the profession	Support a culture that promotes common ethical values
Ensure clinical and environmental safety	Promote the utilization of evidence-based practice	Evaluate the quality of work against professional standards	Safeguard individuals and the community from poor practice

Further reading

Blais K, Mayes J, Kozier B. *Professional Nursing Practice, Concepts and Perspectives*. Prentice-Hall: New Jersy 2005.

Davies, C, Filay, JL. *Changing Practice in Health and Social Care*, Sage Publications: London, 2000.

Accountability

Originally accountability referred to the compliance with the established norms of financial management. More recently, the meaning of accountability has broadened to include the achievement of performance targets, such as those outlined in the Strategy for Mental Health, and with norms external to the organization, such as the Human Rights Act.

Within health care environments there are three clear levels of accountability:

Personal accountability

At its most general, accountability is about an individual who is responsible for a set of activities explaining or answering for their actions. In a hierarchical environment such as the Health Service, it is associated with delegated authority, and is distinct from responsibility. For example, the Chief Executive is ultimately accountable for the organization, but is not responsible for individual actions of staff or service users (called vicarious liability).

Professional accountability

Here there are two strands to accountability, firstly to the service user, and secondly to colleagues. Traditionally, accountability has focused on competence, and on legal and ethical conduct as determined by professional bodies, such as the Nursing and Midwifery Council or the General Medical Council. These bodies establish the content areas that determine competence, but it is not possible for them to monitor an individual's practice. Colleagues are therefore accountable for enforcing professional standards of practice. More recently, accountability to individual service users has become more prominent.

Organizational accountability

This comprises the entire management and control of an organization, including its organizational structure, its business policy, its principles, and guidelines, with both internal and external monitoring being mandatory. It is sometimes referred to as corporate governance or corporate accountability for clinical practice. Within health care, **Clinical Governance** is the major framework through which the organization is held accountable to the public and to the government. This is a systematic approach to maintaining and improving the quality of patient care. It is a multi-disciplinary, multi-agency activity that covers seven domains. These domains are not held in isolation but are networked throughout the organizations to produce a seamless service.

Helen Waldock, Health and Social Care Advisory Service

Domains of clinical governance

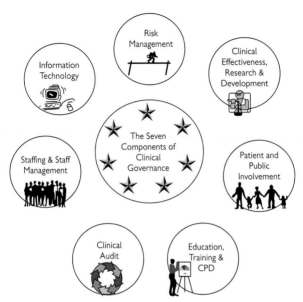

Fig.1.2 Domains of clinical governance http://www.cqc.org.uk/.

Further reading

McSherry, R, Graham-Brown, R. *Clinical Governance: a guide to implementation for Healthcare Professionals*. Blackwell Publishing: Oxford, 2002.
Tiley, S, Watson, R. *Accountability in Nursing and Midwifery*, Blackwell Publishing: Oxford, 2003.

Case management skills

Case management in mental health is synonymous with care management and care coordination. In terms of practice, it is integrated within the CPA system as the process for identifying and addressing an individual's needs within the resources available. The role is carried out by a qualified mental health professional from any discipline. It is central to the care of an individual with mental health problems, with the focus on person centred planning.

The aim of case management is to reach positive outcomes with the service user as effectively and as efficiently as possible, to avoid duplication of services, and to provide fair and equitable access to assessment and services. To support this, there are national directives to provide:

- A single point of entry to mental health services, usually via a community mental health team.
- A unified health and social care assessment within the CPA framework.
- An identified case manager or care coordinator responsible for all agencies involved.
- Access to the support of health and social services through a single point.

Core skills for case management include:
- Assessment, care planning, and documentation skills.
- Effective communication.
- Ability to work with individuals and families or carers.
- Ethical decision-making, including confidentiality.
- Working in groups and teams.
- Leadership skills.
- Intervention skills: influencing, interviewing, enabling, involving.
- Navigational skills: systems, procedures, protocols, eligibility criteria.
- Creative and lateral thinking.
- Analytical skills.
- Emotional intelligence.

Helen Waldock, Health and Social Care Advisory Service

The core role of a case manager

Three whats?	Three hows?
COLLECT data from service user, family, and others involved	COP – define and negotiate the non-negotiable
CREATE a care plan with the service user	COACH – teach new skills to service user and other agencies
COORDINATE with care partners to ensure delivery of the care plan	CONSULTANT– provide information for education and to enable others to make informed decisions

Efficacy of case management

There is little formal research into the efficacy of case management although emerging results indicate:

- Increased numbers remaining in contact with services.
- Increased numbers admitted to psychiatric hospital.
- Possible increases in the length of stay in hospital.
- Some improvement in compliance, medication, and activities.
- No significant improvement of mental state, social functioning, or quality of life.
- Potentially more expensive than traditional case work.

Further reading

Building Bridges – a guide to arrangements for inter-agency working for the protection of severely mentally ill people. HSG(95)96 Department of Health 1995. The Stationery Office London.

Care management and assessment – Practioners Guide. Department of Health 1991 The Stationery Office London.

Effective Care Coordination in Mental Health – Modernising the CPA. Department of Health. The Stationery Office London 1999.

Values and attitudes for professional practice

A value is a belief or an ideal to which an individual is committed. It is an important part of the base or foundation of a profession, and is often connected to the reasoning behind practice, procedure, and policy. Attitudes reflect the values of an individual or an organization, and can be a positive or negative response to an object, person, concept, or a situation.

Values and attitudes can be organized around seven key concepts and can form the basis for a profession's philosophy:

- *Altruism* – unselfish concern for the welfare of others.
- *Dignity* – valuing the inherent worth and uniqueness of an individual.
- *Equality* – individuals are perceived as having fundamental human rights and opportunities, and should be treated with fairness and impartiality.
- *Truth* – requires adherence to accurate facts when working with service users, colleagues, and the public.
- *Justice* – placing value on the upholding of moral and legal principles such as fairness, equality, truthfulness, and objectivity.
- *Freedom* – refers to the exercise of informed choice, independence, and self direction.
- *Prudence* – the ability to govern and discipline oneself.

Attitudes and values are learnt as an individual travels through life, from friends, family, leaders, influential people, experience, culture, race, and religion. The formation of professional values and beliefs is an important part of professional socialization, and will impact on professional practice. The 'Six Pillars of Character'[15] developed by the Josephson Institute of Ethics, identifies the constructs for professional behaviour and practice:

Reference

15 Josephson Institute of Ethics. Six Pillars of Character. Josephson Institute of Ethics: www.josephsoninstitute.org California.

Further reading

Green, C. Critical Thinking in Nursing: case studies across the curriculum. Prentice Hall: New Jersey, 2000.

Katz, JR, Carter C, Bishop J, Kravits S. Keys to Nursing Success. Prentice Hall: New Jersey. 2003.

Helen Waldock, Health and Social Care Advisory Service

Character Attributes (values and attitude)	Description (behaviour)
Trustworthiness	Do what you say you are going to do A person who is trustworthy exhibits the following behaviours: Acts with integrity Is honest and does not deceive Keeps a promise Is consistent Is loyal to those who are not present Is reliable Is credible Has a good reputation
Respect	Treat others the way they treat you A person who is respectful exhibits the following behaviours: Is open and tolerant of differences Is considerate and courteous Deals peacefully with anger/disagreements/insults Treats others the way they want to be treated
Responsibility	Do what you are supposed to do A person who is responsible exhibits the following behaviours: Acts with self discipline Thinks before they act Understands that actions create consequences Is consistent Is accountable
Fairness	Play by the rules A person who is fair exhibits the following behaviours: Is open minded Listens to others Shares information Does not needlessly blame others Is equitable and impartial
Caring	Show you care A person who cares exhibits the following behaviours: Expresses gratitude to others Forgives others Helps people in need Is compassionate
Citizenship	Do your share A person who is a good citizen exhibits the following behaviours: Cooperates Stays informed Is a good neighbour Protects the environment Obeys the law Exhibits civil duty Seeks the common good for most people

The carer's charter

In this context 'carer' does not mean care worker or care staff who are paid to provide care as part of employment, rather those people who look after a relative or friend when they are unwell or distressed. At some point in our life we will all require care of one sort or another, and we will probably all give care at some point.

According to the 2001 census, 5.2 million people were providing unpaid informal care in England and Wales. This number does not take into account young carers or parent carers. Caring is often not the only role these people have; 31% are in full-time employment.

The National Service Framework (NSF) for Mental Health, Standard 6, states that all carers who provide regular and substantial care for a person should:

- Have an assessment of their caring, physical, and mental health needs repeated on at least an annual basis.
- Have their own written care plan which is given to them and implemented in discussion with them.

What carers want

- Well-being for the person being cared for.
- Freedom to pursue their own interests.
- To remain fit and healthy.
- Involvement with, and confidence in the statutory and voluntary services.
- Choice in terms of formal care and support.
- Information to make informed choices and decisions.

Note: the extent of a carer's involvement depends on the consent of the service user, which can raise issues around confidentiality and conflict.

'Caring for Carers' is the National Strategy for England and Wales which has led to the development of local strategies and carers' charters outlining carers' rights, and is based on the following principles:

- Recognition of the carer's role and expertise.
- Giving the advice and information carers need to provide care.
- Recognizing, responding to and incorporating individual needs into the service users care plan.
- Offering help and support when needed.
- Being involved in the planning, development, and evaluation of services.

Local carers' charters will represent the priorities of the carers in their area and may include specifics such as the Mental Health Act or advocacy.

On the Mental Health Act for example:

- Making information on the Mental Health Act freely available, both verbal and written.
- Giving information on your rights under the Mental Health Act.
- Being cared for with respect to the Human Rights Act.

Helen Waldock, Health and Social Care Advisory Service

On advocacy, for example
- Including advocates in your care as you choose.
- Being given information or an explanation of the different forms of advocacy.
- Being informed of any available advocacy schemes and how to access them.

Further reading

Information for carers. 2011. Directgov. www.direct.gov.uk
Department of Health. Carers and Disabled Children's Act. DoH: London, 2000. www.dh.gov.uk
National Institute for Mental Health England. Valuing Carers – The Mental Health Carers Charter;
    A Guide for Carers; Working with Carers. NIMHE: London.
All at: www.nimhe.org

Guidelines for working with users

The government's NHS Plan[16] states that the Health Service should be more patient centred. The NHS and Social Care Act[17] demands that every NHS body has a statutory duty to consult and involve patients and the public in its activities.

In every NHS Trust there is a Patient's Advice and Liaison Service (PALS), to provide help and support for people about the Trusts services. This includes complaints procedures and advice about local voluntary and self-help groups. Independent and statutory forums or groups for patients or service users have been set up, to monitor and review services, as well as to influence the day-to-day management of each Trust.

The Commission for Patient and Public Involvement (PPI) is an independent organization that collects, compares, and promotes information picked up through local networks, PALS, and Patient Forums. They have set national standards for the involvement of patients, and provide training to ensure that local volunteers and representatives are able to meet these standards.

Principles for good practice:

- Be clear about what is wanted from service users and carers, as well as being clear about the role and responsibilities of others, professionals, carers, voluntary organizations, and so on.
- Be respectful of each other, as all have the right to express their own view.
- Be inclusive, by involving a diverse group that reflects the local population.
- Be flexible by adapting work practices, and accept that from time to time people's health may affect their ability to work.
- Be accessible by avoiding the use of jargon and using plain English.
- Offer resources and practical and emotional support to enable people to fulfil their role.
- Avoid tokenism, and enable people to give support and encouragement to others.
- Involve people at all stages of service delivery, development, and evaluation.

By working with service users, NHS Trusts can:

- Help ensure that services are more effective and efficient.
- Inform commissioners about gaps in services.
- Provide feedback on how service users experience local services.
- Provide a better picture of service users' experiences, perceptions, and priorities.
- Ensure users get appropriate responses which meet their needs, and not the needs of the organization.
- Encourage the commissioning and development of a range of service provision options and choices.

Helen Waldock, Health and Social Care Advisory Service

Key areas for working with service users are:
- Involvement in service delivery and care including prioritization in care planning, where users actively participate in their Care Programme Approach (CPA) assessment.
- Involvement in strategic planning, e.g. involving both individuals and groups in activities for local improvement plans.
- Support and training for service users e.g. enabling the acquisition of skills and knowledge to support full participation on an equal footing in relation to mental health services and policy.
- Developing user-led and managed projects and forums, e.g. establishing user forums at a team level, or within a ward or community setting.
- Welcoming user feedback, e.g. involvement in the monitoring and evaluation of local services through the governance systems.
- Involving service users in the training, employment, and evaluation of staff.

References

16 Department of Health. The NHS Plan. DoH: London, 2000.
17 Department of Health. NHS and Social Care Bill. DoH: London, 1990.

Further reading

Tait L, Lester HE. Encouraging user involvement in mental health services. *Advances in Psychiatric Treatment* **11**: 168–75, 2005.

Ethics

Ethics is the general term for what is described as the science of morality. Philosophically, ethical behaviour is that which is right or good. In this instance, it is behaviour that conforms to professional practice. Ethics refers to principles that define behaviour as right, good and proper. Such principles do not always indicate a single 'moral' course of action, but provide a means of evaluating and deciding among competing options.

Ethical behaviour forms the basis of mental health care. There are two main sources of ethical policy guidance for mental health practitioners:
1. The Code of Professional Conduct for Nurses and Midwives from the Nursing and Midwifery Council (NMC), is specifically for nurses.[18]
   The NMC has also produced specific guidelines for mental health. These are:
   • Guidelines for the administration of medication (2002).
   • Guidelines on practitioner-patient relationships and the prevention of abuse (2002).
2. The Code of Practice to the Mental Health Act (2007). This was designed specifically to enable those with the authority to detain people under the Act, to behave in a morally and ethically responsible manner.

There are seven core values shared by all health care regulatory bodies that govern the ethical behaviour of practitioners:
• Respect the patient, the client, or service user as an individual.
• Obtain consent before giving any treatment or care (consent is an ongoing consideration and should be sought before every intervention).
• Protect confidential information.
• Cooperate with others in teams.
• Maintain professional knowledge and competence.
• Be trustworthy.
• Act to identify and minimise risk to patients, clients, or users.

Ethics is about putting principles into actions. Consistency between what we say we value, and what our actions say we value, is a matter of personal integrity.

Helen Waldock, Health and Social Care Advisory Service

The process of ethical decision-making requires:

Commitment	Consciousness	Competency
The desire to do the right thing regardless of cost to self – emotional, material, or physical	The awareness to act consistently and apply moral convictions to daily behaviour, in keeping with professional principles	The ability to collect and evaluate information, to develop alternatives, to see potential consequences and risks

Making ethical decisions: things to ask yourself:
- Does your decision conflict with any core ethical values?
- Think of someone whose moral judgement you respect. Would they make the same decision?
- How will your decision affect others?
- Are your actions legal? Have you checked?
- Are there regulations, rules, policies, or procedures that restrict your choices or actions? Have you read them?
- Would your decision be perceived as unethical?
- How would your decision look if it were reported in the media?
- Would you be proud of your decision if your child, sibling, or parent found out? Would you want them to make the same decision?
- Could you honestly defend your decision?
- Will you sleep soundly tonight?

Reference
18 Nursing and Midwifery Council. Code of Professional Conduct. NMC London: 2002. See also www.nmc.org for other guidelines.

Further reading
Department of Health. Good Practice in Consent. DoH: London, 2001 (HSC2001/023).
Jones, RM. *Mental Health Act Manual*, 8th edn. Swet & Maxwell: London, 2003.

The essence of care

The essence of care is about improving the aspects of care that are most important to service users. It is a patient-focused benchmarking toolkit that was first launched by the Chief Nursing Officer for England and Wales in 2001. Following its implementation across several pilot sites, the tool-kit was simplified, reviewed, and relaunched in 2003. It supports the Clinical Governance Framework.

As the essence of care is contained in the portfolio of the Chief Nursing Officer, it is often viewed as being wholly within the domain of Nursing. This is not the reality, as the benchmarks or standards are applicable to all employees and all departments, not just the professions working within health and social services.

The essence of care is a continuous quality improvement cycle, using statements of best practice, and it is focused on patients or service users. The areas of care where standards have been set and benchmarking applies are:

• Continence, bladder, and bowel care
• Personal and oral hygiene
• Food and nutrition
• Pressure ulcers
• Privacy and dignity
• Record keeping
• Safety of all service users with mental health needs in acute mental health and general hospital settings
• Principles of self-care
• Communication.

These are not stand-alone areas and are often used in groups, e.g. continence care would be assessed at the same time as privacy and dignity.

Each of these areas is divided into specific items (factors) which are considered to achieve the overall benchmark or standard. Each factor is assessed using the continuous quality cycle.

Continuous quality cycle

The patient focus of each of these areas is maintained by having a service user, carer, or a representative as part of the overall process for comparing the performance of each clinical area in relation to the statement of best practice. This is referred to as the 'comparison group'. Areas then share good practice to ensure an overall high standard.

Helen Waldock, Health and Social Care Advisory Service

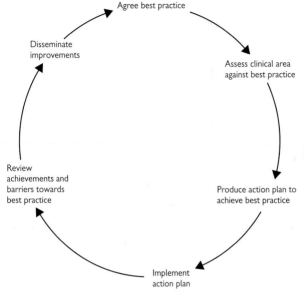

Fig.1.3 Continuous quality cycle.

Further reading

Department of Health. The New NHS: modern, dependable. The Stationery Office: London, 1997.
Department of Health. A first class service: quality in the new NHS. DoH: London, 1998.
Human Rights Act (1998). The Stationery Office: London, 1998. www.hmso.gov.uk/acts
The Essence of Care: Patient focused benchmarking for health care practitioners 2003 DOH London.

The Care Programme Approach (CPA)

The CPA, introduced in 1991, is one of the key processes underpinning the NSF for Mental Health. It is a 'whole systems' (integrated health and social care) approach to clinical effectiveness. The CPA aims to ensure that, where possible, the right intervention happens at the right time and in the right place to promote an individual's optimum mental health. Multidisciplinary team working is fundamental to the CPA process. The CPA aims to ensure that the following points of good practice in mental health are adhered to:

- Arrangements for assessing the health and social care needs of people in mental health services are systematic; including a mental state, a risk assessment, a carer's assessment, and a vulnerable children's assessment where applicable.
- A care plan is formulated with the service user; health and social care needs and action to be taken by the services are identified, clarified, and recorded. Where a need is identified and there is no service provision available, this is recorded on an unmet needs register.
- A care coordinator (a qualified mental health professional) is appointed to keep in close touch with the service user, and to monitor their care plan.
- There are regular reviews of the care plan involving the service user and all agencies involved.

There are two levels of CPA:

Standard: for individuals with a recognized mental health problem and a low risk rating, who are able to manage their mental health problem, have supportive social circumstances, and are active participants in their own care. They may require the intervention of one agency or discipline or low-key support from more than one agency or discipline.

Enhanced: for individuals with a recognized mental illness resulting in multiple care needs and requiring multi–agency involvement. They are more likely to have co-existing physical or mental health problems, disengage with services and present a higher risk to themselves or others. They will require a higher level and intensity of intervention. Care plans at this level will include a crisis plan.

The CPA is applicable to all people using secondary mental health services regardless of whether they are living at home, are homeless, in hospital, in prison or in residential care. As an individual's mental health needs change, it is possible to move from the standard to enhanced level of CPA and visa-versa. This would be done with involvement from the multidisciplinary team.

Helen Waldock, Health and Social Care Advisory Service

Further reading

Carpenter, J, Sbaraini, S. *Choice, Information and Dignity: involving users and carers in care management in mental health.* The Policy Press: 1997.

NHS and Community Care Act (DoH London). 1990.

The patients charter good practice in mental health services a collection of good practice in the provision of community mental health services 1997. Department of Health, NHS Executive. The Stationery Office London.

Department of Health 2001 An audit pack for monitoring the Care Programme Approach. DoH London.

The Single Assessment Process for older adults (SAP)

The single assessment process was introduced in the NSF for Older People in 2001.[19,20] It aims to ensure that older people's health and social care needs are assessed accurately and at the right time, and that information is not duplicated. There is no particular sequence to the assessment process – the emphasis is on the professional exercising clinical judgement in conjunction with the service user. The aim is that just one professional, where possible, completes and coordinates the assessment.

Domains of SAP

All SAP assessments will cover:
- User's perspective; needs, issues, expectations, strengths, and abilities.
- Clinical background; previous conditions, diagnosis, history of falls, and medication use.
- Disease prevention; blood pressure monitoring, nutrition, diet, fluids, vaccination history, alcohol and smoking history, exercise pattern, and screening uptake.
- Personal care and physical well-being; personal hygiene, dressing, pain, oral health, foot health, tissue viability, mobility, elimination, and sleep patterns.
- Senses; sight, hearing, and communication.
- Mental health; cognition, including orientation, memory and dementia, depression, reactions to loss, and emotional difficulties.
- Relationships; social contacts, leisure, hobbies, work, and learning.
- Carer support and strength of caring arrangements; including the carer's perspective.
- Safety; abuse, neglect, fear of crime, and safety in public.
- Immediate environment and resources; care of home and managing daily tasks, such as food preparation, cleaning, and shopping.
  Housing – including, location, access, amenities, heating, and access to local facilities.

Stages in SAP

1) Contact assessment
The initial contact between an older person and a service provider, where significant needs are first described or suspected. Basic personal information is gathered, the nature of the presenting problem is established and the presence of wider health or social care needs are explored.

2) Overview assessment
All or some of the domains identified in the SAP process may be explored, leading to a more rounded assessment and identification of need, deficits, abilities, and strengths.

Helen Waldock, Health and Social Care Advisory Service

3) Specialist assessment

The exploration of a specific need. A specialist assessment will confirm the presence, extent, cause, and likely prognosis of a health or social care condition, for example, a mental health problem. Links may be made to the interactive nature of multiple pathology and social situations.

4) Comprehensive assessment

This can involve pulling together the information gleaned from all stages of the assessment, especially when there has been more than one specialist assessment. Alternatively, it would be completed for people who need intensive or prolonged support such as admission to residential care.

5) Care planning

Following assessment, the information is used as the basis for a single plan that addresses all the domains assessed, including the carers' assessment. This care plan is then reviewed at regular intervals, at least once a year.

6) Care programme approach

Where significant mental health or mental illness needs, such as schizophrenia or dementia are identified, the CPA would be applied. This is outlined in standard 7.5 of the NSF for older people.

References

19 Department of Health. SAP assessment scales. DoH: London, 2003. www.dh.gov.uk
20 Department of Health. National Service Framework for Older People 2001. DoH: London.

Further reading

Department of Health. The community care assessment directions. DoH: London, 2004. www.dh.gov.uk/policyandguidance
Department of Health. Guidance on the Single Assessment Process for Older People 2002. DoH: London www.dh.gov.uk/publications

The National Service Framework for Mental Health

The National Service Framework for Mental Health (1999) is a long-term strategy, and a landmark in the development of mental health services across England for adults up to the age of 65 years. It clarifies what the National Standards are for service provision and what they aim to achieve. This document directs the changes and modernization needed to bring mental health services into the twenty-first century.

Aims

- Ensure that health and social services promote mental health and reduce discrimination and social exclusion associated with mental health problems.
- Deliver better primary mental health care, and to ensure consistent advice and help for people with mental health needs, including primary care services for individuals with severe mental illness.
- Ensure that each person with severe mental illness receives the range of mental health services they need and that crises are anticipated and prevented where possible.
- Ensure that people in crisis receive prompt and effective help, and timely access to an appropriate and safe mental health place or hospital bed, including a secure bed, as close to home as possible.
- Ensure health and social services assess the needs of carers who provide regular and substantial care for those with severe mental illness, and provide care to meet their needs.
- Ensure that health and social services play their full part in achieving the target of reducing the suicide rate by one fifth by 2010 as directed in 'Saving Lives: our Healthier Nation.'

Standards

All NSF standards are monitored at a local and national level, leading to national performance tables.

Standard 1 – Mental health promotion

- Promote mental health for all, working with individuals and communities.
- Combat discrimination against individuals and groups, and promote their social inclusion.

Standards 2 and 3 – Primary care and access to services

Service users who contact their primary health team with a common mental health problem should:

- Have their mental health needs identified and assessed.
- Be offered effective treatments, including referral to specialist services for further assessment, treatment, and care if they need it.
- Be able to make contact with local mental health services 24 hours a day and receive adequate care.

Helen Waldock, Health and Social Care Advisory Service

- Be able to use NHS Direct for first level advice and referral to specialist help-lines or to local services.

Standards 4 and 5 – Effective services for people with SMI

- Receive care that optimizes engagement and anticipates or prevents a crisis thereby reducing risk.
- Have a copy of their written care plan which:
  - a) States the action to be taken in a crisis by the service user, their carer, and their care coordinator.
  - b) Advises the GP how they should respond if the service user needs additional help.
  - c) Is regularly reviewed by the care coordinator.
  - d) Enables them to access services 24 hours a day, 365 days per year.

Service users who are assessed as needing a period of care away from their home should have:

- Timely access to an appropriate hospital bed or place which is:
  - a) In the least restrictive environment, and consistent with the need to protect them and the public.
  - b) As close to home as possible.
- A copy of a written care plan, agreed on discharge, which sets out their care and rehabilitation, identifies their care coordinator, and specifies the action to be taken in a crisis.

Standard 6 – Caring about carers

All carers or people who provide regular and substantial care for a person on CPA should:

- Have an assessment of their caring, physical and mental health needs repeated on at least an annual basis.
- Have their own written care plan given to them, and implemented with them.

Standard 7 – Preventing suicide

Local health and social care services should aim to prevent suicides by:

- Combining all the above standards into a local delivery plan based on local need.

And in addition:

- Support local prison staff in preventing suicides among prisoners.
- Ensure that staff are competent to assess the risk of suicide among individuals.
- Develop a local system for suicide audit, to learn lessons and take any necessary action.

The full document is available at www.dh.gov.uk.

Further reading

All documents are available in PDF format on the Department of Health (UK) website at www.dh.gov.uk

A First Class Service: Quality in the new NHS, 1998.

Saving Lives: Our Healthier Nation, 1999.

Modernising mental health services, 2002.

The NHS Plan, 2000.

The NHS Plan: a progress report, 2003.

The National Service Framework for Older People

The National Service Framework for Older People was launched in England in 2001. It provides the drive and focus for a ten year strategic development plan of all older people's services. The framework informs the culture and attitude of all professionals across all disciplines and is recognized as a speciality area in its own right.

The Framework has four underlying principles:
- Respecting the individual.
- Intermediate care.
- Providing evidence based specialist care.
- Promoting an active, healthy life.

The aims of the Framework are to:
- Ensure older people are never discriminated against in accessing NHS or social care services as a result of their age.
- Ensure that older people are treated as individuals, and receive appropriate and timely packages of care which meet their needs as individuals, regardless of health and social care boundaries.
- Provide integrated services to promote faster recovery from illness, prevent unnecessary hospital admissions, support timely discharge, and maximize independent living.
- Ensure older people receive the specialist help they need in hospital and that they receive maximum benefit from having been in hospital. Reduce the incidence of stroke in the population and ensure that after a stroke, people have prompt access to integrated stroke services.
- Reduce the number of falls which result in serious injuries, and ensure effective treatment and rehabilitation afterwards.
- Promote good mental health in older people, and to treat and support those older people with dementia and depression.
- Extend the healthy life expectancy of older people.

Standards

All NSF standards are monitored at a local and national level, leading to national performance tables.

1) Rooting out age discrimination

Services will be provided, regardless of age, on the basis of clinical need alone. Social care services will not use age in their policies or eligibility criteria, to restrict access to available services.

2) Person-centred care

NHS and social care services treat older people as individuals and enable them to make choices about their care. This is achieved through the single assessment process, integrated commissioning arrangements, and integrated provision of services, including community equipment and continence services.

Helen Waldock, Health and Social Care Advisory Service

● *Intermediate care*
●lder people will have access to a new range of intermediate care ser-
●ces at home, or in designated care settings, to promote their indepen-
●ence. These enhanced services from the NHS and local authorities will
●m to prevent unnecessary hospital admissions and will provide effective
●habilitation services to enable early discharge from hospital. They also
●m to prevent premature or unnecessary admission to long-term resi-
●ential care.

● *General hospital care*
●lder people's care in hospital is delivered through appropriate specialist
●are and by hospital staff who have the right set of skills to meet their
●eeds.

● *Stroke*
●he NHS will take action to prevent strokes, working in partnership with
●ther agencies where appropriate.

● *Falls*
●he NHS, working in partnership with local authorities, will take action to
●revent falls and, as a result, reduce fractures or injuries in their popula-
●ons of older people.

● *Mental Health in older people*
●lder people who have mental health problems will have access to
●tegrated mental health services, provided by the NHS and local
●uthorities to ensure effective diagnosis, treatment and support for them-
●lves and their carers.

● *The promotion of health and an active life in older age.*
●he health and well being of older people is promoted through a
●o-ordinated programme of action led by the NHS with support from
●cal authorities.

●he full document is available at www.dh.gov.uk. Including examples of
●ervice models and care pathways.

urther reading

●ll documents are available on the Department of Health (UK) website at www.dh gov.uk
●arers and Disabled Childrens' Act, 2000.
●ational Service Framework for Older People: report of progress and future challenges, 2003.
●eep Well, Keep Warm Campaign, 2004.
●are Quality Commission www.cqc.org.uk.

The biological context of mental health

Recent years have seen many changes to the provision of services and therapies for people suffering from mental illness, but there is still a slant towards the biological context of mental health.

Historical context

In primitive times, people believed that mental illness was created by evil spirits entering and taking over the body. Their expulsion was facilitated by a healer, medicine man, or spiritualist via magic or reincarnation.

Ancient civilizations, notably the Romans, Greeks, and Arabs, believed the mentally ill should be treated humanely, sedated with opium, but with good hygiene, good nutrition, activity, and social occupation. The Greek physician Hippocrates was the first to attempt to classify mental illness. Controversies about the approaches to treatment were apparent ranging from the drilling of a person's skull to let the spirits out, to good counsel (direction and advice).

After the fall of the Roman Empire – around 500–1450 AD – mental illness became surrounded by witchcraft, superstition, magic, and fear. Some were locked away in asylums, some were hidden by their families while others were left to fend for themselves.

In the 14th–17th centuries the mentally ill were thought to pose a risk to society. They were put in prison or in asylums and were often subject to cruel regimes, such as being locked in cages or chained to walls for containment. The first mental hospital, The Bethlem Royal, was established in the UK. People could visit, and for a small fee observe the inmates.

In the 18th–19th centuries, social changes included urbanization and impoverishment on a large scale. The asylums or madhouses were closely associated with the workhouses, and were presided over by a medical superintendent – despite the awareness of 'moral treatment' (pioneered by William Tuke, where restraint was kept to a minimum and people were engaged in occupational tasks). In 1845 the Lunatics Act was introduced, and the approach to mental illness was consolidated with the introduction of the new sub-specialty of medicine, called Psychiatry. The psychiatrist became the responsible guardian of the lunatic, thus medical doctors sought to improve their knowledge about the cause and treatment of mental illness. At this time a physiological explanation was the most common rationale for mental illness.

In the 20th century the asylum population continued to grow, until in the later half of the 20th century it was decreed that the asylums should close. The introduction of phenothiazines (major tranquilizers) reinforced the position of the psychiatrist as treating mental illness, while attendants and nurses contained the patients. Within the field of psychiatry, interest in the biological causes of mental illness remained dominant, with the introduction of new forms of treatment with fewer side-effects.

Helen Waldock, Health and Social Care Advisory Service

In the 21st century the nature or nurture debate continues. There is now recognition that behaviour is the product of both, with each contributing to the development of mental health and mental illness. There is an increasing evidence base to support non-medical interventions alongside the role of the psychiatrist. The discovery of the genome is likely to bring the greatest advances to psychiatry over the next decade, although how this will impact is not yet known. Medical science continues to dominate in terms of economics, and social status, with more resources being allocated to medical research and consultants continuing to manage resources (beds), whilst contributing to the care of an individual, although this is gradually being challenged by the growth in the service user movements and the thrust of current mental health policy.

Further reading

Breggin, PR. *Toxic Psychiatry*. Harper Collins: London, 1993.

Lomax, M. *The Experience of an Asylum Doctor*. George Allen & Unwin: 1921 London.

Rogers, A, Pilgrim, D. *Experiencing Psychiatry: Users views of services*. Macmillan: London, 1993.

Rogers, A, Pilgrim, D. *Mental Health Policy in Britain* Palgrave Macmillan UK 2001.

The socio-cultural context of mental health

Sociology refers to the study of the social lives of humans, groups, ar societies. It is concerned with social rules and processes that bind ar separate people, not only as individuals, but as members of association groups, and institutions. It is relevant to today's health care institution whether they in a hospital or in a community, as they help us understan how we got to where we are.

Ivan Illich, a well known author of an informal series of controversi critiques of the institutions of 'modern' culture, used the concept c 'iatrogenesis' to describe illnesses caused by medical practice.[21] Th concept describes the ways in which the activities of doctors may hav harmful results, for example the ill effects of prescribed medicatio Another theme of Illich's work is the mis-allocation of resources, wher the highest investment is allocated to technology or high prestig medicine such as cardiac surgery, leaving the 'Cinderella services' such a mental health and care of the elderly suffering. Some would argue tha this is still the current situation in the UK. Illich has been criticized fo underestimating the advances in modern health care.

Talcott Parsons, a sociologist who attempted to integrate all the socia sciences into a science of human action, stressed the importance of healt for the smooth running of society.[22] He developed the concept of the 'sic role' involving certain rights and obligations, which should restore the sic person to health as soon as possible (see below). There is much to thin about when this is applied to mental health.

Rights and obligations of the 'Sick Role'

Obligations	Rights
Person must wish to recover as soon as possible	Person is relieved of usual responsibilities and tasks
Person must seek professional advice and follow prescribed treatment	Person is accorded sympathy and support

Whilst recognizing that not all illnesses are sufficiently severe enough tc fit into the sick role, Parsons describes ways in which society expects ar ill person to behave and which can account for society's attitude to those who do not conform.

Inequalities in health

Inequalities in health were first brought into the public domain with the publication of the Black Report in 1980. This showed that the lower the social class you were, the more likely you were to become ill or die prematurely. Whilst the focus was not on mental health, the factors concerning physical health directly impact on mental health; the more

Helen Waldock, Health and Social Care Advisory Service

economically advantaged you are the better your health and the greater your life chances.

There are three broad types of inequality in mental health:

- Inequality in access to health care, e.g. access of refugees to primary health care or treatment for PTSD.
- Inequality in health and health outcomes e.g. there is a 6 year difference in average life expectancy for people living in different London boroughs.
- Inequalities in the determinants of health, access to the means of financial reward: the better educated the more likely you will have a better income therefore better housing, diet, and so on e.g. 70% of those with a psychotic disorder are unemployed.

Different groups and categories of people have very different experiences of the determinants of health. Some are well known, such as gender, age, social class, ethnicity, geographical area. Others such as disability, single parenthood, quality of school, age of housing, type of road user, are less obvious. Inequalities can become entrenched when these categories overlap e.g. a combination of age, ethnic group, and area. In these circumstances, there can be a snowballing effect leading to pockets of deprivation and increased *rates of mental illness, such as are seen in some deprived inner city areas*

References

21 Illich, I. Medical Nemesis: the exploration of health. Calder & Boyars: London, 1957.
22 Parsons, T. The Social System. Routledge: London, 1951.

Further reading

Townsend, P, Davidson, N. *Inequalities in Health – The Black Report*. Penguin: 1986. UK.
The Black Report www.sochealth.co.uk

Mental health promotion

Standard one of the NSF for mental health

Mental health services and staff have a direct interest in promoting positive mental health and well-being in individuals, the family and the work place. Mental health promotion involves any action to enhance the mental well-being of an individual, families, communities, and organizations. It is important to recognize that everyone has mental health needs, whether or not they have a diagnosis of mental illness. Mental health programmes that target the whole community will also benefit those who have mental health problems.

Mental health promotion is essentially concerned with
- How individuals, families, organizations, and communities think and feel.
- The factors that influence how we think and feel, individually and collectively.
- The impact this has on overall well-being.

Mental health promotion works at three levels:
- Strengthening individuals – or increasing emotional resilience through interventions designed to promote self esteem, life and coping skills, relationship and parenting skills.
- Strengthening communities – increasing social inclusion and participation, improving local environments, developing health and social services to support mental health, anti-bullying strategies in schools, work place health, community safety, childcare and self-help networks.
- Reducing structural barriers to mental health – through initiatives to reduce discrimination and inequality by promoting access to education, meaningful employment, housing services, and support for those who are vulnerable.

At each level, interventions may focus on strengthening factors known to protect mental health (e.g. social support, job control) or to reduce factors know to increase risk (e.g. unemployment, violence).

The benefits of mental health promotion are:
- Improving physical health and well-being.
- Providing capability to cope with mental distress in life.
- Preventing or reducing the risk of mental health problems, notably behavioural disorders, depression and anxiety, substance misuse.
- Assisting recovery from mental health problems.
- Reducing the stigma and discrimination associated with having mental health problems or using mental health services.
- Strengthening the capacity of communities to support social inclusion, tolerance and participation and reducing vulnerability to socio-economic stressors.
- Increasing mental health awareness.
- Improving health at work, increasing productivity and reducing sickness absence.

Helen Waldock, Health and Social Care Advisory Service

Community strategies are usually coordinated by a local strategic partnership including health, primary care, education, transport, voluntary sector, social services, and local government, and are available at local town halls and libraries.

Further reading

MacDonald, T. *The Social Significance of Health Promotion*. Routledge: London, 2003.
Tudor, K. *Mental Health Promotion: paradigms and practice*. Routledge: London, 1996.

Transcultural mental health nursing

Transcultural nursing is a humanistic and scientific area of study. It focuses on differences and similarities among cultures with respect to health and illness. It aims to use knowledge of people's cultural values beliefs and practices to provide culturally specific or culturally congruent nursing care.

Culture refers to the norms and practices of a particular group that are learned and shared and that guide thinking, decisions, and actions. Cultural values are an individual's desired or preferred way of acting or knowing something, sustained over a period of time, and which govern actions or decisions.

Culturally diverse nursing care is an optimal mode of health care delivery. It refers to the variability of nursing approaches needed to provide culturally appropriate care, incorporating an individual's cultural beliefs, values, and practices.

It is relevant in the UK because:
- Minority ethnic groups report higher scores of psychological distress.
- Rates of psychotic illness are twice as high in African-Caribbean people than in their white counterparts.
- Ethnic minorities are six times more likely to be detained under the mental health act.
- Women born in East Africa have a 40% higher suicide rate than those born in the UK.
- Irish people have suicide rates 53% in excess of other minority ethnic groups.

To be culturally competent, the nurse needs to understand their own and their patient's world view, but to avoid stereotyping and misapplying scientific knowledge *e.g. interpretation of somatic symptoms*. Different cultures have different perceptions of illness and disease and their causes, and this affects their approaches to health care. Culture also influences how people seek health care and how they behave towards health care providers. How people are cared for and how they respond to this care is greatly influenced by culture. Health care providers must have the ability and knowledge to communicate with all their patients and to understand health behaviours influenced by culture. This ability and knowledge can reduce barriers to the delivery of health care.

There are five essential elements that contribute to an organization becoming culturally competent:
- Valuing diversity.
- Having the capacity for cultural self-assessment.
- Being conscious of the dynamics inherent when cultures interact.
- Having a workforce that reflects the local population to enhance cultural knowledge.
- Having developed adaptations of service delivery reflecting an understanding of cultural diversity e.g. female only clinics.

Helen Waldock, Health and Social Care Advisory Service

Major challenges to transcultural care include:
- Recognizing clinical differences among people of different ethnic and cultural groups.
- The challenges of communication; working with interpreters, nuances of words in different languages.
- Ethical challenges; while western medicine is the most dominant in the world, it does not have all the answers. Respect for the belief systems of different cultures, and the effects of those beliefs on well-being are crucial.
- The effect of an authority figure is not always apparent; but many people are wary of caregivers. Some may have been victims of atrocities at the hands of authorities in their homelands.

As individuals and caregivers, nurses need to learn to ask questions sensitively and to show respect for different cultural beliefs. More importantly, they must listen carefully to patients.

Further reading

Cross, T, Baxron, B, Dennis, K, Issacs, M. *Towards a Culturally Competent System*, vol. 1. Georgetown University: Washington DC, 1989.

Minarik, PA. *Culture and Nursing: a pocket guide California*. Rittenhouse Book Distributors: 1997.

Models of mental health nursing

Early models of nursing evolved in the context of economic, societal, and technological changes. Today, the systems of health care organization and nursing care delivery continue the challenge of adaptation in a rapidly changing service.

Systems of mental health nursing

- *Functional nursing*; technical tasks are assigned to staff according to the complexity of the task and the knowledge and skill of the nurse.
- *Team nursing*; a team of nurses deliver care to a group of patients who are assigned to each team member according to the complexity of the patients' needs. A team leader is accountable for coordinating care and delegating to the team.
- *Primary nursing*; a registered nurse is accountable for the care planning from admission to discharge, promoting continuity, and delegating to an associate nurse as required.
- *Case management*; a collaborative approach with the nurse as the co-ordinator, not necessarily providing direct patient care.

Aspects of all four approaches are used depending on the environment, the work load, and the individual needs of patients.

The nursing process

The nursing process is a systematic, goal-directed, flexible and rational approach to care. It ensures consistent, continuous, quality nursing care and provides a basis for professional accountability. The steps of the nursing process are cyclic, overlapping and interrelated.
1. Assessment (of patient's needs).
2. Diagnosis (of human response needs that nursing can assist with).
3. Planning (of patient's care).
4. Implementation (of care).
5. Evaluation (of the success of the implemented care).

Theories and models of nursing

Nursing models are conceptual models, constructed of theories and concepts. They are used to help nurses assess, plan, and implement patient care by providing a framework within which to work.

There are four concepts or paradigms that are fundamental to all nursing models and theories, these being man, health, environment, and nursing. The relationship between these paradigms is explored with the beliefs of the person writing the theory thereby guiding the focus of the theory. Within mental health, relationships are acknowledged as being the fifth paradigm. There are over forty models of nursing to choose from, and the skill of choosing the right one is to explore the belief and value

Helen Waldock, Health and Social Care Advisory Service

ystems underpinning them. In mental health the four most commonly used models are:

Imogene King: the general systems framework[23]

King's conceptual framework includes three types of dynamic interacting systems. These are: personal systems (represented by the individual), interpersonal (represented by dyadic interactions), and social systems (represented by broader connections such as the family or health services). This model focuses on goal attainment, acknowledging that each bring their own perceptions and judgements to an interaction.

Dorothea Orem: self-care framework[24]

Orem's model focuses on an individual's ability to perform self-care. Self-care activities vary depending on individual circumstances. Self-care requisites can be divided into universal (applicable to all e.g. breathing), developmental (a particular point in life e.g. pregnancy), or health deviation requisites (when unwell). Self-care deficits are identified with the nurse and the patient working together in a wholly compensatory, partially compensatory, or supportive educative system to address the deficits.

Rosemarie Parse: man-living-health[25]

Parse's theory views human beings as an open system. Using three core principles she describes man (generic term) as a unique individual with unique reactions to illness. The nurse's role is to become fluent in the uniqueness of the individual accepting their language, values, beliefs, desires, pace of life and so on, and through practice enable the individual to move forward to live a fulfilled life as determined by themselves.

Hildergard Peplau: the theory of interpersonal relations[26]

The nurse and the patient work together toward solutions for everyday encounters. Peplau identifies four sequential phases in the nurse-patient relationship: orientation, identification, exploitation, and resolution. The nurse fulfils different roles throughout the stages of the relationship, teacher, resource, counsellor, leader, technical expert, and surrogate.

All theories and models have their strengths and weaknesses. It is worth referring to the original texts to get the accurate meaning.

References

23 King, IM. A Theory for Nursing: systems, concepts, process New York. A. Wiley Medical Publications: 1981.
24 Orem, D. Nursing: concepts of practice. Mosby: St Louis, 1995.
25 Parse, R. Man Living Health: A theory of nursing. Wiley: New York, 1981.
26 Peplau, HE. Interpersonal Relations in Nursing. GP Putnam: New York, 1952. Reprinted 1991, Springer: New York.

Mental health nursing in context

From the beginning of time, people with mental health problems, mental disorders, or what was defined as socially deviant behaviour, have received some form of care or control.

From asylum to community

Asylums housed the 'insane' from the 12th century, where they suffered degradation, repression, and cruelty. In the 17th century, the pioneer Philippe Pinnel in France, and William Tuke in the UK introduced reform, unchaining the 'lunatics' and creating havens for the insane. Physical restraints were replaced with moral constraints based on reason supported by meaningful work, social and recreational activities within a domestic type environment. This marked the beginning of changing attitudes towards the insane.

During the 19th century, the asylums were rapidly expanded, catering for thousands of people, and quickly became overcrowded and custodial in nature, with many allegations of malpractice. County authorities were expected to provide their own asylums, for the care or incarceration of the insane. Private institutions had existed before this, and provided the only care available. Throughout this period, private institutions continued to exist and be founded for so-called idiots and imbeciles, who were usually those who today would be said to have learning disabilities. The county asylum structure was nationalized in 1948, when the institutions were absorbed into to the National Health Service

In 1926, a Royal Commission investigated the lunacy laws resulting in the Mental Treatment Act coming into being; it defined categories of voluntary and temporary patients, and by 1959 the Mental Health Act put medical professionals in control, with a strong emphasis on community involvement.

In 1961 the government of the time declared that the asylums must close, and by the 1960s there was a decline in asylum numbers due to:
- Gross overcrowding.
- Deterioration in the fabric of the buildings.
- Increasing labour costs.
- The view that medication could control symptoms.
- The increasing role of the consultant psychiatrist.
- The increased influence of the anti-psychiatry movement.
- Scandals and public enquiries highlighting neglect and suffering.
- Government policy that stated mental hospitals must close and local facilities be developed.

This has remained the approach of all national policy to the current time. Many of the large institutions did not finally close their doors until the 1990s.

The 2007 Mental Health Act protects the rights of the detained patient.

From attendants to nurses

All branches of nursing arose under the patronage of the medical profession. Initially, attendants in institutions were there for their personal and moral qualities; they were expected to have physical strength, be sober, set a

Helen Waldock, Health and Social Care Advisory Service

positive example and offer guidance. For this, they had their meals with the patients, slept in rooms off the wards, and worked 15 hours a day. As a result, many of them became as institutionalized as their charges.

It was not until the late 19th century that consideration was given to the education of the attendants. This came in the form of a handbook from the Royal Medico-Psychological Association (RMPA), known as 'The Instruction of Attendants on the Insane'. This later formed the basis of the first recordable qualification in mental health nursing.

Due to overcrowding in the asylums, bureaucratic nurse patient hierarchies became the norm. These relied on strength and intimidation rather than friendliness and common sense. An uneasy relationship between the general hospital nurses and the attendants began to develop as the governing body, the British Nursing Association (BNA), refused entry to those who had completed their RMPA training on the grounds of social standing, as general nursing was then a middle class occupation.

It was not until the General Nursing Council (GNC) (predecessor to the UKCC and NMC) started its own courses for psychiatric nursing that the attendants were permitted onto the national register. This made little difference to career pathways, as most asylum matrons were general nurses. This has been ameliorated to some extent with the introduction of Project 2000 with the shared common foundation programme.

The decline of the asylums brought changes for nurses. Many of them were resistant to their closure as this was a direct threat to their economic stability. Even in the 1950s, many lived in the grounds of the institution around which their social life revolved.

But this was a time of opportunity; many nurses who believed in their profession moved into innovative roles in the district general hospital psychiatric units, day hospitals, outpatient departments, and after care services. This led to the placement of community psychiatric nurses in primary care, a role that did not survive as government policy was to focus services on those who were deemed SMI, although this is being reversed with the implementation of the NSFMH.

Mental health nursing today

The current government drive towards integrated care and primary mental health care has led to a variety of post registration qualifications, and to the development of a mental health practitioner who does not have to be a registered nurse. Conflict remains within mental health nursing about the future of the profession. This is not just in relation to other branches of nursing, but it relates to the unanswered question of 'do you need to be a mental health nurse to provide mental health care now that there is a move away from the medical model towards a more socially inclusive model?'

Further reading
Goffman, E. *Asylums*. Penguin Books Ltd 1991 London.

McMillan, I. Years of Bedlam Nursing, *Times* **92**(47) 62–3, 20 Nov, 1996.

Nolan, P. *History of Mental Health Nursing*. Nelson Thornes Ltd: 1998 Cheltenham UK.

Nolan, P. Annie Altschul's Legacy to British Mental Health Nursing. *Journal of Psychiatric and Mental Health Nursing* **6**(4): 267–72, 1999.

Rehabilitation and recovery

Recovery for each person is an individual journey and therefore unique. At some point in our lives we all need the support of another. Knowing yourself, your own signs and symptoms is an important step to wellness regardless of whether you have a mental illness or not.

The concept of recovery is having a substantial impact on service users, families, mental health researchers, and service delivery. It was introduced in the writings of service users in the 1980s, who had recovered to the extent of being able to write about their experiences, coping with symptoms, getting better, and gaining an identity.

There is no single definition of recovery, nor a single way to measure it, but the overreaching message is that hope and restoration to a meaningful life are both possible despite a serious mental illness. Recovery does not always mean cure but involves less interference of symptoms in everyday life.

Recovery is different to rehabilitation, which is seen as a specialist service, as opposed to a process or concept. Rehabilitation combines pharmacological and social support to service users and families in order to improve their lives and their functional capacity. Recovery does not refer to any specific service, but to the experience of gaining a new and valued sense of self and purpose.

Principles of recovery:
- It concerns the whole of an individual's life; this includes their relationships, friends, family, housing, money, work, education, social activities and life, medication, and therapies. The CPA provides the framework for this, providing a coordinated approach and using experts where necessary.
- It concerns personal growth and development; assessment should not only consider symptoms and problems, but strengths and abilities. Services need to fit around the user, rather than have the user fit into the services.
- Recovery is ongoing; there is no time limit to support, although this may vary as an individual fluctuates. The role of maintenance support provided by a coordinator or support worker is important – this is a meaningful long-term relationship that may 'hold' a person through a difficult time.
- It concerns the wider context of social inclusion outside mental health services; including meaning in life, work, home relationships, culture, and beliefs. The role of the professionals is to enable access to what people want, empowering individuals to take part in their own lives.
- Access to peer support is seen as valuable; this may be via self-help groups, or voluntary organizations such as Mind. The way forward is via public and patient involvement in designing and delivering services.

Helen Waldock, Health and Social Care Advisory Service

The impact of recovery is felt most by users and their families, who are energized by the message of hope and self-determination. Having a more active role in treatment, research, social and vocational functioning, and personal growth strikes a responsive chord in users of services. Harbouring more optimistic attitudes and expectations may improve the course of the illness yet direct empirical evidence to support recovery is still in its infancy.

Further reading

Jacobson, N. *In Recovery: the making of mental health policy*. Vanderbilt University Press: 2004.
Moxley, DP. *Sourcebook of Rehabilitation and Mental Health Practice*. Kluwer Academic Publishing USA: New York 2003.
Newbiggin, K, Wells, A, West, A. *Working for Mental Health*. Health and Social Care Advisory Service: 2004. London.

The Mental Health Act 2007

The detention of patients into mental health services is governed by the Mental Health Act (England and Wales) 2007. The Mental Health Act (MHA) 2007 is essentially an amendment to the MHA 1983. The table below outlines the main provisions of the Mental Health Act 2007.

Section number and purpose	Maximum duration	Can patient apply to MHRT?	Automatic MHRT hearing?	Can nearest relative apply to MHRT?	Do consent to treatment issues apply?
2 Admission and treatment — application may be made by the nearest relative or an Approved Mental Health Professional (AMHP), and supported by 2 medical recommendations	28 days, not renewable	Within first 14 days	No	No	Yes
3 Admission for treatment — application may be made by a nearest relative or an AMHP, supported by 2 medical recommendations	6 mths. May be renewed for 6 mths, then annually	Within first 6 mths, then in each period 1 yr	Yes – at 6 mths, then every 3 yrs (yearly if under 16) if no application	No	Yes
4 Emergency admission for assessment made by at least one medical recommendation	72 hrs. Not renewable but 2nd medical recommendation can change to s2	Yes, but only if s4 is converted to s2	No	No	No
5(2) Doctors' or Approved Clinician's holding power	72 hrs. Not renewable	No	No	No	No
5(4) Nurses' holding power	6 hrs. Not renewable, but doctor or Approved Clinician can change to 5(2)	No	No	No	No

7 Reception in guardianship	6 mths. May be renewed for 6mths, then yearly	Within first 6 mths, then in each period of 1 yr	No	No	No
16 Dr re-classifies the mental disorder	For the duration of the detention	Within 28 days of being informed	No	No	No
17 Supervised Community Treatment (SCT) – provisions for people to be discharged from inpatient detention under a Community Treatment Order (CTO)	6 months, may be renewed for 6 months, then annually	Within first 6 mths, then in each period	Yes – at 6 mths then every 3 years	Yes	Yes
18 Transfer from guardianship to hospital	6 mths. May be renewed for 6 mths, then annually	Within first 6 mths, then in each period	Yes – at 6 mths, then every 3yrs (yearly if under 16) if no application	No	Yes
25 Restriction of discharge by nearest relative	Variable	No	No	Within 28 days of being informed	
135 Warrant to search for and remove patient	72 hrs. Not renewable	No	No	No	No
136 Police power in public places to remove person to place of safety	72 hrs. Not renewable	No	No	No	No

Further reading

Jones R. *The Mental Health Act Manual: 11th edition.* Sweet and Maxwell, London, 2007.
Department of Health. *Reference Guide to the Mental Health Act 1983.* TSO, London, 2008.

Chapter 2 from the Oxford Handbook of
Children's and Young People's Nursing

Edited by

Edward Alan Glasper
Professor of Child Health Nursing,
School of Nursing and Midwifery,
University of Southampton, UK

Gillian McEwing
Senior Lecturer, Faculty of Health and Social Care,
University of Plymouth, UK

Jim Richardson
Principal Lecturer, School of Health Care Sciences,
University of Glamorgan, Pontypridd, UK

OXFORD
UNIVERSITY PRESS

Care of the child/young person and family

Working with families   206
Communication with the child and family   208
Family nursing   210
Working with siblings   212
Using nursing models in practice   214
Partnership model of nursing   216
How to write a care plan   218
Evaluation of care   220
The importance of play   222
Diversionary/normal play   224
Preparation and post-procedural play   226
Directed and hospital role play   228
Guided imagery   230
Education and the ill child   232
Patient and parent information and education   234
Dealing with parental aggression   236
Writing a patient information leaflet   238
Normal physiological values in children   241

Working with families

Introduction

Families contribute greatly to the care and wellbeing of the child, but to do so effectively must be considered part of the healthcare team. The nature of interaction between the family and professionals will impact upon team functioning. Developing positive relationships is a complex demanding task which, to be successful, requires respect for each other's knowledge, skills, and expertise.

Paternalism

- Professionals, with the best intentions, decide what is best and expect compliance.
- Power lies with professionals.
- Assumptions are made which may be incorrect.
- The family has a limited controlled contribution to care.
- The family may feel frustrated at their perceived lack of input.
- The family may be relieved that they do not have to make decisions.

Collaboration

- Partnership, where power is shared with child/family, increases family choices.
- Decision making meets a family's need to be included in care delivery and increases the prospect of compliance.
- There is a danger that the family may feel overwhelmed and abandoned by professionals.

Empowerment

- The family is educated and informed regarding condition, treatment, and care.
- They are encouraged to participate in care delivery.
- Support is provided in a non-judgemental way.
- The family feels prepared for their role in care delivery.
- Family wishes are taken into account when care is planned.

Important points

Team working:
- Role clarity is crucial.
- Be consistent, confusion/resentment arises when the family is part of the team one minute and then disregarded the next.
- The family should not be pressured into carrying out care they feel unprepared or unable to do.
- If truly collaborative, child/family decisions are accepted even if different to yours.

Communication

- Acknowledge that often the child/family know what is best for them.
- Be truthful at all times.
- Give the family time to assimilate information and make decisions.
- Speak to family members as individuals, as well as part of a group.
- Remember to respect confidentiality of all family members.

Irene McTaggart, University of Dundee

Further reading

Booth, K., Luker, K. (ed.) (1999). *A practical handbook for community health nurses: working with children and their parents*. Blackwell Science, Oxford.

Smith, L. (ed.) (2002). *Family centred care: concept, theory and practice*. Palgrave, Basingstoke.

Communication with the child and family

Definition
Communication is a two-way multifaceted process, consisting of verbal and non-verbal strategies. Communication takes place on an informal and formal basis, throughout which it is just as important to observe and listen as it is to talk.

General points
Purpose:
- to gain information
- to give information
- to establish a therapeutic relationship
- social.

Set scene
- Ensure privacy.
- Avoid interruptions, e.g. phones, staff.
- Organize furniture avoiding confrontational arrangement, e.g. chairs at an angle, not face to face.
- Allow for personal space, e.g. leg room.
- Do not position chairs in front of window, reduces non-verbal aspect of communication, while backlight may be discomforting for those facing it.

Plan
Consider:
- purpose
- developmental level of recipient(s)
- stage of child's illness/condition
- emotional state of child/family, and their readiness for communication.

Explain to child/family purpose of discussion; allow them preparation time if possible.

Implement
Verbal
- Adjust vocabulary/tone to gain maximum understanding.
- Speak clearly, express yourself unambiguously.
- Use layman's language, not technical jargon.
- Give small amounts of information at a time.
- Minimize barriers between you and the child/family.

Non-verbal
- Open, friendly, professional approach.
- Avoid judgemental facial expressions, body posture.
- Use appropriate responses, e.g. facial expression, touch.
- Encourage dialogue by eye contact, nodding, etc.

Irene McTaggart, University of Dundee

- Use diagrams and leaflets.
- Observe for signs of discomfort, change subject, and revisit later if possible/necessary.
- Respond to verbal and non-verbal cues; do not rush to fill silences.

Evaluate
- Summarize discussion or ask child/parents to do so; checks/reinforces understanding.
- Ensure child/family do not feel pressurized to give a *correct* answer.
- Give child/family an opportunity to ask questions, state concerns, etc.

Follow-up
- Arrange further discussion if necessary, e.g. Tuesday, not 2.30 pm Tuesday; avoids potential deterioration of relationship if emergency occurs.
- Encourage child/family to:
  - write down any concerns arising in interim
  - ask questions any time to avoid excess worry or delay.

Important point
It is just as important to know when not to ask a question as when to ask it.

Useful website
Organization for parents of babies requiring special care:
🖥 www.bliss.org.uk

Further reading
Arnold, E., Boggs, K.U. (2003). *Interpersonal relationships: professional communication skills for nurses*, 5th edn. W.B. Saunders, St Louis.
Hargie, O., Dickson, D. (2004). *Skilled interpersonal communication: research, theory and practice*, 4th edn. Routledge, London.

Family nursing

Conceptual clarification

Represents a paradigm shift from family-centred care to family nursing focus.

There is ongoing debate within the profession as to what constitutes 'family nursing' and a little understanding of nursing interventions that might begin to address family needs. The extent to which we have developed family nursing in paediatric practice is debatable.

Family nursing can be perceived as:
- a philosophy of care
- an ethos of care
- an approach to care.

The family

- Definitions are diverse and often unclear. It is a dynamic concept which is culturally influenced.
- Understanding of family systems is fundamental to understanding family nursing.

Family systems

- Parts of a family are related to each other.
- One part of the family cannot be understood in isolation from the rest of the system.
- Family functioning is more than just the sum of the parts.
- A family's structure and organization are important in determining the behaviour of family members.
- Changes (e.g. change in overall health status) in one family member create changes in other family members, which in turn create a new change in the original member.
- Family health has been reported to be a significant factor in the child's recovery from illness and/or adjustment to disability.

Family assessment

In order to practise family nursing, it is necessary first to conduct a comprehensive family assessment. Four intrinsic elements in family nursing assessments include:
- having a human caring presence
- acknowledging multiple perceptions
- respecting diversity
- valuing each person in the context of family.

Each of the above is consistent with family nursing systems, in that all members are involved in the assessment process.

Child health nurses need to critically appraise various family nursing assessment tools available for possible adoption in their practice context.

Gary Mountain, University of Leeds

Family nursing interventions

Family systems nursing targets the cognitive, behavioural, and affective domains of family functioning. Interventions that meet these three domains of family functioning may assist the family in finding new solutions to their problems arising from such changes in health status.

Typical interventions

- Behaviour modification
- Contracting
- Case managing/coordinating
- Collaborative strategies
- Empowering/participating
- Family advice
- Environmental modification
- Family crisis intervention
- Networks/self-help groups
- Information and technical expertise
- Role modelling
- Role supplementation
- Teaching strategies

The above list is by no means exhaustive and points to synonyms, related roles, and prerequisites for family nursing.

Further reading

Neabel, B., Fothergill-Bourbonnais, F., Dunning, J. (2000). Family assessment tools: a review of the literature from 1978–1997. *Heart and Lung*, **29**(3), 196–209.

Friedman, M.M., Bowden, R.V., Jones, E.G. (2003). *Family nursing: research, theory and practice*, 5th edn. Prentice Hall, Upper Saddle River, NJ.

Working with siblings

Siblings of all ages are affected by having an ill brother or sister, especially if this illness is chronic.

Young children

Parents report that they feel that babies, toddlers, and pre-school siblings miss out on the normal cuddles and prolonged contact that they would have from mum, as she is constantly caring for her ill child. One parent's solution to this was to ensure that another carer attended to her sick child for a full day once a week so she could give undivided attention to her other son on his special day. Other relatives or care team members may be available to give parents time to devote to siblings.

Older children

As children get older, parents report that they are often angry, frustrated, ashamed, attention seeking, and naughty.

Children under 10 years of age may not understand what is happening with their sibling. They may feel they are at risk of getting the disease or that they have caused the illness in some way. They may feel embarrassed and confused as they see their sibling is different to others. Parents need to acknowledge the feelings that their well child has, and discuss with the child how difficult it is to live with a poorly sibling, allowing them to feel free about discussing their feelings.

Adolescents

Adolescents may struggle with their own need for independence and may feel guilty about not wanting to be available for care giving. They need to be reassured that their life does not revolve around caring for their sibling and that they should be attentive to their own needs. Most children of any age like to feel useful, but the burden of care should not be on their shoulders.

Interventions

In a study looking at psychosocial support for siblings of children with cancer, Murray and John (2002) reported that the most helpful interventions were emotional and instrumental support, followed by informational and appraisal support. It was noted that the greatest difficulty siblings remembered was being left out and not being able to share their feelings.

Support

Respite, especially in children's hospices, is a valuable asset to allow siblings more access to family activities, as the care team takes over some of the parents' care roles.

Support groups, e.g. SIBS, are available to provide centres where children of all ages can meet, socialize, and discuss concerns. They provide short breaks and holidays, enabling siblings to meet others in their situation.

Jackie Imrie, Central Manchester and Manchester Children's University Hospitals NHS Trust

Further reading

Murray, L.T.C., John, S. (2002). A qualitative exploration of psychosocial support of children with cancer. *Journal of Pediatric Nursing*, **17**(5).

Post, C.E. (1991). When the youngest becomes the oldest. *Exceptional Parent*, March.

www.sibs.org.uk

Using nursing models in practice

Models of nursing

Models are representations of reality. Like a model of a building, a nursing model shows how parts fit together to make a whole. The universal *concept model* of nursing has four elements:
- person
- environment
- health
- nursing.

Definitions of these concepts and the relationships between them differ in the many models that exist to represent different approaches to nursing.

A *process model* widely used in nursing consists of the steps taken to plan individualized care:
- assessment
- planning
- intervention
- evaluation (the nursing process).

Choosing a model

Consider what the model is supposed to represent.
- Does it fit with your view of nursing? Is it culturally appropriate?
- What is it for, i.e. what aspects of nursing, person, health, and environment does it describe? Does that fit with what you want to use it for?
- Has the model been evaluated for use in your care setting?
- Is it understood by, and acceptable to, the child, young person, and family?

Models in use

A team of nurses used the Casey partnership model to decide on audit criteria. They evaluated the quality of the support provided for children and families and found that support needs were not assessed, supportive care was not planned systematically, nor was it evaluated.

Community nurses in East London used the model to argue for better translation services, making the case that they could not teach and support families in care without good translation.

When nurses in an acute ward were provided with a nursing model their records no longer described care in terms of medical diagnosis but reflected the model, including:
- continuity of usual care by parents
- support for family members
- impact of illness and hospitalization
- participation by parents in nursing and medical care.

Anne Casey, Royal College of Nursing

Evaluation

As with any aspect of practice, use of nursing models should be evaluated. Begin with your reasons for using a model and then assess whether the model is meeting your needs. Does the model help you to:

- think about, describe and improve your practice?
- teach students about practice?
- direct research and audit?
- argue for resources and facilities?

Further reading

Pearson, A. (2005). Nursing models for practice, 3rd edn. Butterworth Heinemann, Oxford.
Mason, G., Webb, C. (1997). Researching children's nurses' clinical judgments about assessment data. *Clinical Effectiveness in Nursing*, **1**, 47–55.

Partnership model of nursing

Principles

Partnership nursing is based on recognition of, and respect for, the child/
young person and family's rights and preferences, as well as their knowledge about, and expertise in, (their own) care and treatment. It involves
the following:

- ongoing provision of information, teaching, and support to enable them
  to be involved in decision making, care, and treatment to the extent
  that they wish to be.
- negotiation of choices and care responsibilities, balancing the child/
  young person and family's needs and preferences with available
  resources and professional views of what is needed.

Partnership is an approach to child- and family-centred care; it differs from
family involvement in that there is no assumption that the child and family
will be involved.

Practice

Assess
- Ask the child; ask the parents/carer.
- Invite the child/parent to observe and measure; observe and measure.
- Confirm your impressions and conclusions with the child and
  parents, especially their view of priorities.

Plan
- Agree goals with the child and parents.
- Discuss possible actions and assist them in making choices.
- Agree plan for what needs to be done, who will do it,
  when and how.
- Plan for regular shared review of the plan, care responsibilities,
  and teaching and support needs.

Implement
- Perform direct care as planned (child, parents, nurse).
- Facilitate learning and information sharing.
- Provide support and supervision.
- Monitor progress and re-assess as planned (child, parents, nurse).
- With consent, refer to other professionals and coordinate care.

Evaluate
- Invite the child and parents to observe and measure outcomes and
  report their experience of care.
- Review and reflect on the care process from the child and family
  perspective and from the professional nursing perspective.

Outcomes

Evaluation and audit of the partnership model for nursing children and
young people address the following questions.

Anne Casey, Royal College of Nursing

Did the child/young person and family feel that their views and preferences were heard and their knowledge and experience respected?

Were they involved in decisions, care, and treatment to the extent they wished to be?

Did they feel adequately informed and supported in making decisions and carrying out care/treatment?

Further reading

Casey, A. (2005). Assessing planning care in partnership. In *A Textbook of Children's Nursing*, (ed. E.A. Glasper and J. Richardson). Churchill Livingstone, London.

How to write a care plan

What is a care plan?

- A nursing care plan is a written structured plan of action for patient care based on a holistic assessment of patient requirements, the identification of specific problems, and the development of a plan of action for their resolution.
- Care plans are designed to provide the organizing frame for the planning, provision, and evaluation of nursing care, and they operate as a vehicle for communication and a record of care given.
- The Nursing and Midwifery Council (NMC) views record keeping as an essential aspect of nursing care and not a distraction from its provision. It is a professional requirement for nurses to construct and maintain accurate care plans.

The structure of a care plan

- The structure of a care plan is dependent on the nursing model on which it is based, and as there are many models, there is also a wide range of formats for a nursing care plan. Whichever nursing model the care plan is based on, it should involve all four elements of the nursing process, i.e. the assessment, planning, implementation, and evaluation of nursing care.
- The nursing care plan must be factual and accurate. It should be seen as a structured tool for documenting holistic care, including a balanced assessment of patient need.
- The care plan should contain sufficient detail for a nurse to care for the patient without further information.

How to write a care plan

- Following the nursing assessment, the nurse must identify the patient's needs and document accordingly.
- A plan must be written for each identified need, consisting of a nursing diagnosis (what the problem/need is), expected outcome(s) and/or goals, nursing interventions and rationales required to meet the outcome, and a time at which the plan should be reviewed.
- The intended goal may not be a return to full health but should be appropriate to the patient and the individual circumstances.
- There may be more than one goal for each diagnosis, and each goal should have a set of interventions/rationales required for its achievement.
- The nurse caring for the patient should follow each care plan, which should be assessed and evaluated following every intervention or change in the patient's condition.
- Care plans should remain contemporary—they must be reviewed regularly and rewritten or changed to accurately reflect the patient's current needs.

Paula Flint, Central Manchester and Manchester Children's University Hospitals NHS Trust

Date	Problem number	1

01.01.06	**Nursing Diagnosis**: Sally Smith has pain related to removal of drain from abdomen

Patient Goal: Sally will experience no pain or reduced level of pain acceptable to her

Nursing interventions/*rationales*

1. Administer analgesics as prescribed *for pain*
2. Do not wait until pain is occurring in *order to prevent pain from occurring*
3. Avoid palpating area unless necessary to *minimize risk of pain*
4. Allow Sally to find own position of comfort unless contraindicated
5. Perform nursing procedures and activities (e.g. dressing changes) after *analgesia to minimize risk of pain occurring*
6. Monitor effectiveness of analgesics *to ensure Sally is receiving and has been prescribed adequate and appropriate pain relief*
7. Discuss all care and treatment with Sally and encourage her participation in care *to minimize her distress and anxiety and allow the opportunity for Sally to inform staff if she is experiencing any pain*

Nursing Evaluation

Date

Evaluation of nursing care following care plan 1

Sign & print name and designation

Further reading

Nursing and Midwifery Council (2005). *Guidelines for records and record keeping.*
 www.nmc-uk.org
Foster, E., Harrison, M. (2000). Setting up a collaborative care plan. *Nursing Standard*, **15**(8), 40–3.
Mason, C. (1999). Guide to practice or 'load of rubbish'? The influence of care plans on nursing practice in five clinical areas in Northern Ireland. *Journal of Advanced Nursing*, **29**(2), 380–7.

Evaluation of care

In order to measure the effectiveness of the care that is delivered, and to justify the contribution that we as nurses make to the patient experience, evaluation of that care is essential to identify whether the goals or outcomes of that care have been achieved.

Evaluation involves
• Comparison of the outcome with the original goal or outcome statement.
• If the goal or outcome is not achieved, then reassessment and re-formulation of the nursing outcomes or goals for the child.

The evaluation of care cannot take place if there is no statement or tool to measure it against. For example, how can you evaluate the effectiveness of analgesia that you administered to a child if you have no nursing outcome statement with which to compare it?

Evaluation skills are similar to assessment skills, and are intrinsically linked. By continually evaluating the care delivered to the child, predictions and effectiveness of interventions will become known to both the nurse and the child, thus affording the child choice in his/her future care.

Evaluation of care is an ongoing process and it is an essential component of the nursing process. This may be referred to as formative evaluation, with summative evaluation taking place once the nurse is no longer involved in the care of the child. In evaluating the care given and its effectiveness, the nurse must also critically examine the implementation of the care given, to identify if it was delivered by the most effective means and what it was like for the child and family. Any difficulties encountered in carrying out the plan of care should be documented, as should any changes to the plan of care. Nursing records serve to protect the patient and should contain an accurate account of the treatment given and the care planned and delivered.

Although it is the final part of the nursing process, it is a continual activity, and best practice should advocate the involvement of the child and family so that assumptions will not be made about the effects of care; thus making evaluation objective and empowering the child and parent.

Further reading
Aggleton, P, Chalmers, H. (2000). *Nursing models and nursing practice*, 2nd edn. Macmillan Press, Basingstoke.
Nursing and Midwifery Council (2005). *Guidelines for records and record keeping*. NMC, London.

Liz Gormley-Fleming, University of Hertfordshire

The importance of play

Play can be described as the engagement in activities for pleasure rather than for a serious or practical purpose. It is a source of enjoyment for both the player and the observer of play activity.

Play is the language of children, an essential tool through which they attain knowledge about themselves and the world around them. Play is a rich learning medium, and the ability to play develops earlier in children than the ability to communicate through language, making it a valuable communication tool for children of all ages.

For children there are no extrinsic goals in play activity. Nevertheless play makes an important contribution to normal growth and development. Play and playing are vital parts of children's lives, and through play children learn how to learn and how to do things.

The child uses play:

- for physical development (e.g. fine and gross motor skills, strength, and stamina)
- for social development (e.g. social skills and social behaviours, control of aggression)
- for moral development (e.g. learning to take turns, to win and lose, not to cheat, self-control, and consideration for others)
- for psychological development (e.g. the development of self-awareness and self-actualization)
- for cognitive development (Piaget linked play to cognitive development)
- for problem solving
- as a communication tool (e.g. to demonstrate misconceptions about information received)
- to normalize the environment
- to practise adult behaviours and skills
- for language development
- for distraction from anxiety-provoking situations
- to master/make sense of the environment (play helps children to understand the world in which they live and to differentiate between what is real and what is not)
- to have fun!

Play is an important outlet for anxiety, frustration, emotional tension, and fear, and it enables the child to make sense of anxiety-provoking situations such as invasive medical procedures. In this sense play becomes therapeutic and is emotionally enhancing for the child.

Margaret Chambers, University of Plymouth

Further reading

Piaget, J. (1963). *The origins of intelligence in children*. Norton, New York.
LeVieux-Anglin, L., Sawyer, E. (1993). Incorporating play interventions into nursing care. *Pediatric Nursing*, **19**(5), 459–63.
🖳 www.nncc.org/Curriculum/better.play.html

Diversionary/normal play

- In order to enable medical/nursing staff to examine a child in the way that is least traumatic for the child, time needs to be given to build a relationship of trust through play.
- Play can then be used for distraction, should unpleasant invasive procedures be required.
- Ensure that the activity is developmentally age appropriate, taking into account any special needs the child may have.
- The effect on parents is reduced stress. They are more relaxed, which improves communication.

Children need to be able to access play wherever they are. Play is their way of making sense of the world and coping with their feelings. Play areas provide a safe child-friendly environment in which they are surrounded by familiar things that provide them with a link to home. This creates an environment away from the clinical areas, which is conducive to building relationships and trust with play staff.

The play provided needs to be age and ability appropriate, taking into account special needs, and must also be appropriate for black and ethnic minority children. Staff need to take account of language and communication barriers as well as religious beliefs.

Taking time to build a relationship with parents and children can prove invaluable in gaining trust and identifying the most appropriate and effective activities.

It is important to gain as much information from parents as possible at admission with regard to the child's special toy and any special vocabulary they may have. In addition, it is important to take into account any previous bad experiences the child may have had in hospital and any knowledge of any abuse or neglect the child has experienced.

Include parents and siblings wherever possible. This also has the benefit of creating a home-from-home environment.

Where access to the play room/teenage room is available, children/young people can be provided with an opportunity to self-select activities of their choice. When children are unable to access play independently, the necessary support needs to be provided to enable them to access play. In the event that the child is unable to access the playroom, every effort should be made to identify the favoured activities and provide them at the bedside.

Suggested distraction tools
Infants:
- tactile soothing
- cuddling
- music tapes

Pam Iles, Southampton University Hospitals NHS Trust

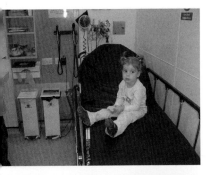

Toddlers:
- blowing bubbles/feathers
- pop-up toys and books
- songs or rhymes

Pre-school children:
- *Where's Wally?* books/posters
- songs and rhymes
- puppets

School-age children:
- joke books
- counting games
- songs and rhymes
- puppets
- kaleidoscopes (with/without glitter wand)
- guided imagery
- games consoles

Further reading

National Association of Hospital Play Specialists (2002). *Guidelines for professional practice: Distraction therapy*. National Association of Hospital Play Specialists.

Preparation and post-procedural play

Understanding what is happening is important to help children/young people and parents relax and accept treatment.

Parents do not always prepare their child for hospital, but all children should be prepared in a way that is appropriate to their cognitive ability, taking into account any special needs and/or cultural and/or religious beliefs.

Illness, accidents, or invasive medical investigations can all bring the emotional challenge of:
- the threat of physical harm
- separation from one's parents and other trusted people
- the threat of strange and unforeseeable experiences
- uncertainty about acceptable behaviour
- relative loss of control and personal autonomy.

Preparation play

A range of quality play helps in preparing children/young people for procedures. This can be achieved through attending a pre-admission club, which will introduce children to the environment and equipment. They will have an opportunity to become familiar with the surroundings, including the theatre waiting room and the recovery room for those children who are to undergo surgery. The familiarization of hospital equipment and routines reduces stress and anxiety, helping the child/young person to come to terms with his/her condition.

Play specialists, in conjunction with the health care team, can develop presentation programmes for children undergoing surgical, clinical, and diagnostic procedures, to develop their understanding of what is going to happen, thus reducing fear.

Role play is particularly useful when enabling children who do not have the necessary language and/or cognitive skills to develop an understanding of the procedure and familiarize them with the equipment.

Good-quality preparation play in the radiotherapy department, for example, enables children, who would otherwise need a general anaesthetic to keep still for treatment, to lie still without fear.

Post-procedural play

Post-procedural play is particularly important for children admitted as emergencies. Post-procedural play should be offered and should include:
- praise; certificates and/or stickers will reinforce this
- an evaluation of the coping strategies used
- an opportunity to express feelings following the procedure
- planning, if future admissions are necessary.

Pam Iles, Southampton University Hospitals NHS Trust

Further reading

Journal of the National Association of Hospital Play Staff, Spring/Summer 1994.

National Association of Hospital Play Specialists (2002). *Guidelines for professional practice*. National Association of Hospital Play Specialists.

Directed and hospital role play

P participation in play introduces normality into a strange setting
L lessens the impact of pain and anxiety
A allows the child/young person to work through feelings and fears, so that hospitalization can become a positive experience
Y yields results: recovery is faster and the in-patient stay is reduced

Being in hospital can be a frightening experience. Directed play enables the child to regain some control over what is happening by acting out his/her feelings and fears. Hospital role play involves playing with clinical equipment in order to gain familiarity and reduce fantasies about it. Gaining the child's/young person's confidence/trust enables medical, nursing staff to observe the patient's reactions and to pick up and deal with fears and misconceptions. In order to achieve this, an attractive and inviting child-friendly environment is required, where children can feel confident and safe to explore and investigate the equipment and activities provided. For example, dolls that children can use to insert a central line enable them to ask questions, develop their understanding of the procedure that they will undergo, and reduce fears. Role play creates a relaxed forum where children, parents, and siblings are free to take their time and ask questions and develop their understanding in a non-judgemental environment. This activity is best carried out whenever possible by a member of the play staff in a non-clinical area, where children are in surroundings that are familiar to them and with people whom they know are safe (not going to undertake any painful procedures).

The effect on the child of skilled directed role play is to reduce fears and anxiety. The child will then be more responsive to procedures and treatments, thus aiding the medical/nursing staff in carrying out what would otherwise be a very distressing procedure. This is particularly important where the child may have to undergo the treatment on more than one occasion. Any distress that is experienced by the child initially will be compounded with each episode experienced. This will make the work of those carrying out the procedure stressful and time consuming. The effect of not making time for role play results in the child potentially having a bad experience. It is extremely difficult to regain a child's trust once this has happened, and it will take substantially more time for the play specialist to develop the child's understanding and acceptance of the treatment/ procedure he/she is required to undergo.

Further reading

Sylvia, K. (1995). Play in hospital: When and why it is effective. *Current Paediatrics*, **3**, 247–9.
Barry, P. (2000). *A child's recollection of hospital.* National Association of Hospital Play Specialists.

Pam Iles, Southampton University Hospitals NHS Trust

Guided imagery

Guided imagery is a 'therapeutic technique that allows two people to communicate on a reality that one of them has chosen to describe through the process of imaging.

It can be used with children in hospital as a form of pain management.

Before the imagery can start, it is important to carry out an assessment of the child you hope to use this technique with. You need to look at:
- age/cognitive level of child
- what type of pain they may be experiencing, e.g. procedural, anxiety, chronic
- emotional state of the child
- expectations of the child (remember always to be realistic and do not make promises)
- any existing coping strategies the child may use
- environment
- staff to be involved. At least two people are needed: one to carry out the procedure and the other to guide the imagery at an appropriate point
- organization of procedure

Guided imagery technique
- Building a rapport and gaining the child's trust.
- 'I know a way we could help to make this easier. Would you like to try?'
- Child to identify what they would like to imagine (should be something fun!).
- Start by getting the child to do some deep breathing and progressive muscle relaxation.
- Child begins to describe imagery.
- You begin to guide and be guided by child's imagery.
- Ask questions such as, What can you see? What's happening now? Is anyone there with you? Tell me what it looks like.
- Always inform the child what is happening while they are in imagery, e.g. the tourniquet is going on now, we are going to remove the dressing now.
- Reinforce imagery when necessary.

Always round off imagery:
- Ask the child if he/she would like to finish his/her imagery.
- Encourage him/her to take a big deep breath in and out slowly.
- Think backwards from 4 to 1 (younger children count 1–4).
- Open his/her eyes slowly.
- Wiggle toes and fingers.

Ask the child how he/she feels and encourage him/her to sit still for a few moments, as he/she may feel a little 'funny'.

Joanne Groves, Southampton University Hospitals NHS Trust

Guided imagery response indicators
- Eyes closed (not always at first)
- Eye movements under closed lids
- Slowing of breathing
- Relaxed, absence of muscle tension
- Speech normal—calm
- Easy flowing description of imagery

Points to consider
- Guided imagery can be used with children from an age when they are able to use their imagination. It may not be suitable for children with special needs.
- Imagery can be guided by play specialists, nurses, doctors, and parents, as long as, when it is used during a procedure, there is at least one other person to carry out the procedure.
- Remember to review each case. It will not work for everybody. What was easy to focus on? What were the goals? How can I improve the outcome?

'Guided imagery, a form of relaxed focused concentration is a natural and powerful coping mechanism.'

Further reading
🔲 www.guidedimageryinc.com
🔲 www.phoenixchildrens.com

Education and the ill child

Children with medical conditions have an increased likelihood of experiencing, at some time, a constellation of factors that may directly or indirectly place their education at risk. The importance of school for children with chronic diseases cannot be underestimated.

If education is to be effective for children with medical conditions, education authorities, schools, and staff must make positive responses to these issues. Section 19 of the 1996 Education Act says that 'each local education authority shall make arrangements for the provision of suitable education at school or otherwise than at school for those children of compulsory school age who, by reason of illness ... may not for any period receive suitable education unless arrangements are made'. Because each case is unique, it is not possible to quantify this.

Most establishments are ill-prepared in terms of experience, professional development, knowledge, skills, and attitudes, to take up and sustain the challenge in an in-depth way.

When parents are considering their child's education, they are mindful not only of academic and performance-related matters, but also of care, medical, and quality-of-life issues. For a family whose life is totally affected and controlled by the child's illness, the quality of the child's school life assumes an enormous significance.

Some children go through their entire schooling suffering the effects of their condition and experiencing difficulties. Schools should not underestimate the difference they can make to the child's quality of life. With careful planning, appropriate activities, and sensitive teaching, the school can make a significant contribution. Teachers and support staff can be content in the knowledge that their input has the double benefit of being therapeutic and educational.

It is important that a holistic approach is adopted by all working with the family and its individual members. Sick children do not exist in isolation; they are members of a family group that functions as a unit. All members of the family are affected by the illness.

There are many other reasons why an ill and disabled child may not be able to attend school but still benefit from home tuition, such as a susceptibility to serious chest infections, difficulties over school transport, or supervision problems at school associated with distressing, unpredictable, and possibly life-threatening symptoms.

Home tuition for children with degenerative disorders, for example, is not an extension of school per se but rather is a unique service provision, a specially crafted resource to meet the needs of a child and family living under difficult, stressful, and peculiar circumstances.

Jackie Imrie, Central Manchester and Manchester Children's University Hospitals NHS Trust

Patient and parent information and education

The provision of adequate information is an essential prerequisite to the formation and development of a trusting relationship between practitioner, child, and family. It is, therefore, extremely important that all information provided should be clear, factual, and aimed at empowering and enabling the family in relation to their understanding, consent, and participation.

This may include the creative use of verbal communication, non-verbal communication, abstract communication, and aids such as leaflets, books, and posters, or interactive methods such as videos, CDs, DVDs, and computers with internet access.

All information provided needs to be good quality, based on up-to-date evidence, and adapted to take account of the age, development, and level of understanding of all involved.

This will require knowledge and skills on the part of the practitioner, not only in relation to their understanding of child development and interpersonal communication strategies, but also the ability to assess and evaluate information needs and understanding. Linked to this, it must never be assumed that parents lack knowledge in relation to their child or their child's condition. With the increasing influence of the internet, it follows that children and their parents now have improved access to information which can, in many cases, lead to an expert knowledge and understanding on their part. It is important that practitioners do not perceive this as a threat to their own expertise. Rather, it should be viewed as a basis on which to develop communication strategies based on partnership, mutual trust, and respect. In this way further exploration and explanation of specific issues can be provided and appropriate skills acquired by all, with guidance given towards reliable sources of good-quality information.

Factors to note when providing information include the following.
- Information should be appropriate in its presentation and linked to the age, ability, and level of understanding of those involved.
- Verbal information should be clear and factual and spoken at a normal pace.
- Technical terms or jargon should be avoided and explanations should be simple and uncomplicated.
- Adequate time should be allocated; include time for questions and discussion.
- Not all information will be understood at first and back-up material, such as leaflets, videos, or books, should be provided for reinforcement and further explanation.

Elaine Mahoney, University of Glamorgan

Further reading

HMSO (2001). *Learning from Bristol: the report of the public inquiry into children's heart surgery at the Bristol Royal Infirmary 1984–1995*. CM5207(1). HMSO, London.

Matthews, J. (2006). Communicating with children and their families. In *A textbook of children's and young people's nursing*, (ed. A. Glasper and J. Richardson). Elsevier, London.

Dealing with parental aggression

In today's society, having the skills to manage anger, aggression, and violent behaviour successfully is very important for a children's nurse. However, prevention of the occurrence and escalation of these situations will be more satisfying and productive for all involved. Where prevention has not been possible and aggression or violence is a reality, nurses must have the ability to utilize high-level interpersonal skills in order to effectively relate to the individuals involved.

It is important that you can:
- define and differentiate between anger, aggression, and violence
- understand the possible causes of anger, aggression, and violence
- identify what signs to look for
- understand how to respond
- develop the skills required to prevent and deal with situations as they occur.

Factors that can lead to families becoming angry and aggressive can include:
- staff shortages and increased workload that lead to a reduction in the time you can spend with families
- unrealistic expectations of the family
- poor planning and prolonged waiting times
- poor communication
- lack of appropriate information
- inadequate resources
- inappropriate discharge planning.

In relation to this, an important aspect is the ability of the children's nurse to become self-aware. Self-awareness will enable you to learn about your own behaviour and reactions. This, in turn, will lead to an understanding of how your own behaviour is perceived by others and how, in certain circumstances, if responses are deemed to be inappropriate, this may contribute to increasing the frustration and anger experienced by the family. Along with the development of self-awareness, you must strive to incorporate some of the basic principles of communication. Communication involves content and context factors, and situations may escalate if one person misinterprets or misunderstands what the other person has said or done.

It is also essential that you learn to become tuned in and perceptive to the possible predisposing factors and emotions that can lead to a person becoming frustrated, angry, or aggressive. These may include:
- fear—for the welfare of the child or of the environment
- stress and anxiety
- feelings of loss of control
- blaming themselves and feelings of guilt for their child's illness
- perceived inappropriate waiting times
- insufficient information.

Elaine Mahoney, University of Glamorgan

By developing this understanding, the skills and strategies aimed at calming the situation and preventing escalation can be more successfully applied. These include:

- effective listening
- remaining calm and actively engaging with the family
- demonstrating empathy and understanding of the situation
- being responsive but remaining in control
- being aware of the environment and personal safety.

Arnold, E., Underman Boggs, K. (2003). *Interpersonal relationships: communication skills for nurses,* 4th edn. WB Saunders, St Louis.
Hollinworth, H., Clark, C., Harland, R., Johnson, L., Partington, G. (2005). Understanding the arousal of anger: a patient-centred approach. *Nursing Standard,* **19**(37), 41–7.

Writing a patient information leaflet

Written and other information resources play an increasingly important role in the care of families with sick children. A fundamental component of the NSF is the giving of information, which is complete and clearly communicated. All healthcare staff who treat children should receive training in communicating with young people and their parents.

Production of local information

Writing a patient information leaflet may appear superficially easy but the reality is that it cannot just be typed on a word processor one evening using a home computer.

- Readability formulae can help writers of patient information leaflets to assess how well their writing can be understood by the reader. The FOG and standard measure of gobbledegook (SMOG) indices are widely available for this. Remember that the average reading age of UK adults is at the level of the *Sun* newspaper.
- Keep sentences short, using simple explanations.
- Use familiar, but avoid unnecessary, words.
- Use action verbs and terms your reader can picture.
- Make sure the leaflet is comprehensible, usable, and easy to navigate.

Before rushing to your computer

- Know your purpose. What do you want to achieve?
- Know your target audience. Who are you writing for, a child or a carer?
- Know your subject. If you do not, get help.
- Know the setting under which your intended audience will read the leaflet.

Make sure your information leaflet contains:

- Awareness information.
- Information that allows the reader to optimize the purpose of the leaflet.
- Principles information which gives, for example, real concrete information on how certain drugs work.

The style of patient information leaflets

- Use informative headings.
- Personalize the leaflet by using personal pronouns such as 'I, we, or you'.
- Use decisive, clear, and unambiguous language.
- Describe actions positively ('give only after meals', or 'give only if wheezing').
- Only use familiar words and avoid professional jargon.
- Use short paragraphs with strong topic sentences.
- Use simple visual images and 12-point type.
- Leave lots of white space.

Alan Glasper, University of Southampton

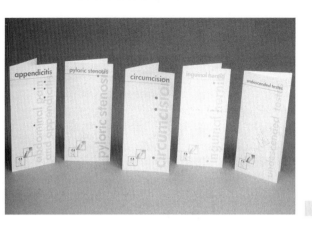

Remember to always:

- Base your leaflet on best evidence.
- Have it peer reviewed.
- Use families to pilot and develop the leaflet.
- State explicitly by using a date when the leaflet should be updated.

Further reading

Glasper, A., Burge, D. (1992). Developing family information leaflets. *Nursing Standard*, **25**, 24–7.
Glasper, E.A., McWilliams, R. (1998). Developing a centre for health information and promotion.
  In *Innovations in paediatric ambulatory care*, (ed. E.A. Glasper and S. Lowson). Macmillan,
  Basingstoke.

Test	Reference range (conventional units)
17-Hydroxyprogesterone (17-OHP)	0.4–4 nmol/L
Acidity (pH)	7.35–7.45
Ammonia	15–50 µg of N_2/dL
Amylase	53–123 units/L
Calcium	8.5–10.5 mg/dL (normally slightly higher in children)
Chloride	98–106 mEq/L
Creatinine kinase	60–300 units/L (Infant /child)
Creatinine	20–80 µmol/L
Glucose	3 – 6 mmol/L
Haemoglobin	12–18 g/dL
Iron	10–30 µg/dL (lower in infants)
Magnesium	0.6 –1.0 mmol/L
Osmolality	280–296 mOsm/kg water
Phosphatase	50–160 units/L (normally higher in infants and adolescents alkaline)
Potassium	3.5–5.0 mEq/L
Proteins	
Total	6.0–8.0 g/dL
Albumin	3.5–5.0 g/dL
Globulin	2.3–3.5 g/dL
Pyruvic acid	0.3–0.9 mg/dL
Sodium	135–145 mEq/L
Thyroid-stimulating hormone (TSH)	0.5–6.0 µunits/mL
Urea nitrogen	2.5–6.5 mmol/L

Normal physiological values in children

Age (years)	Pulse (bpm)	Respiratory rate (breaths/min)	Systolic blood pressure (mmHg)
<1	110–160	30–40	70–90
1–2	100–150	25–35	80–95
2–5	95–140	25–30	80–100
5–12	80–120	20–25	90–110
>12	60–100	15–20	100–120

Pulse
Most serious illness or injury is associated with tachycardia, but may also result from anxiety, excitement, pyrexia, or pain. Hypoxia causes tachycardia in older infants and children, but prolonged or severe hypoxia will result in bradycardia. Bradycardia in children may indicate raised intracranial pressure, but is generally considered an ominous and pre-terminal sign.

Respiratory rate
Rates are higher in infancy, because of an increased metabolic rate and oxygen consumption, and decrease with age. Regular reassessment is necessary because rates change dramatically depending on activity. Tachypnoea is indicative of airway/lung disease or metabolic acidosis and is usually the first indicator of respiratory distress. A slow respiratory rate indicates fatigue, cerebral depression, or a pre-terminal state.

Blood pressure
Accurate blood pressure recordings depend on the use of the right size cuff. The width should cover >80% of the upper arm, and the cuff bladder should cover >40% of the arm's circumference.

Predicted systolic blood pressure can be estimated using the following formula: blood pressure = 80 + (age in years x 2).

Hypertension may be the cause or result of coma or raised intracranial pressure. Hypotension in children is a late and pre-terminal sign, suggesting cardiac arrest is imminent.

Temperature
Normal body temperature is 36.8°C. A fever usually indicates infection as the source of the illness, but may be the result of prolonged convulsions or shivering. A child with a high temperature (over 38.5°C) or who is cold (below 32°C) must be seen urgently.

Normal core temperature by age
Under 6 months	37.5°C
7 months–1 year	37.5–37.7°C
2–5 years	37.0–37.2°C
Over 6 years	36.6–36.8°C

Further reading
Advanced Life Support Group (2005). Advanced paediatric life support: the practical approach. 4th edn. Blackwell.

Jevon, P (2004). Paediatric advanced life support: a practical guide. Butterworth Heinemann.

Ruth Trengove, South Devon Healthcare NHS Trust

Chapter 1 from the Oxford Handbook of

Learning and Intellectual Disability Nursing

Edited by

Prof Bob Gates

Project Leader
Learning Disability Workforce Development
South Central Strategic Health Authority

and

Dr Owen Barr

Head of School
School of Nursing
University of Ulster

OXFORD
UNIVERSITY PRESS

The nature of intellectual disability

Introduction 246
Identifying intellectual disability 248
Degree of intellectual disability 250
Definition of intellectual disability 252
Incidence and prevalence of intellectual disability 254
Diagnosing intellectual disability 256
Causes and manifestations of intellectual disability 258
Common conditions among people with intellectual disability 260
Defining intellectual disability nursing 262
The purist form of nursing 264
Principles and values of social policy and their effects on intellectual disability 266
Holism and working across the life span 268

Introduction

In this chapter the term intellectual disability (ID) will be defined. It will be shown that ID is identified by the presence of a significantly reduced ability to understand new or complex information (impaired intelligence) with the reduced ability to cope independently (impaired social functioning), which started before 18yrs of age.[1]

The chapter outlines that there is general agreement that 3–4/1000 of the general population will have a severe ID, and that 25–30/1000 of the general population will have a mild ID.

Also outlined are the various ways in which a diagnosis, or assessment, of ID is made. A range of known causes and manifestations of ID will be provided.

Above all else it will be emphasized that people with ID, regardless of the impact of their disabilities, share a common humanity with that of their fellow citizens in their communities, and in the wider society in which they live. Most people desire love and a sense of connection with others; they wish to be safe, to learn, to lead a meaningful life, to be free from ridicule and harm, to be healthy, and free from poverty, and in this respect people with ID are no different to any of us.

All health and social care workers, especially ID nurses, have a professional responsibility to bring about their inclusion, into their communities, by adhering at all times to a value base that respects them as fellow citizens.

This value base leads this chapter to conclude by articulating the nature of ID nursing, and how this group of professionals work to support the whole person throughout their lives when they are in need of such support.

1 DHSSPS (2005). *Equal Lives*. DHSSPS: Belfast.

Identifying intellectual disability

It is essential to stress at the outset of this section that each person with an ID is a unique human being. Like everyone else, each person has their own personality along with a profile of abilities and disabilities that can only be understood in the context of their culture, history, and relationships.

ID manifests in a number of different ways for each individual.

Intellectual profile

Fundamental to ID is a difficulty in learning and processing information. The following intellectual abilities may be impaired:

Verbal abilities

- Memory—including immediate recall of people, objects or events, and the ability to store and process information
- Comprehension—this means understanding situations, knowing socially accepted norms and being able to weigh up possible options
- Language—vocabulary may be limited and some people may not understand words at all. Others may recognize words but struggle to understand more subtle meanings
- Abstract thinking—people may find it hard to separate themselves from the thing they are thinking about. Hypothetical situations are particularly difficult.

Non-verbal abilities

- Speed of processing—an individual may take a long time to work out what is going on in a situation
- Reasoning—shapes, patterns and numbers may be confusing and people can find it hard to put things in order
- Coordination – there may be difficulty in coordinating movement or using fine motor skills.

Coping with everyday life

These difficulties in intellectual function can have an impact on a person's ability to cope with everyday life. This means that a person may have a range of difficulties that require support:

- Self care—including everything from getting up, washing, and dressing, through to going to bed
- Domestic skills—looking after clothes, cooking, and cleaning are all included here
- Community living skills—getting out and about, managing simple social interactions, and using shops and public services
- Communication—getting on with people and being able to communicate needs and wishes
- Work and leisure—using time purposefully, having fun, and pursuing personal goals.

Behavioural phenotypes

As will be seen later, most people with ID have a general ID that manifests in the ways shown above. There are a number of people with specific syndromes, and these syndromes may be associated with a particular profile of verbal and non-verbal abilities. For example people who are on the autistic spectrum of disorders are characterized by specific difficulties with social communication and information processing. Information about specific syndromes is important, therefore, in understanding and predicting possible manifestations of ID.

Additional needs

People with ID are more likely to have a range of additional needs. Of particular note are:

- Sensory impairments
- Gastro-oesophageal reflux disorder (GORD)
- Epilepsy.

Context

As mentioned above, each person with ID presents with a history and background, and it is essential to understand these alongside the immediate disabilities. People with ID are likely to be receiving support from their family or from other carers, and these people will have a key role to play in any assessment or intervention.

Further reading

American Association for Mental Retardation (2002). *Mental Retardation, Definition, Classification and Systems of Support.* 10th edn. AAMR: Washington.

Hogg J, Langa A (2005). *Assessing Adults with Intellectual Disabilities: A Service Providers Guide.* Blackwell Publishing: Oxford.

Prasher V, Janicki M (2002). *Physical Health of Adults with Intellectual Disabilities.* Blackwell Publishing: Oxford.

Degree of intellectual disability

For many years, ID has been divided into a number of categories to reflect its nature and extent. These tended to range from 'borderline' through 'mild', 'moderate' and 'severe', to 'profound'. This represents one understanding of ID but there are others. This understanding uses the World Health Organization classification system that defines the degree of disability according to how far an individual is from the normal distribution of IQ for the general population. Using this system, an individual who consistently scores more than 2 Standard Deviations (SD) on an IQ test, that is, a measured IQ of <70, is said to have ID. Individuals whose IQ is 50–69 are generally identified as having mild ID (F70); those with an IQ of 71–84 are said to be on the borderline of intellectual functioning; moderate ID (F71) is identified when the IQ is 35–49; the term 'severe intellectual disability' (F72) is reserved for people whose IQ is 20–34; finally, the term 'profound intellectual disability' (F73) refers to those with an IQ of <20. There are also other classifications. These are not identified here but most rely on the use of standardized tests offering high validity and reliability. An alternative approach is based on a model of ID that sees it as an interaction between a person, the support they receive, and the environment they are in (Fig.1.1). For example:

Andrew has very significant ID. He has to use a wheelchair, he cannot speak or understand words, and he has not been able to look after even his most basic needs. He needs a great deal of support to provide his basic care, and to understand what he is trying to communicate. He also needs an environment with special equipment, and opportunities to get out and meet new people, which he loves to do.

Elizabeth has Down's syndrome and can communicate very well with words. She looks after herself and can cope well in the community. She has to do things one at a time and can get overwhelmed if she feels there is too much to do. Elizabeth needs someone to visit her once a day to make sure she has remembered everything, including her epilepsy medication, and to make sure she is not getting overwhelmed. She needs an environment where she has just one task at a time to get through the day, and the opportunity to meet her family at least once a week.

These examples show that each individual has a unique profile of ID that impacts on everyday life in different ways. Assessment of the degree of ID will identify the level of support a person needs, as well as the kind of environment and opportunities that they need.[1] There is a system for categorizing the amount of support people need on 4 levels:

- Intermittent—this is time limited support at key times in life such as loss of key relationships or transition
- Limited—consistent need of support for specific tasks, such as employment training; still time limited

- Extensive—regular long-term direct support in at least one setting
- Pervasive—constant high-intensity support across all settings.

To this is added an assessment of the kind of environment a person needs, and the opportunities that are important for them to be healthy and to achieve their personal goals. It is always important to remember that quality of life and relationships are very important to everyone whatever the degree of ID.

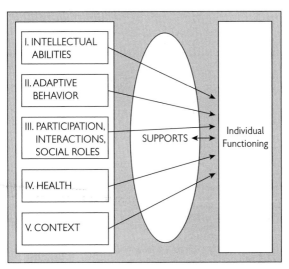

Fig. 1.1 American Association for Mental Retardation (2002). *Mental Retardation, Definition, Classification and Systems of Support.* 10th Edn. AAMR: Washington.

Reference and further reading

1 American Association for Mental Retardation (2002). *Mental Retardation, Definition, Classification and Systems of Support.* 10th edn. AAMR: Washington.

Hogg J, Langa A (2005). *Assessing Adults with Intellectual Disabilities: A Service Providers Guide.* Blackwell Publishing: Oxford.

Definition of intellectual disability

ID has been understood from a number of different theoretical perspectives. Three key perspectives have led to modern definitions of ID:

Sociological—people who fall outside accepted norms and expectations in society. From this perspective intellectual disability can be seen as deviance, where the task of services is to enable people to be included in community life. The alternative is to see ID as a subculture that is distinct and different from other groups in society. Here services are intended to empower and support the group.

Medical—this focuses on the possibility that there is an underlying disease or pathology that might at some point be identified, understood, and treated as a medical condition. There is also a controversial notion that prevention of ID might be an important and valid aim.

Statistical—here it is assumed that any aspect of human behaviour can be measured and will have a mean and standard deviation. In the case of ID there are two aspects of measurement—intelligence as measured by intelligence tests to arrive at an IQ, and adaptive behaviour: the ability to cope with the challenges of everyday life. People with ID are defined as those who fall below one SD below the mean on these measures.

These perspectives have produced a common understanding that ID is defined as an interaction between the person and the community. A person may have significant deficits but cope well in the right environment and with the right support. Minor difficulties can be massively handicapping in a world where the person is isolated and unsupported.

These ideas have led to an accepted definition of ID in the UK. There are 3 main components:

• A significant lifelong difficulty in learning and understanding
• A significant difficulty in learning and practising the skills needed to cope with everyday life
• That there is evidence that these difficulties started before adulthood.[1,2]

These definitions have been worded very carefully from a political perspective but they are not sufficiently precise for professional practice. It is important, therefore, to add the internationally accepted definition of ID, the latest revision of which was drawn up in the USA in 2002. The same social model is used and ID refers to:

"Substantial limitations in present functioning. It is characterized by significantly sub average intellectual functioning, existing concurrently with related limitations in two or more of the following applicable adaptive skill areas: communication, self care, home living, social skills, community use, self direction, health and safety, functional academics, leisure and work. Mental retardation manifests itself before age 18."

Intellectual function is generally measured by intelligence tests, but although this may be necessary it is not sufficient to define ID. Coping with everyday life is broken down into 10 key areas, of which 2 must be significantly impaired.

The rigid application of assessments based on this definition is not helpful. Rather it is important that practitioners consider the individual circumstances of each person, including culture, personal history, socio-economic, and psychological factors. There is increasing attention now being paid to the role of economic factors in determining ID in general and health inequalities in particular.

Further reading

American Association for Mental Retardation (2002). *Mental Retardation, Definition, Classification and Systems of Support.* 10th edn. AAMR: Washington.

1 Department of Health (2001). *Valuing People: a New Strategy for Learning Disability in the 21st Century.* Cmnd 5086. HMSO: London.

2 Scottish Executive (2000). *The Same as You: a Review of Services for People with Learning Disabilities.* Scottish Executive: Edinburgh.

3 American Association for Mental Retardation (2002). *Mental Retardation, Definition, Classification and Systems of Support.* 10th edn. AAMR: Washington.

Incidence and prevalence of intellectual disability

Calculating the incidence of ID is difficult because there is no way of detecting the vast majority of those infants who have ID at birth. Therefore to arrive at any estimate one has to use cumulative incidence, and this has been calculated at 8yrs of age as 4.9/1000 for severe ID and 4.3/1000 for mild ID.[1]

It is only the obvious manifestations of ID that can be detected at birth—e.g. Down's syndrome, and for these conditions it is possible to calculate incidence.

It is more usual, therefore, to refer to the prevalence of ID, and where there is no obvious physical manifestation at birth, diagnosis must be delayed in order to await significant developmental delay along with other manifestations to diagnose ID; therefore, it is more common to talk about prevalence.

Prevalence is concerned with an estimation of the number of people with a condition, disorder or disease as a proportion of the general population.

If IQ is used as an indicator of intellectual disability, then it can be calculated that 2–3% of the population is likely to have an IQ <70. Given that a large proportion of the people with such an estimated IQ never come into contact with a caring agency, it is more common to refer to 'administrative prevalence', which refers to the number of people provided with some form of service from caring agencies.

Historically, there has been a general consensus that the overall prevalence of severe learning disabilities is approximately 3–4/1000 of the general population.[2]

The Department of Health has suggested that mild learning disability is quite common; prevalence has been estimated to be in the region of 20/1000 of the general population. In the UK it has been further calculated that, of the 3–4/1000 population with an intellectual disability, ~30% will present with severe or profound learning disabilities. Within this group it is not uncommon to find multiple disabilities, including physical and/or sensory impairments, or disability as well as behavioural difficulties.

Emerson et al., drawing on extensive epidemiological data, have confirmed the estimation of prevalence for severe learning disabilities.[1] They state it to be somewhere in the region of 3–4/1000 of the general population. The prevalence rate Emerson et al. give for the intellectually disabled population referred to as having mild ID is much more imprecise. It is estimated that it might be 25–30 people/1000 of the general population. Based on these estimates it can be assumed that there are some 230,000–350,000 persons with severe ID, and possibly 580,000–1,750,000 persons with mild ID in the UK.

There is a slight imbalance in the ratio of males to females in people with both mild and severe learning disabilities, with males having slightly higher prevalence rates. Also there is some evidence of slightly higher prevalence rates among some ethnic groups, and this includes Black Groups in the USA, and South Asian Groups in the UK.[1]

Further reading

Grant G, Goward P, Richardson M, Ramcharan P (2005). *Learning Disability: a Life Cycle Approach to Valuing People.* Open University Press: Milton Keynes.

Learning About Intellectual Disabilities and Health ⊞ http://www.intellectualdisability.info

1 Emerson E, Hatton C, Felce D, Murphy G (2001). *Learning Disabilities: The Fundamental Facts.* The Foundation for People with Learning Disabilities: London.

2 Department of Health (2001). *Valuing People: a New Strategy for Learning Disability for the 21st Century.* CM 5086. HMSO: London.

Diagnosing intellectual disability

That this section concerns the diagnosis of ID would seem to imply that people with ID are the preserve of the medical model: this is not so. In the context of this section it will be shown that sometimes identifying an ID is arrived at in a number of ways and by different professionals, and this may or may not include a medical diagnosis.

Diagnosing or identifying intellectual disabilities

The vast majority of parents will have no evidence that their child will have ID before the birth. Only a minority of parents have advance warning, possibly from screening investigations such as blood tests and ultrasound scans, or diagnostic investigations such as amniocentesis, chorionic villous sampling or other tests undertaken because the parents are perceived as being at a high risk. [1]

Unless a definite physical abnormality or characteristic signs (as in children with Down's syndrome) are present at birth, or a traumatic delivery has taken place, ID is seldom suspected or diagnosed at birth. A diagnosis can vary from the confirmation of the presence of a specific condition (e.g. Down's syndrome) to a much broader diagnosis of developmental delay with no specific condition identified.

ID is usually identified during childhood or sometimes later during adolescence, but in order to meet most criteria for being classified as intellectually disabled this should be before 18yrs of age, or if identified later in life there should be sufficient evidence available that this started before 18yrs. Those children with severe or profound ID are likely to be more noticed as having learning disabilities at a younger age than those with mild to moderate ID. Therefore ID is most often diagnosed in early childhood when a child fails to reach 'normal' developmental milestones.

During this period, parents may have expressed concerns over the nature of their child's progress and suspect that a problem exists. It is unprofessional and potentially dangerous if those in contact with the parents at this time (e.g. GP, health visitor, paediatrician or other nurses) dismiss parental concern and label them as 'overanxious' or 'overprotective'. Such judgements are prejudicial and negate parents' concerns subsequently; they have no place in family centred services.[1] Rather a regular check should be kept on the child's progress, more frequently than the usual screening checks, and records kept. It is a relief to both parents and professionals, after a period of observation, to be able to show that the child is reaching normal milestones. The prospects of active family involvement will be damaged in the short term, and possibly for several years, when a diagnosis of ID is confirmed despite repeated concerns having been previously raised only to be dismissed or largely ignored.

Finally it is important to identify the nature and extent of ID and either exclude or include other more specific developmental disorders that are sometimes present, for example ASD, ADHD, or dyspraxia (developmental coordination disorder).

Conclusion

Identification of the cause of ID and the provision of an early diagnosis are crucial to:
- limit the feelings of self blame that may be experienced by some parents of children with ID
- reduce the possibility of inadequate adaptation by the parents to their child and thereby hopefully avoid rejection.

Other reasons for identifying the presence of ID and diagnosis include a need to:
- understand the possible manifestation of the identified condition over a defined period of time
- identify the range of therapeutic approaches that may be used to ameliorate the effects of the condition, including the mobilization of specific resources
- establish, in some cases, the degree of risk to other family members of the condition reoccurring in their siblings and offspring.

Further reading

Grant G, Goward P, Richardson M, Ramcharan P (2005). *Learning Disability: a Life Cycle Approach to Valuing People.* Open University Press: Milton Keynes.

Overview of Learning (Intellectual) Disability in Children ⬚ http://www.intellectualdisability.info/

1 Barr O (2007). Working effectively with families of people with learning disabilities. In: Gates B (Ed). *Learning Disabilities: Toward Inclusion.* 5th edn. Churchill Livingstone: Edinburgh, 567–598.

Causes and manifestations of intellectual disability

ID is a major health condition thought to affect an estimated 150,000 infants/year either born with, or later diagnosed as having ID.[1] The reported frequency of ID varies across studies, but overall rates of 1–3% of the general population have been found, with a male:female ratio of 1.3:1, mainly attributed to X-linked ID.[2]

In 40–80% of individuals with ID the cause cannot be determined.[1] The aim should be to try to establish any cause of ID so that accurate information about any diagnosis reached can be given, as well as precise rather than empiric recurrence risks.[2]

ID can result from experiences in the prenatal environment that interfere with brain and CNS development and functioning. ID is a feature of hundreds of congenital conditions, but 5–15% are thought to result from genetic disorders. Abnormalities associated with chromosomes and/or genes can often disrupt physical and/or intellectual development.

ID can result from a combination of the following factors:

Genetic abnormalities

Genetic abnormalities may be subdivided into chromosomal, single gene, multifactorial, mitochondrial, and/or somatic cell disorders. Recognized Mendelian patterns of inherited disorders include autosomal dominant, autosomal recessive and X-linked.

Exposure to environmental agents/teratogens

Environmental agents that cause disruption in normal prenatal development are known as teratogens. Fetal development can be disrupted by teratogenic exposure to chemicals, drugs or diseases.

Chemicals: Examples of chemicals with known teratogenic effect include excessive radiation, smoking, and alcohol.

Drugs: Examples of drugs include so-called 'recreational' illegal substances and also prescribed drugs, which may have teratogenic effects (e.g. thalidomide or phenytoin).

Diseases: Examples of diseases with known teratogenic effect include rubella.

It is now recognized that an embryo may be susceptible to virtually any substance if exposure to the substance is sufficiently concentrated. A number of broad generalizations have emerged from research into teratogens, for example, some individual embryos and pregnancies are more *susceptible* to exposure, and/or there may be developmental periods which are *critical or sensitive* with regard to specific teratogen exposure.

Intrauterine or birth trauma

Where there is a clear biological cause of ID, for example, oxygen deprivation at birth or placental insufficiency.

Prematurity

ID caused by premature birth due to interruption of the normal course and duration of maturation in the uterine environment or due to trauma(s) experienced in the perinatal period following premature birth.

Postnatal developmental period

ID may be caused in the immediate postnatal period, if there is interruption, disruption or damage of a sufficient, significant level to the normal course of development. Examples would include infections such as meningitis, or trauma such as severe or intractable epilepsy or head injury.

1 Wynbrandt J, Ludman MD (2000). *Genetic Disorders and Birth Defects*. Facts on File Inc.: New York.

2 Firth HV, Hurst JA (2005). *Oxford Desk Reference. Clinical Genetics*. Oxford University Press: Oxford.

Common conditions among people with intellectual disability

Genetic diseases and disorders with associated ID may be subdivided into chromosomal, single gene, multifactorial, and mitochondrial disorders. Recognized Mendelian patterns of inherited single gene disorders include autosomal dominant, autosomal recessive and X-linked inheritance.

Chromosomal disorders

The normal chromosome complement is 46 chromosomes occurring in pairs. Pairs 1 to 22 are called autosomes and are common to both genders. The 23rd pair are the sex chromosomes because they relate to gender. Thus normal male chromosome complement is 46 XY whereas female chromosome complement is 46 XX. An abnormal chromosome complement can be the result of loss, duplication, or rearrangement of genetic material.

Aneuploidy is the condition in which the chromosome number in the cells of an individual is not an exact number of the typical chromosome complement of 46 XX or 46 XY. There may be a full extra chromosome, called trisomy, or there may be a complete loss or absence of a chromosome, called monosomy.[1] Examples of trisomy include trisomy 21 (Down syndrome), trisomy 18 (Edwards syndrome), or trisomy 13 (Patau syndrome). An example of monosomy that may be but is not always associated with ID is monosomy X (Turner syndrome).

Single gene disorders

Genes located on the X chromosome are referred to as X-linked genes and those on the autosomes as autosomal genes. Of each of the pairs in a chromosome set, one is derived from each parent, so each pair of chromosomes will have a comparable gene located at the same position on each chromosome pair, which may be referred to as alleles. Therefore, with the exception of the X and Y chromosomes in males, each gene is present in two copies, one from each parent. A gene mutation indicates a changed or altered gene.[2] These principles of dominant, recessive and X-linked inheritance patterns reflect Mendelian laws of inheritance.[2]

Autosomal dominant—a gene mutation in one of a pair of genes, which produces an abnormal characteristic despite the presence of the other normal or unaltered copy, is referred to as dominant. Examples of autosomal dominant disorders often associated with differing degrees of ID include Apert syndrome, myotonic dystrophy (early onset and congenital cases frequently associated with ID, though adult onset infrequently associated with ID), tuberous sclerosis.

Autosomal recessive—a gene mutation that causes an abnormal characteristic only when present in both copies of a gene is referred to as recessive. Examples of autosomal recessive disorders causing, or often associated with, differing degrees of ID include galactosaemia, Sanfilippo syndrome, Tay–Sachs disease, phenylketonuria.

X-linked—The sex chromosomes consist of two X chromosomes in a normal female, and one X and one Y chromosome in a male. Therefore females have two copies of each X chromosome gene, one from each parent, but males have only one copy of each gene on the X chromosome. Mutations on the X chromosome may be described as dominant or recessive. X-linked dominant mutations may manifest obvious clinical effects in both males and females, whereas X-linked recessive mutations usually manifest in males but have minimal, or no, effect on (carrier) females. Examples of X-linked disorders causing, or often associated with, differing degrees of ID include fragile X syndrome, Coffin–Lowry syndrome, adrenoleucodystrophy.

Multifactorial/polygenic disorders

In multifactorial/polygenic disorders, both genetic and environmental factors combine to influence the manifestation of the disorder. Such disorders, although frequently exhibiting familial clustering and raised recurrence risks in relatives, do not conform to Mendelian laws of gene transmission. Examples of multifactorial disorders include neural tube defects, orofacial clefting, and pyloric stenosis.

Mitochondrial disorders

Mitochondria of cells contain DNA, which has unique features that distinguish it from nuclear DNA. Mitochondrial DNA is exclusively maternally inherited, with few, very rare, exceptions. Paternal mitochondria enter the egg on fertilization only in miniscule proportions and are usually rapidly eliminated early in embryogenesis.[3] Examples of mitochondrial inherited disorders include MERRF and MELAS.

Further reading

Harper P (2004). *Practical Genetic Counselling*. 6th edn. Arnold: London.

1 Field RC, Stansfield WD (1997). *A Dictionary of Genetics*. 5th edn. Oxford University Press: Oxford.

2 Jones KL (2006). *Smith's Recognizable Patterns of Human Malformation*. 6th edn. Elsevier Saunders: Philadelphia.

3 Firth HV, Hurst JA (2005). *Oxford Desk Reference. Clinical Genetics*. Oxford University Press: Oxford.

Defining intellectual disability nursing

Twelve years ago Gates provided the first comprehensive definition of ID nursing that stated its purpose to be:

'To skillfully assess the social and health care needs of people with intellectual disabilities and/or their families, in order to assist them to live as independently as possible. The nurse will achieve this by marshalling skills as manager, enabler and co-coordinator of services, and will demonstrate that her evidence based interventions lead to health maintenance and/or gain. The nurse will practice her craft autonomously yet interdependently with other colleagues from a variety of other academic disciplines and service agencies in a variety of settings, in partnership with people with intellectual disabilities to assist them to lead valued life styles. This role will require her to develop and refine her knowledge and competence in a range of skills in order to meet the changing needs of people with intellectual disabilities.' [1]

What is intellectual disability nursing?

'Learning disability nursing is a person-centred profession with the primary aim of supporting the well-being and social inclusion of people with learning disabilities through improving or maintaining physical and mental health'.[2]

What do intellectual disability nurses do?

Nowadays much of the care planning and delivery of ID nursing no longer takes place in the old long-term ID hospitals, rather it occurs in a landscape of complex service provision that includes: residential care homes, independent living homes, supported living, and people with ID living in their own home as well as family homes.

Also to be found are larger service configurations and/or very specialist settings such as treatment and assessment services and challenging behaviour units. They may also reside in other specialist health or social care settings such as hospices or homes for older people.

Wherever people with ID live, if they are in receipt of nursing care, whether this comprises short intensive nursing interventions or long periods of care and support, then this care should be guided by a care plan. ID nurses must be competent in preparing robust, professionally prepared care plans based on a systematic nursing assessment. Much evidence exists of the positive contribution of ID nurses to the lives of some people with ID.[3] The authenticity and validity of such a claim continue to be validated by the many examples of excellent practice highlighted in the recently published *Good Practice in Learning Disability Nursing*.[2]

Intellectual disability nursing today

ID nurses currently work in a wide range of organizational settings that include: NHS, local authority, private, statutory, and third sector. Typically they are likely to work in inter-professional teams and for a variety of agencies. Recent changes are beginning to dictate a range of new roles that are undertaken by ID nurses, for example nurses working in healthcare teams such as in acute hospitals, mental health services, and primary care. In England the *Good Practice in Learning Disability Nursing* publication[2] has asserted that most ID nurses still employed by the NHS can be described as working in one of three practice areas:

- Health facilitation—supporting mainstream access
- Inpatient services—for example, assessment and treatment, and secure services
- Specialist roles—in community teams.

Other, broader developments in health care roles, such as the modern matron and nurse prescribing openings, have provided new opportunities in ID services. Also to be found are ID nurse consultant roles who are able to offer valuable clinical, supervisory expertise along with regional and national professional leadership.

Further reading

Turnbull J (2004). *Learning Disability Nursing*. Blackwell Publishing: Oxford.

Department of Health (2007). *Good practice in learning disability nursing*. Department of Health: London. ☐ http://www.dh.gov.uk/en/Publicationsandstatistics/Publications/PublicationsPolicyAndGuidance/DH_081328

Northway R, Hutchinson C, Kingdon A (2006). *Shaping the Future: A Vision for Learning Disability Nursing*. UK Learning Disability Consultant Nurse Network: UK. ☐ http://www.ntw.nhs.uk/uploads/documents/doc203.pdf

1 Gates B (Ed) (1997). Understanding learning disability. In: *Learning Disabilities* 3rd edn. Churchill Livingstone: Edinburgh, 16–17.

2 Department of Health (2007). *Good Practice in Learning Disability Nursing*. Department of Health: London.

3 Alaszewski A, Gates B, Ayer S, Manthorpe G, Motherby E (2000). *Education for Diversity and Change: Final report of the ENB-funded project on educational preparation for learning disability nursing*. Schools of Community and Health Studies and Nursing. The University of Hull: Hull.

The purist form of nursing

The context of intellectual disability nursing

The practice setting for ID nursing is located in a complex landscape of service provision. This includes, for example, residential care homes, independent living homes, supported living arrangements, and people with ID living in their own homes as well as family homes. There are also larger service configurations and very specialist settings such as treatment and assessment services, challenging behaviour units, as well as specialist health or social care settings, such as hospices for children with life-limiting conditions, or homes for older people. ID nurses work with people from birth through to death, who require a range of supports throughout their lives that will range from none, or minimal, support through to intensive holistic nursing aimed at meeting the multidimensional needs of people with ID. This is why ID nursing is often referred to as the purist form of nursing; unlike our colleagues in other branches of nursing, we do not concentrate on specific manifestations of physical ill health or trauma, nor do we just focus on mental health and well-being, or children, or childbirth for that matter; rather we offer support to people with ID and their families that is all embracing and quite literally from the cradle through to the grave.

The purist approach

In order to offer comprehensive nursing interventions that meet the multidimensional needs of people with ID, it is necessary to adopt a structured approach. A comprehensive needs assessment (physical, psychological, social, spiritual, and emotional) has to be completed. If a nurse is required to work with someone with ID and their families, it is necessary that their needs are assessed and incorporated into an individual care plan, taking their desires, wishes, and aspirations into account. The nurse must work closely with the client's family, care providers, and other professionals, as this broad approach may bring very important and essential information to light for assessment, as well as care plan development, its approach, delivery, and management. This is followed by construction of a written care plan that is then implemented and followed, with ongoing review and evaluation. It is this very structured approach, with partnership working and a consideration of the multidimensionality of people coupled with person-centred planning, that allows us to make claim, as well as others to validate, that what we do is the purist form of nursing.

A modelled approach

In response to social and political influences, the arena of ID care models and that of care planning, have changed considerably; so, therefore, has the practice of ID nurses.[1] For example, during the last century, ID services were dominated by a medical model of care that emphasized the biological needs of people and the need to 'cure' physical problems in order to allow a person to function in society. Most people with ID have now moved out of long-stay hospitals, but there remains a concern that the powerful effects of the medical model continue to influence care provided in smaller community based residences. Klotz has argued that the use of the medical model has pathologized and objectified people with

ID, leading to them being seen as 'less human'.[2] Therefore, nurses need to consider adopting a nursing model to guide their care in practice, to ensure that what they offer is holistic and is the purist form of nursing. It must be remembered, therefore, that the use of such a model must hold the person with ID as central to the care-planning process, and that the nurse must be mindful they use such a model to promote what is best for that person. There are numerous nursing models that can be adapted and used in a variety of health and social care settings. Some nursing models, such as Orem's self-care[3], Roper's (2002) activities of daily living,[4] and Aldridge[5] are all well known and seemingly most used in ID nursing. It should be remembered that they may not be seen as relevant or ideal for all people with ID, but they can generally be adapted relatively easily and then become ideal frameworks for the assessment of health as well as more general needs.

Further reading

Gates B (2006). *Care Planning and Care Delivery in Intellectual Disability Nursing*. Blackwell Science: London.

1 Alaszewski A, Motherby E, Gates B, Ayer S, Manthorpe J (2001). *Diversity and Change: The Changing Roles and Education of Learning Disability Nurses*. London: English National Board.

2 Klotz J (2004). Sociocultural study of intellectual disability: moving beyond labelling and social constructionist perspectives. *British Journal of Learning Disabilities* **32**, 93–4.

3 Orem DE (1991). *Nursing: Concepts of Practice*. St Louis: Mosby.

4 Roper N, Logan W, Tierney A (2002). *The Elements of Nursing*, 4th edn. Churchill Livingstone: Edinburgh.

5 Aldridge J (2004). Intellectual disability nursing: a model for practice. In: Turnbull J (Ed). *Learning Disability Nursing*. Blackwell Publishing: Oxford.

Principles and values of social policy and their effects on intellectual disability

Since 2000, each of the countries of the UK has published substantial reviews of their policy guiding the development and delivery of ID services.[1,2,3,4] These highlight the importance of supporting people as individuals, and giving due regard to their human, civil and legal rights.

Scotland: *Same as You?*[1]

- People should be valued. People are individuals and they should be asked about the services they need and be involved in making choices about what they want
- People should be helped and supported to do everything they are able
- People should be able to use the same local services as everyone else, wherever possible
- People should benefit from specialist social, health, and educational services
- People should have services that take account of their age, abilities, and other needs.

England: *Valuing People*[2]

Legal and civil rights—all services should treat people with ID as individuals with respect for their dignity, and challenge discrimination on all grounds including disability. People with ID will also receive the full protection of the law when necessary.

Independence—the starting presumption should be one of independence, rather than dependence, with public services providing the support needed to maximize this. Independence in this context does not mean doing everything unaided.

Choice—this includes people with severe and profound disabilities who, with the right help and support, can make important choices and express preferences about their day-to-day lives.

Inclusion—enabling people with ID to do ordinary things, make use of mainstream services, and be included fully in the local community.

These original principles were revised in 2009, placing a greater emphasis on the outcomes that need to be achieved:[5]

Personalization—people have real choice and control over their lives and services.

What people do during the day (and evenings and weekends)—helping people to be properly included in their communities, with a particular focus on paid work.

Better health—ensuring that the NHS provides full and equal access to good quality healthcare.

Access to housing that people want and need, with a particular emphasis on home ownership and tenancies.

Making sure that change happens and the policy is delivered, including making partnership boards more effective.

Wales: *Fulfilling the Promises*[3]

- Provide comprehensive and integrated services to achieve social inclusion, be person-centred, and improve empowerment and independence
- Ensure effortless and effective movement between services and organizations at different times of life
- Be holistic in approach and delivery, taking into account an individual's preferences, hopes and lifestyle, and ensure a range of appropriate advocacy services is available for people who wish to use them
- Be accessible in terms of service users and their carers and families having full information, and have fully developed collaborative partnerships to deliver flexible services that have been developed on evidence of their effectiveness, and have transparency for costs
- Be delivered by a competent, well informed, well trained, and effectively supported and supervised workforce
- The early completion of the National Assembly's resettlement programmes to enable all people to live in the community.

Northern Ireland: *Equal Lives*[4]

Citizenship—people with ID are individuals first and foremost, and each has a right to be treated as an equal citizen.

Person-centred—people with ID should be supported in ways that take account of their individual needs.

Participation—people with ID should be consulted about the services they want. They should be actively involved in making choices and decisions affecting their lives.

Interdependence—people with ID should be valued and encouraged to contribute to the life of the community.

Equality—people with ID should be able to use the same services and have the same entitlements as everyone else.

1 Scottish Executive (2000). *The Same as You? A Review of the Services for People with Learning Disabilities.* Scottish Executive: Edinburgh.

2 Department of Health (2001). *Valuing People. A New Strategy for Learning Disability for 21st Century.* Department of Health: London.

3 Welsh Office (2001) *Fulfilling the Promises.* Welsh Assembly: Cardiff.

4 Department of Health, Social Services and Public Safety (2005). *Equal Lives.* Department of Health, Social Services and Public Safety: Belfast.

5 Department of Health (2009). *Valuing People Now. A New Strategy for People with Learning Disabilities* Department of Health: London.

Holism and working across the life span

Holistic nursing for health

Holistic approaches to nursing seek to promote nursing interventions that adopt a whole-person approach. This means providing nursing that responds to the various dimensions of being, and these typically include attention to the physical, emotional, social, economic, and spiritual needs of people.

Working holistically across the life span

Being healthy is a positive state of being that we all seek. We are constantly exposed to factors throughout our lives that have the potential to compromise our health. Thus the health of all individuals, but in particular those with ID, is susceptible to health loss. To seek health gain and health maintenance for this group will sometimes require the support of an ID nurse.[1] Throughout the life span from childhood to old age, and even in end of life care, ID nurses can be found supporting people with ID, and wherever they practice they must remember that holistic care planning and delivery form an essential part of their everyday practice. ID nurses can enable people with ID to obtain good quality care. But in order to do this they must reflect on their practice and use the best possible evidence to meet the multidimensional needs of people—thus providing person-centred holistic care. ID nurses have many dimensions and responsibilities within their role; however, supporting people with ID to reach their goals in the form of living their lives as fully and independently as possible is by far the most vital. As registered professionals they have a duty of care, and they have to act within the best interests of their clients at all times. This necessarily includes the planning and delivery of care that attends to the holistic nature of the people they are supporting.

Further reading

Allan E (1999). Learning disability: promoting health equality in the community. *Nursing Standard* 13(44), 32–37.

Journal of Holistic Nursing. Available at 🖳 http://jhn.sagepub.com/

---

1 Gates B, Beacock C (Eds) (1996). *Dimensions of Learning Disability*. Baillière Tindall: London.

Chapter 1 from the Oxford Handbook of **Midwifery**

SECOND EDITION

Edited by

Janet Medforth

Senior Midwifery Lecturer and Lead Midwife Educator
Faculty of Health and Well Being
Sheffield Hallam University, UK

Susan Battersby

Independent Lecturer/Researcher Infant Feeding, UK

Maggie Evans

Freelance Lecturer and Consultant in Midwifery
and Complementary Therapies, UK

Beverley Marsh

Senior Midwifery Lecturer, Faculty of Health and Well
Being, Sheffield Hallam University, UK

Angela Walker

Lecturer in Midwifery, Contraception and Sexual
Health and Independent/Supplementary Nurse/Midwife
Prescribing; Clinic Nurse Co-ordinator, Contraception
and Sexual Health Service, Derbyshire Community Health
Services NHS Trust, Chesterfield, UK
Previously Senior Midwifery Lecturer,
The University of Sheffield (retired)

OXFORD
UNIVERSITY PRESS

Introduction

Definition of a midwife 272
Role of the midwife 273
Principles for record keeping 274
Statutory midwifery supervision 276
Role of supervisor of midwives (SOM) 277
Role of the LSA and LSA midwifery officer 278
Drug administration in midwifery 280

Definition of a midwife

The official definition of a midwife comes from the International Confederation of Midwives (ICM):

'A midwife is a person who, having been regularly admitted to a midwifery educational programme, duly recognised in the country in which it is located, has successfully completed the prescribed course of studies in midwifery and has acquired the requisite qualifications to be registered and/or legally licensed to practise midwifery.

The midwife is recognised as a responsible and accountable professional who works in partnership with women to give the necessary support, care and advice during pregnancy, labour and the postpartum period, to conduct births on the midwife's own responsibility and to provide care for the newborn and the infant. This care includes preventative measures, the promotion of normal birth, the detection of complications in mother and child, the accessing of medical care or other appropriate assistance and the carrying out of emergency measures.

The midwife has an important task in health counselling and education, not only for the woman, but also within the family and the community. This work should involve antenatal education and preparation for parenthood and may extend to women's health, sexual or reproductive health and child care.

A midwife may practise in any setting including the home, community, hospitals, clinics or health units.'

(Adopted by the International Confederation of Midwives Council meeting, 19 July, 2005, Brisbane, Australia. It supersedes the ICM 'Definition of the Midwife' (1972) and its amendments of 1990).

This definition tells us that midwives have a very diverse role and it is one that is expanding to meet the needs of modern society.

There are a number of little known facts about what midwives do and these are just a few examples from the Association of Radical Midwives:

- The midwife is the senior professional attendant at over 75% of births in the UK.
- Midwives can give total care to mother and baby from early pregnancy onwards, throughout childbirth, and until the baby is 28 days old.
- Midwives may legally set up in practice and advertise their midwifery services, either alone or in partnerships.
- It is not necessary to be a nurse in order to become a midwife, although many practising midwives also hold nurse qualifications in addition to their midwifery registration.
- Midwives are the only professionals concerned solely with maternity care. The only other people legally allowed to deliver babies are doctors (who need not have had specialist training in this field).

---

1 International Confederation of Midwives. Core documents. Available at: ℬ www. internationalmidwives.org/Documentation/Coredocuments/tabid/322/Default.aspx (accessed 10.3.10).

Role of the midwife

The role of the midwife can be summed up in just two words: 'delivering babies'! This is the common view of the public and other professionals of what midwives do.

The Royal College of Midwives (RCM)—our professional organization— dedicated to promoting midwifery, and supporting mothers and babies by helping midwives in their professional sphere, says the following about the role of the midwife:

'A midwife does more than just deliver babies. Because she is present at every birth, she is in a position to touch everyone's life. A midwife is usually the first and main contact for the expectant mother during her pregnancy, and throughout labour and the postnatal period. She helps mothers to make informed choices about the services and options available to them by providing as much information as possible.

The role of the midwife is very diverse. She is a highly trained expert and carries out clinical examinations, provides health and parent education and supports the mother and her family throughout the childbearing process to help them adjust to their parental role.

The midwife also works in partnership with other health and social care services to meet individual mothers' needs, for example, teenage mothers, mothers who are socially excluded, disabled mothers, and mothers from diverse ethnic backgrounds.

Midwives work in all health care settings; they work in the maternity unit of a large general hospital, in smaller stand-alone maternity units, in private maternity hospitals, in group practices, at birth centres, with general practitioners, and in the community.

The majority of midwives practice within the NHS, working with other midwives in a team and other health care professional and support staff. Midwives can also practise independently and there is a small group of midwives who do so.

In any one week, a midwife could find herself teaching antenatal classes, visiting women at home, attending a birth, providing parenting education to new mothers or speaking at a conference on her specialist area. So there is more to the role than delivering babies, even though this is a very important aspect of the work of the midwife.'

In 2008 in England there were 672 807 livebirths. This is an increase of 2.7% from the previous year. In the same year there were 19 639 full-time equivalent midwives working in the National Health Service (NHS). This represents that for each of these working midwives there were 34 births, however not all working midwives offer the full range of services to women. This is because midwives fulfil many varied roles such as managerial or other specialist roles.

Principles for record keeping

Record keeping is an integral part of midwifery practice, designed to assist the care process and enhance good communication between professionals and clients. The Nursing and Midwifery Council (NMC; 2009)[1] has published guidelines for record keeping, the main recommendations of which are given below.

The principles of good record keeping apply to all types of record, regardless of how they are held. These can include:

- Handwritten clinical notes
- Emails
- Letters to and from other health professionals
- Laboratory reports
- X-rays
- Printouts from monitoring equipment
- Incident reports and statements
- Photographs
- Videos
- Tape-recordings of telephone conversations
- Text messages.
  Patient and client records should:
- Be factual, consistent, and accurate
- Be written as soon as possible after an event has occurred
- Be written clearly and so that the text cannot be erased
- Be dated accurately, timed, and signed, with the signature printed alongside the first entry
- Not include jargon, abbreviations, meaningless phrases, or offensive subjective statements
- Identify problems that have arisen and the steps taken to rectify them
- Be written with the involvement of the mother
- Provide clear evidence of the care planned, decisions made, care delivered, and information shared with the mother.
  Alterations or additions should be dated, timed, and signed so that the original entry is still clear.

Record keeping is part of the midwife's legal duty of care and should demonstrate:

- A full account of the assessment, and any care planned and provided for mother and baby
- Relevant information about the condition of the mother/baby and any measures taken in response to needs
- Evidence that all reasonable steps have been taken to care for the mother/baby and that their safety has not been compromised
- Any arrangements made for continuing care of the mother/baby.
  You need to assume that any entries you make will be scrutinized at some point. It is normal practice for mothers to carry their own records in the antenatal period and have access to their postnatal notes while under the care of the midwife.

Other members of the team involved in the care of the mother and baby will also make entries into the care record, and information about the mother and baby is shared on a need-to-know basis. The ability to obtain information while respecting the mother's confidentiality is essential.

Midwives should at all times give due regard to the way in which information systems are used, issues of access to records, and keeping their personal and professional knowledge and skills for record keeping responsibilities up to date.

It is a requirement of the NMC Midwives Rules and Standards (2004) that records are kept for at least 25 years.[2]

1 Nursing and Midwifery Council (2009). *Record Keeping: Guidance for Nurses and Midwives* London: Nursing and Midwifery Council.

2 Nursing and Midwifery Council (2004). *Midwives Rules and Standards*. London: Nursing and Midwifery Council.

Statutory midwifery supervision

Statutory supervision of midwives provides a system of support and guidance for every midwife practising in the UK and is a legal requirement.[1] The purpose of supervision of midwives is to protect women and babies by:
- Promoting best practice and excellence in care
- Preventing poor practice
- Intervening in unacceptable practice.
  The practising midwife's responsibilities are to:
- Ensure the safe and effective care of mothers and babies
- Maintain fitness to practise
- Maintain registration with the NMC.
  Your responsibility in maintaining current registration with the NMC is to:
- Identify and meet the NMC requirements for PREP
- Meet at least annually with your named supervisor of midwives
- Notify your intention to practise annually to the local supervising authority (LSA) via your named supervisor of midwives (SOM)
- Have a working knowledge of how NMC publications affect your practice.[2]

---

1 The Nursing and Midwifery Order (2001). *Statutory Instrument 2002/253*.

2 Nursing and Midwifery Council (2008). *Modern Supervision in Action*. London: Nursing and Midwifery Council.

Role of supervisor of midwives (SOM)

The potential SOM is nominated by peers and supervisors in their place of work and must undergo a selection process led by the LSA midwifery officer and university programme leader and which must include a user representative. The midwife must:

- Have credibility with the midwives she/he will potentially supervise and with senior midwifery management
- Be practising, having at least 3 years' experience, at least one of which shall have been in the 2-year period immediately preceding the appointment
- Be academically able
- Have demonstrated ongoing professional development.[1,2]

Having successfully completed the preparation programme, the midwife must then be appointed by the LSA midwifery officer as a supervisor to the LSA and to whom the SOM is responsible in that role.[2] Good communication skills and an approachable manner are essential to the role. Each supervisor is responsible for supervising a maximum of 15 midwives.

SOMs:

- Receive and process notification of intention to practise forms
- Provide guidance on maintenance of registration
- Work in partnership with mothers and midwives
- Create an environment that supports the midwife's role and empowers practice through evidence-based decision making
- Monitor standards of midwifery practice through audit of records and assessment of clinical outcomes
- Are available for midwives to discuss issues relating to their practice and provide appropriate support
- Are available to mothers to discuss any aspects of their care
- Arrange regular meetings with individual midwives at least once a year, to help them evaluate their practice and identify areas of development
- Investigate critical incidents and identify any action required
- Report to the LSA midwifery officer serious cases involving professional conduct, and when it is considered that local action has failed to achieve safe practice
- Contribute to confidential enquiries, risk management strategies, clinical audit, and clinical governance.

1 Nursing and Midwifery Council (2006). *Standards for the Preparation and Practice of Supervisors of Midwives.* London: NMC

2 Nursing and Midwifery Council (2004). *Midwives Rules and Standards: Rules 9–16.* London: NMC.

Role of the LSA and LSA midwifery officer

The LSA is a body responsible in law for ensuring that statutory supervision of midwives and midwifery practice is employed, within its boundaries, to a satisfactory standard, in order to secure appropriate care for every mother.[1]

Each LSA appoints an LSA midwifery officer to undertake the statutory function on its behalf. This must be a suitably experienced SOM,[1] who has the skills, experience, and knowledge to provide expert advice on issues such as structures for local maternity services, human resources planning, student midwife numbers, and post-registration education opportunities.

The functions of the LSA are to:
- Appoint supervisors of midwives and publish a list of current supervisors
- Ensure that every practising midwife has a named SOM
- Determine the appropriate number of supervisors to reflect local circumstances
- Receive the annual notification of intention to practise from all midwives within the LSA boundary and forward the completed forms to the NMC
- Operate a system to ensure that each midwife meets the statutory requirements for practice
- Provide continuing professional development and updating for all SOMs for a minimum of 15h in each registration period
- Ensure that systems are in place to investigate alleged suboptimal care or possible misconduct, in an impartial and sensitive manner
- Determine whether to suspend a midwife from practice
- Where appropriate, proceed to suspend a midwife from practice whom it has reported to the NMC
- Investigate and initiate legal action in cases of midwifery practice by unqualified persons.

1 Nursing and Midwifery Council (2004). *Midwives Rules and Standards: Rules 9–16*. London: NMC.

Drug administration in midwifery

Under the Medicines Act (1968), medicines can only be supplied and administered under the directions of a doctor. Midwives are exempt from this requirement in relation to certain specified medicines, provided they have notified their intention to practise, and the drugs are for use only within their sphere of practice. This allows midwives to supply and administer these drugs without the direction of a doctor.

Changes to the midwives exemptions list came into force on 1 June 2010; these changes will ensure appropriate and responsive care can be given to women safely as part of a midwife's normal sphere of practice, and especially during emergencies.

The medicines to which this exemption applies are as follows:
- Diclofenac
- Ergometrine maleate
- Hydrocortisone acetate
- Miconazole
- Nystatin
- Phytomenadione
- Adrenaline
- Anti-D immunoglobulin
- Cyclizine hydrochloride
- Diamorphine
- Ergometrine maleate
- Hepatitis B vaccine
- Hepatitis B immunoglobulin
- Lidocaine
- Lidocaine hydrochloride
- Morphine
- Naloxone hydrochloride
- Oxytocins, natural and synthetic
- Pethidine hydrochloride
- Phytomenadione
- Prochloperazine
- Carboprost
- Sodium chloride 0.9%
- Gelofusine
- Haemaccel
- Hartmann's solution.

Midwives can also supply and administer all non-prescription medicines, including all pharmacy and general sales list medicines, without a prescription. These medicines do not have to be in a patient group direction (PGD) for a midwife to be able to supply them.

Patient group directions

PGDs are detailed documents compiled by a multidisciplinary group of a local trust or hospital. They allow certain drugs to be given to particular groups of clients without a prescription to a named individual.

This arrangement is very useful as it allows the midwife to give a drug listed in the PGD to a woman without having to wait for a doctor to come and prescribe it individually. The midwife is responsible for following the instructions related to dosage and contraindications provided in the PGD.

Examples of drugs included in a PGD are:

- Dinoprostone (Prostin gel) for induction of labour. 1mg or 2mg gel can be repeated after 6h. Give a lower dose if cervix is favourable
- Ranitidine 150mg tablets.

It is recommended that if a drug is on the midwives exemption list it does not need to appear in a PGD. Under medicines legislation there is no provision for 'standing orders', therefore these have no legal basis.

The NMC has published *Standards on Medicines Management* (2008)[1] which includes, dispensing, storage and transportation, administration, delegation, disposal, and management of adverse events and controlled drugs. Registered midwives must only supply and administer medicines for which they have received appropriate training.

There is clear instruction on the role of the midwife in *directly supervising student midwives during drug administration* and that only a registered midwife may administer a drug which is part of PGD arrangements. Student midwives may administer any medicines that have been prescribed by a doctor (including controlled drugs), or those on the midwives exemptions list (with the exception of controlled drugs).

Further reading

Medicines for Human Use (Miscellaneous amendments) Order 2010. Available at: ℘ www.opsi. gov.uk/si/si2010/uksi_20101136_en_1 (accessed 17.6.10).

Department of Health (2010). CNO letter to SHA Directors of Nursing implementation of Medicines for Human Use (Miscellaneous Amendments) Order 2010 Midwives Exemption List. Available at: 🖳 www.dh.gov.uk/prod_consum_dh/groups/dh_digitalassets/documents/digitalasset/dh_116516.pdf (accessed 17.6.10).

Nursing and Midwifery Council (2009). Supply and/or Administration of Medicine By Student Nurses and Student Midwives in Relation to Patient Group Directions (PGDs). Circular 5/2009. London: NMC.

1 Nursing and Midwifery Council (2008). *Standards for Medicines Management*. London: NMC.

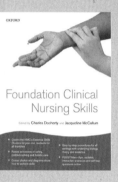